Winter Pasture

Winter
Pasture

One Woman's Journey
with China's Kazakh Herders

Li Juan

Translated by Jack Hargreaves and Yan Yan

ASTRA HOUSE | NEW YORK

Originally published in the Chinese language as *Dong Mu Chang* by New Star Press
© 2012 Thingkingdom Media Group.

For information about permission to reproduce selections from this book,
please contact permissions@astrahouse.com.

Astra House
A Division of Astra Publishing House
astrahouse.com
Printed in the United States of America

Publisher's Cataloging-in-Publication Data

Names: Li, Juan, 1979-, author. | Hargreaves, Jack, translator. | Yan, Yan, translator.
Title: Winter pasture : one woman's journey with China's Kazakh herders /
Li Juan; translated by Jack Hargreaves and Yan Yan.
Description: New York, NY: Astra House, A Division of Astra Publishing House, 2021.
Identifiers: LCCN: 2020917189 | ISBN: 978-1-6626-0033-3 (Hardcover) | 978-1-6626-0034-0
(ebook) | 978-1-6626-0035-7 (trade audio) | 978-1-6626-0040-1 (library audio)
Subjects: LCSH Li, Juan—Travel—China. | Kazakhs—China—Xinjiang Uygur
Zizhiqu—Social life and customs. | Nomads—China—Xinjiang Uygur Zizhiqu—
Social life and customs. | Minorities—China—Xinjiang Uygur Zizhiqu—Social life
and customs. | China, Northwest—Description and travel. | Herders. | BISAC
Classification: LCC DS793.S6213 L5323 2020 | DDC 951.6—dc23

First edition
10 9 8 7 6 5 4 3 2 1

Design by Richard Oriolo
Map illustration and design by Jonathan Roberts
The text is set in Walbaum MT Std.
The titles are set in Flecha L ExtraLight.

Contents

Translators' Note

Li Juan's experiences in the winter pasture have her traveling, living, and working with a family of Kazakh herders, who along with their new neighbors are carrying on a way of life their people have practiced in the region for centuries. With the coming of each season, they migrate with their families, yurts, and livestock to the pastureland that will offer the most favorable climate and the most grass for the coming months, moving north to higher altitudes from winter to spring to summer, and south, back to lower altitudes, from summer to fall to winter. But the year that Li Juan has chosen to accompany these nomadic pastoralists, she is told on more than one occasion, will be the last. After millennia of grazing vast swathes of land, moving from one spot to the next to allow for the grasses' recovery and regrowth, overgrazing has now officially been deemed a problem. The reason for this—and the herders' feelings about it—remains unclear. Regardless, the herders must settle. They will henceforth live along the Ulungur River, around what have long been the spring and fall pastures, where the government has called for land to be reclaimed for cultivation and for aid to be given to the newly relocated herders to help them adjust to their new lives.

Another age-old Kazakh tradition, besides transhumance, is handicraft and textiles. Specifically, felt-based textiles. Living with a hundreds-strong flock of sheep means ready access to plenty of wool, which the herders use to make thread and felt. They use these materials to make carpets, wall hangings, mats, bags, and bands (*bau*, бау) for securing parts of the yurt frame together or to the ground. Various examples of these felt products feature in Li Juan's daily life on the winter pasture, spread, hung, and piled throughout the earthen burrow. In Chinese, Li Juan simply refers to them as "wall hangings" and "patterned rugs" or "patterned mats," depending on which surface they decorate or cover. In this English translation, we have opted to include the romanized versions of their Kazakh names. *Syrmak* (сырмак), which are used as both carpets and wall hangings, are made by quilting ornamental patterns of multicolored felt onto a plain white, brown, or gray felt—a *kiiz* (кииз). *Teke-met* (текемет) are carpets made by pressing and rolling dyed-wool patterns. *Ayak-kap* (аяк-кап) are small embroidered felt bags, and *tus-kiiz* (тускииз) are cotton wall hangings that bear intricate patterns embroidered using tambour stitch. Of the process for making these, Li Juan provides only glimpses—Sister-in-law's questionable dyeing process or Sayna sketching a ram's horn pattern with soap to teach her young daughter how to stitch—so we encourage readers to look up how the finished products look. The same goes for the foods and the central tablecloth and main seating area (*dastarkhān*, дастарқан), for which Li Juan simply gives Chinese equivalents, but for which we have added the Kazakh. On the map that follows, the place-names used are, on the whole, Kazakh renderings, for examples: Dopa in Kazkh, Dure in pinyin, 杜热镇; Akehara in Kazakh, Akehala in pinyin, 阿克哈拉村. Note also that this map is an illustration of the area, rather than a precise representation, and not to scale.

Many thanks to Altinbek Guler for providing translations into English and transliterations into the Latin alphabet of all the Chinese renderings of Kazakh found in the original text.

Lastly, it might help with navigating the narrative to know that since the regions where Li Juan lives, in her everyday life and during her stay with the Cumas, are a confluence of Chinese and Kazakh culture, some of the place-names in this translation are in romanized Kazakh and others in Mandarin pinyin. Also, the characters might be one year younger than stated in the book. We are unsure if their age is based on the Gregorian calendar or the East Asian reckoning, which puts a person at the age of one at birth.

—Jack Hargreaves and Yan Yan
August 2020

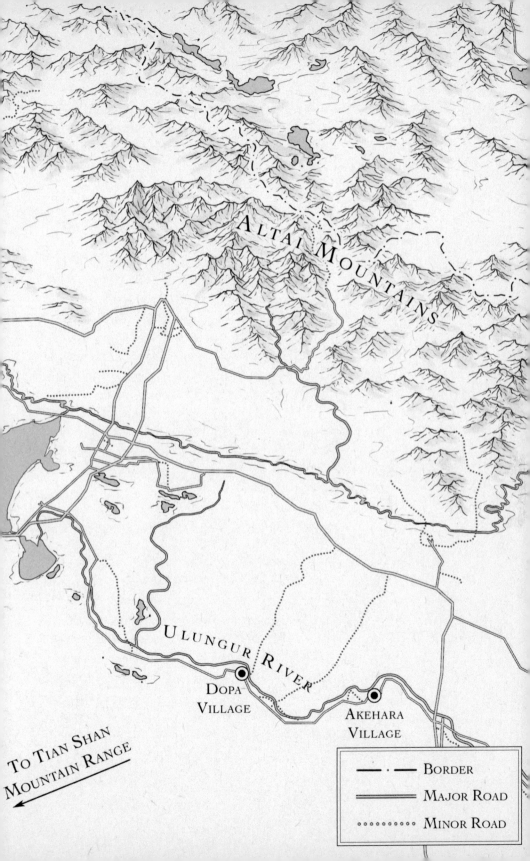

Winter Pasture

PART

ONE

Winter Burrow

1.

In the Beginning

FROM THE MOMENT I released my second book, my mother started bragging to the whole village that I was an "author." But our neighbors only ever saw me, day after day, muck-faced and mussy-haired, chasing after ducks from one end of the village to the other. They all expressed their incredulity. Even as my mother kept going on and on about it, when they turned to look, they'd catch sight of me scurrying along a ditch as fast as my slippers could carry me, hollering and brandishing a stick. Not at all as advertised, quite undignified really.

Eventually, some of them came around to believing her. Eighteen miles from the lower reaches of the Ulungur River, the government was establishing a new herder village named "Humuzhila." One of the villagers approached my mother to ask me to become the "assistant village head," with a salary of two hundred yuan per month. To emphasize that it was a good deal, he said the village head himself only earned four hundred yuan.

Deeply offended, my mother proudly declared, "My daughter would *never* agree to that!"

The visitor looked perplexed and asked, "Didn't you say she's a writer?"

In short, I am something of an enigma in Akehara village, where I live with my mother. I am suspicious for four main reasons: one, I'm unmarried;

two, I don't have a job; three, I don't visit our neighbors much; and four, I'm not what they would consider "proper."

But this winter, I decided to embark on an adventure truly worthy of an author—I would follow the migrating herds deep into the desert south of the Ulungur while observing and noting every last detail of nomadic life in the dark and silent winter. My mother didn't waste a minute before spreading this news to anyone who would listen—to further emphasize how extraordinary I was. But how were we even to begin to explain my work to the herders? This was the best she could come up with: "She will write. Take all your comings and goings, your work 'n' stuff, and write it all down!"

The herders let out a collective "ooooh" of understanding before lowering their heads to mutter, "What's there to write about?"

In any case, word of a Han girl bound for the winter pasture quickly reached the herding teams across Kiwutu township. My mother began to select a family that would agree to take me along.

At first, my ambitions were grand. I wanted to spend the winter in a destination that was at least two hundred and fifty miles away, which would mean over a dozen days by horseback, so that I could get a taste of the hardest, most unforgiving aspects of nomadic life. But all the families who were planning to journey more than ten days refused to take me along for fear that I'd be nothing but trouble. More importantly, as the day of the great migration approached, my ambition dwindled. Think about it: to sleep on the frozen ground only to wake a mere four hours later for two whole weeks. Before daybreak, every day, I would have to grope my way through the darkness to start the journey ahead. Herding sheep, keeping up with the horses, keeping the camels in check and grooming calves . . . for my petite eighty-eight-pound frame, two weeks would have been pushing it. So the trip was truncated to a week's journey . . . and finally, a week before we were supposed to leave, I cut the trip down to three days.

AMONG THE HERDER FAMILIES that passed through Akehara village, those who intended to travel only for three or four days belonged to Kiwutu's herder team number three. Mama Jakybay and her family were no exception. I had spent a summer with them, and ideally I would join them again for the winter. But after a few months, a rumor circulated among the herders that I was Jakybay's son Symagul's "Han girlfriend," which made me angry, and Symagul's wife, Shalat, even angrier. For a while, whenever she saw me, her face stretched so long it nearly hit the ground.

Another important reason why I couldn't stay with Mama Jakybay was because no one in her family spoke Mandarin. Communication between us was difficult and led to misunderstandings.

Herding families that did speak a little Mandarin were mainly young married couples, to whom my presence would have been a nuisance. Newly-weds are invariably deeply in love. If at night they were to express that love, then . . . well, how would I get any sleep?

The winter pasture isn't a particular place. It's the name of all the land used by the nomads during the winter, stretching south uninterrupted from the vast rocky desert south of the Ulungur River all the way to the north-ern desert boundary of the Heavenly Mountains (also known as Tian Shan Mountains). It is a place of open terrain and strong winds. Compared to the region to its north, the climate is warmer and more constant. The snow mantle is light enough that the sheep can use their hooves to reach the withered grass beneath. At the same time, there is enough snowfall to provide the herders with all the water they and the livestock need to survive.

The winter pasture is considerably drier and less fertile than the lands the livestock graze in summer. Each family herd grazes an enormous area. The sheer distance this puts between the families means that contact with one another is a rare occurrence. You could almost call it "solitary confinement."

Herders entering the winter pasture search for a depression sheltered from the wind among the undulating dunes. There they dig out a pit up to six feet deep, lay several logs across the opening, and cover it with dry grass as a roof. A passage is then dug sloping down into the hole and a crude wooden door is fitted to complete this winter home: they call it a burrow. Here, a family can return for protection from the cold and wind during the endless winter months. A burrow is never very big, at most a hundred or so square feet comprising one big sleeping platform and a stove, as well a tiny kitchen corner, a tight squeeze. Life inside is spent shoulder to shoulder without any privacy to speak of.

In brief, living in a winter burrow is no vacation, but what other choice did I have?

And so, I eventually settled on Cuma's family.

Cuma could get along in Mandarin and three days was all it took to get to their land. The Cumas were pushing fifty, and their nineteen-year-old daughter, Kama, would accompany me and the migrating herd while her par-ents would drive to the burrow in a truck—it wasn't going to get any better than that!

Frankly, the real reason they took me on was that Cuma had owed my family a good deal of money for several years. His family was poor and it didn't look like they would ever pay us back, so we gave up expecting it. Why not stay with them for a few months and cancel the debt? That was my mother's idea.

Later, when I found myself hoisting thirty pounds of snow, tottering across the desert huffing and puffing like an ox, I couldn't help but sigh: bad idea.

WITH A HOST FAMILY confirmed, I started preparations.

The image of a pack camel trudging under a heavy load led me to begrudgingly reduce my packing to the essentials—yet another bad idea. Only right before I left did I learn that Cuma had rented a truck to haul the luggage—a truck wasn't going to tire no matter how much there was to carry. So Cuma and Sister-in-law brought all kinds of junk with them to the desert.

As a result, for the coming days, I only had two sets of underwear to swap and wash and a single shirt (which became so dirty by the end of the winter that during the final group photo, no one wanted to stand next to me). For warmth, I packed a simple down jacket, a pair of camel-wool long johns, a scarf, a hat, and gloves. I packed two pairs of shoes, but it turned out that one would have been enough. The winter pasture isn't covered in snow, as I had expected, but in sand, which doesn't wear out shoes.

As for the clothes I would wear during the trip, I was better prepared: a sheep-leather army coat with fleece lining and a pair of woolly sheepskin pants. After all, on the coldest of days, spending hours on horseback was never going to be comfortable. Picking out boots was a major undertaking. A herder typically chooses a pair two sizes larger than usual to allow room for two extra pairs of socks. After some deliberation, I went with a pair of boots eight sizes too big. . . . As a result, I had to wear more socks than anyone had ever worn. My small frame in such huge boots was a sight to behold—like I was skating on two canoes.

To make sure my outfit was as reasonable and comfortable as possible, I tried it all on several times at home, adjusting as I went along. A scarf or a neck gaiter? Which hat? Which set of gloves might prove most appropriate? Two days before our departure, I trekked, wind in my face, to the barren parts of the village south of Akehara Road to test each of my potential outfits, using empirical evidence to make my final decision:

My lower half from inside out: cotton long johns, down long johns, camel-wool long johns, airtight cotton padded pants, woolly sheepskin pants.

My top half from the inside out: long-sleeve shirt, thin sweater, thicker sweater, cotton vest, down jacket, sheep-leather army coat.

On top of that, a leather hat, neck gaiter, scarf, mask, and gloves—in terms of resisting the cold, I had faith I had achieved total victory!

The only problem was that, fully clad, I was so bundled up I could hardly breathe. I couldn't raise my arms, turn my neck, or even swallow my saliva. My neck and shoulders were constricted, sore, and heavy. After walking only a couple of times around the house, I was out of breath. The thought of riding a horse for seven or eight hours with over twenty pounds of clothing on my back was a point of serious concern: Would I be crushed to death? But out in the frigid air of the desert, these would be the least of my troubles! Stuck neck, immovable arms, soreness, and fatigue . . . that was overthinking it. Even if I was encased in a suit of concrete, I wouldn't have noticed.

ONE FINAL PIECE of equipment I felt was necessary for the journey was a thermometer. I searched all over Altai City and Koktokay County but couldn't find a portable, low-temperature thermometer anywhere. In the end, I had to settle for a twenty-inch-long unwieldy thing. I told myself, big is good, I won't lose it. Testing it over the next several days back home, I was surprised at how accurate it was. But sadly, the lowest temperature it could measure was negative thirty-one degrees Fahrenheit. When the temperature dropped below thirty, I'd just have to guess.

One last thing to do was get a haircut. My plan was to get a buzz cut because I had a feeling I wouldn't be washing my hair at all for the next few months (actually I did end up washing it a couple of times). Unfortunately, the only hairdresser in the village, Mayra, was off somewhere falling in love. She hardly tended to her business—she was always appearing and disappearing like a ghost. I went to her shop ten times a day, and eight out of ten the door was locked. The other two times, either someone else was midchop or there was no hot water and I was told to come back in an hour. Naturally, when I did return, she was nowhere to be found. I was so annoyed that I chopped off my hair myself before I left. In the following days, whenever we visited other herders, or received visitors, the state of my hair put a big dent in my self-esteem.

Meanwhile, I was determined to learn Kazakh. I was ambitious about it too, wanting not only to speak it, but write it as well. I borrowed a set of Kazakh exercise books and braced myself for battle. But to actually learn it was something else! Even though the Arabic alphabet only has two more letters than the Latin alphabet, it felt like a mighty army of ten thousand horses. One tongue wasn't nearly enough and the letters were full of twists and turns with a thousand appendages, like an unspooled thread that is tangled beyond untangling . . . sigh—*au-to-di-dact*, four syllables that are not nearly as simple as they seem.

REGARDLESS, IT DIDN'T matter how thoroughly I prepared; actually leaving was a whole other issue. If it wasn't Cuma's sheep wandering off one day, it was his camels disappearing the next. The big day continued to be pushed further and further back. On top of that, it was almost the end of November, but it still hadn't snowed. Snow is the only source of water in the desert in winter. Without it, humans and animals can't survive. As a result, the departure date seemed impossibly far away, which made everyone tense and anxious.

To make matters worse, whenever Cuma, the drunk, thought about having to stay sober for the whole winter, he felt sad. So each day, he tried to drown his sorrows in booze and inevitably ended up getting into trouble all over town. This was not a good omen.

Finally, the day of departure was upon us. The previous evening, I moved into Cuma's family's permanent spring and fall encampment five miles down the Ulungur River. As usual, Cuma had drunk himself into a stupor, so my mother had to drive me there on a motorcycle.

The final step before leaving, as per the herders' custom, was to turn my watch back two hours. Until that moment, I had been on Beijing time.

I fell in love with the morning light on the winter pasture.

2.

A Three-Day Journey

O N THE DAY OF DEPARTURE, we rose before dawn and started the final preparations in the wan sunlight, packing, binding the heavy pack to the lead camel's hump, seeing to the horses, and ushering the sheep into a single flock. Cuma's neighbor-to-be on the winter pasture, Shinshybek, along with his brother, Kulynbek, came to lend a hand. At 7:00 a.m., the team was ready to set out. Kulynbek led my horse over to me. He and Shinshybek would be accompanying Kama and me and the migrating herd. With one hand gripping the saddle and the other clutching a fistful of the horse's mane, I strained to pull myself up. After much wiggling around, I found what felt like a stable seat (despite my clothes). Apa (Cuma's mother, who was to stay in the nearby permanent encampment through the winter) came over and tugged on the bottom of my sheepskin pants to cover my ankles. It was exactly the kind of tender gesture that I needed to ease my nerves. The sky chose this moment to come to light. The air was crisp and cold. The sheep were already on the main road a ways off. Riding between them and myself, Kama hollered for me to catch up. After waving goodbye to those who had come to see us off, I sent the horse into a canter with a light kick to its belly and quickly gained on the rest.

For the three-day journey, nineteen-year-old Kama and I would be in charge of the camel team (thirty-some camels), while Shinshybek and Kulynbek would be in charge of the sheep flock (the three families had nearly five hundred sheep combined) and large livestock (over a hundred cattle and horses) for the duration of the trip. Cuma and Sister-in-law (which is what I called his wife), along with the rest of Shinshybek's family, would join us three days later by truck, bringing food, fodder, and ice by the ton. Kulynbek and his family would then head to a different pasture for the winter.

Compared to the sheep flock, our camels could walk quickly, so Kama and I would be arriving at the evening's camp before the two brothers with the rest of the team. After setting up a simple triangular tent, we were to ready hot tea to await their arrival. Meanwhile, the main team would follow our tracks, taking as long as necessary for the sheep, cattle, and horses to nibble on dried grass and snow as they walked. Such a long journey was hard work for everyone; it was only fair to let them satisfy their bellies.

That morning, the camels, sheep, and large livestock all set off at the same pace. After our clamoring team crossed the suspension bridge over the Ulungur River, we continued south, past the road running along its southern bank then up and down a series of rugged hills. From on top of one, we took in the vast undulating landscape surrounding us. An hour later, we had left the villages along the Ulungur River far behind and were venturing deep into the scrublands.

The barren hills before me rolled like waves. There was only the vestige of a thin trail meandering through them. The sun was still rising, the sky was cloudless and blue. Having walked for so long with no break, the herd was growing anxious. The sheep snuggled up to the goats, the lambs followed close to the ewes. The horses refused to walk with the cattle but the cattle insisted on staying close to the horses—it was a game of tag that inevitably led to chaos. The camels without nose pegs were the most unruly. Whenever they found a tuft of grass as thin as a thumb, they stopped to eat, refusing to budge, constantly falling behind as if they hadn't the slightest clue we were on the road far from home. The two men shouted angrily at the animals as they ran to and fro, disciplining the ones that deviated from the path.

The sheep were the most orderly. Heads bowed, they huddled tightly together, afraid to stray from the group by even one step.

The ten or so camels fitted with nose pegs were also obedient. They formed a long line and calmly followed the rope that bound them together. The lead camel, packed with a heavy load, set the pace.

It was my job to steer the camels. Generally, they were friendly, but sometimes they liked to chew on my hat. It was a straightforward task; I just had to hold tightly on to the rope. Even so, I managed to lose them twice. The first time, we had walked barely half a mile when I heard Kama shouting from a distance. That's when I realized that I was holding a rope attached to nothing at all. The second time, I had walked for who knows how long with only a single camel attached to the rope, plodding along at my back. The others were left standing far behind us, wondering why nobody was paying them any attention.

Ah, what could I do. All these layers of clothing had my neck locked in place. I couldn't nod or look up, let alone turn my head to see what was happening behind me (though it must have done wonders for my arthritic neck)—I had to turn my whole horse around.

Speaking of horseback riding, even though the horse was doing all the walking, I still felt tired beyond belief. The main reason was that my hands were too full. I carried a whip, my horse's reins, the camels' rope, the thermometer (for more accurate readings, I kept it in my hand rather than stuffed in my warm pocket), cheese (for a quick snack), a camera, and a camcorder. In addition to losing the camels, I nearly dropped the whip a few times as well. Losing it would have been a real pain. Bundled up as I was, what were the chances that I could reach it? To be safe, I strapped the horse's reins to my wrist, fastened the thermometer to my glove, tied the camel's rope to the horse's reins, wedged the cheese between my teeth, and hung both cameras from my neck. And so it was that I jingled all the way, like a fully decorated Christmas tree.

GIVEN THAT IT WAS only a three-day trek, one camel was all it took to carry the necessary provisions. There were several pieces of bedding, two large wooden tent frames, some felt covers, a kettle, a big sack of food, an iron *oshak* stove, two chimney funnels, sets of bowls and chopsticks, bark from a birch tree (to start fires), and a generous bundle of kindling. In the gravelly scrublands, there is nothing that can be used for firewood, only sparse scrubgrass.

Just before noon, as the temperature rose, the team emerged from the hills into the flat expanse of the rocky desert where withered scrubs shyly dot the earth. The sheep and livestock slowed—it was lunchtime! Kama and I picked up the pace, leading the camels toward the southwestern horizon.

Clouds metamorphosed before our eyes, drifting from east to west. The endless sky, the boundless earth, left us speechless. Compared to the sense of loneliness the moment conjured, our weariness seemed trivial. The wind picked up—heaven and earth were hollering at each other. I had already been wearing my face mask. My scarf was wrapped tightly around my neck gaiter. The earflaps on my big hat were buttoned tightly beneath my chin. The only part of my face that showed through a narrow slit, half a finger wide, were my eyes. The world that appeared before me was shallow and oppressive, but I felt safe. Soon, the lenses on my glasses were misted over by my own breath. The steam thickened until all I could see was Kama's blurry silhouette before me. But there was no need to see—the world offered no obstacles and the horses knew their own way. At first, every so often, I plucked my glasses off to wipe them. But soon, I simply sat on top of my horse and waited for time to pass.

Having passed through the empty and monotonous plain, the landscape began to gradually change. Before us was an expansive salt flat that was slightly lower in elevation. Half an hour later, the camels descended into the western margin of the salt flat, a place that was sheltered from the wind. When I saw Kama slide down from her horse and approach the camels, my heart leaped. We're here! The first day's journey had come to an end.

The moment my feet touched the ground, Kama assigned me my first task: to act like a hitching post. On that flat, empty land, there was nothing else to secure the reins to. With the reins of all the horses and camels in my hands, I plodded to and fro, untethering the camels from one another, unpacking supplies, and erecting the stove. I did what little I could to help until Kama's hands were free. Then the saddles came off, the lead camel was relieved of its pack, and only then were the reins released and the animals allowed to wander free. At first they lingered nearby. Then, gradually, they began to drift out into the desert.

AFTER ONLY A DAY of riding, my face and the backs of my hands were chapped so bad it hurt. I wanted to wash them, but we had no water. The flask that we had brought along contained only a block of ice—not a drop of water would come out. I found the wet wipes that I remembered packing, but they were frozen too, like iron sheets, rock-hard and impossible to pull apart.

Kama went to collect snow as I lit the stove. But the iron chimney funnel had been squashed flat. I scoured the ground nearby for a rock to smash it back into shape, but I couldn't find anything bigger than a walnut. All I could do was stomp on the chimney and squeeze it with my hands until there was an opening wide enough to be wedged onto the stove.

I lit the fire easily enough and Kama returned with half a bag of snow over her shoulder. We had a big tin pot to melt the snow in, except that after a day of being jostled about, a coating of dust and dry twigs had accumulated on the bottom (it sat directly below the kindling in the pack). I wondered how Kama planned to wash it, but she didn't; she simply poured the snow right in.

After the snow melted into water, I carefully washed my hands and face. My hardened skin felt softer, more comfortable. Then I pulled a tube of hand cream out of my pack, but once again, nothing came out—it too had turned into a tube of ice.

While the tea was boiling, the two of us quickly set up the temporary tent. Building the tent was simple; all you had to do was stretch out the two wooden frames, bring the tips together, tie up the top, and throw on the cover. At first, I couldn't see how two flimsy wood lattices could hold themselves upright. But under the weight of the heavy felt cover, what was once loose and flimsy became firm and unwavering.

Underneath us was a thick layer of animal manure. Apparently, people had been stopping there to rest for many, many years.

Next, Kama asked me to fetch a horse. They'd arrived before the sheep. She pointed to the east, which was her way of telling me to bring back a particular large black steed. After accepting the mission, I immediately set off running toward the horses. But after ten yards, I turned back. I needed to remove my sheepskin pants, which were so thick and stiff that I couldn't bend my knees.

With my pants off, I felt as light as a swallow, but my feet were still encumbered by my many socks and colossal boots. Once again, I ran back to change out of my black rubber boots that were eight sizes too big.

Having finally disposed of the restraints that had burdened me all day, my strength was unleashed and I quickly covered a large distance. When I saw the horses, I was stupefied. They were all black, and all very large. I couldn't possibly bring them all back at the same time, so I chose the two blackest and went after them.

Catching horses is easier said than done. Even if I had six more legs, I couldn't have outrun them. Instead, I circled them, trying to block their path . . . but that didn't work either. How exhausting. After a while, panting, I climbed to a higher ground. That's when I saw that the flock of sheep had already crossed into the scrub plain to our north. I gave up on the horse chase and returned to camp, bringing Kama the news. She was still furnishing the tent. As soon as she saw me, she shouted for my help, never bothering to ask about the horses. I still don't know why she had asked me to fetch the horse in the first place. . . .

The sheep appeared on the highland to the north. They were only a half mile away from camp. Kulynbek had left the flock behind, charging toward the rising smoke of our camp. He sang at the top of his lungs as he cracked his whip. He must have been thinking excitedly about the end of the first arduous day of travel. His excitement infected Kama, whose work around the camp grew into a frenzy as her voice quietly accompanied his song.

Though both are the music of nomadic peoples that ring out across the steppes, Kazakh music is different from the music of the Mongols, who we are more familiar with. The latter is soulful and austere, while the former is exuberant, bright, and rhythmic.

Kulynbek rode up to the camp, but he never dismounted. He circled the camp, signaling his satisfaction, and then charged back toward the herd without even stopping for a sip of water.

Once the sheep were accounted for, the men lay down on a slope by the camp to catch their breath. They kicked off their felt overboots (chunky, round things that were impossible to walk in) and gulped down a few bowls of tea to soothe their weariness before jumping straight back on the horses to gather up the scattered herd. Having brought the livestock back to camp, they tied up what needed to be tied up and fettered the hind legs of those that needed fettering. They beat the ones that demanded a beating and scolded the ones that deserved a scolding. It wasn't until the sky was dark that the animals began to quiet down. But even then, they appeared anxious. This was unfamiliar territory after all. At this point, the horses that had been ridden all day were relieved of their saddles. With their hind legs fettered, they wandered off to eat grass for the night. Only then did the men crouch down in the tent where, at last, we sat to enjoy tea without worry.

The bowls, wet from washing, were frozen into a single tower. It took great effort to pry them apart. The milk in a plastic bottle labeled "Nutrition Express" was frozen solid as well. Kama used a small spoon to dig into the frozen bottle and scraped bits of icy milk into everyone's tea. The tea was neither dark nor aromatic, but out in the desert, it was enough to assuage our pitiful bellies. The trick to drinking tea in the cold is to drink quickly, before the tea has a chance to cool. Once cooled, solidified chunks of butter would float in the tea bowl, which made it hard to swallow. I drank as quickly as I could, and before I knew it, I had gulped down five bowls, which meant countless trips to the toilet.

As soon as night fell, I began to feel sleepy, exhausted beyond words. When I thought about the fact that I only had four hours to sleep, I was desperate to crawl under the covers and shut my eyes. But no one else seemed to share my sense of urgency, or perhaps after the arduous day, they still needed time to recuperate. By the dim light of a flashlight, they continued to drink one bowl after another, while the kettle kept at a boil. They spent two hours drinking tea and finished two kettles of water! When they saw that I couldn't stay awake any longer, they told me to sleep. Meanwhile, they remained seated together, silently, around a shaft of light encompassed by the dark night. I slept a little, then suddenly woke up to find them still sitting there, unmoving. It wasn't until later that I understood that only Kama and I could sleep that night—the men couldn't shut their eyes for more than a second. Because we had no sheepdogs with us, it was their duty to keep watch, protecting the herd from wolves. They could do nothing but drink tea in order to make it through the cold, trying night.

When Kama had first put up the tent, I had poked my head in and found quilted felt *syrmak* rugs and wool blankets laid out in the thirty-square-foot space. Could four people really sleep here? Whoever had to sleep near the side of the tent would be the unfortunate one. Of course, that ended up being me.

Sleeping under the stars in the frozen wilderness, I couldn't help but have the jitters. At first, I hadn't planned on taking off my leather coat, but on second thought, I realized wearing thick, stiff clothes to bed might constrict my blood flow, which might actually increase my chances of freezing, so I crawled under the covers in my down jacket and long johns and laid my heavy coat on top of the equally heavy leather blanket. Snuggled under all that weight, I lay motionless. Soon, my feet warmed up.

Ordinarily, covering my head with a blanket would have made me feel like I was suffocating. But that night, I was like a baby bird tucked beneath her mother's wing—safe and sound. This little nest, dark and warm, separated me completely from the cold. It was a universe within a universe, a seed inside an apple.

But going to the toilet in the middle of the night was a tragedy. I was loath to even poke a toe out into the frozen air. It took real determination to pull myself upright. In the dark, I clawed blindly at the tent's felt cover (sleeping at the edge of the tent had its perks after all) before finally finding a flap through which to crawl out. It took a lot of fumbling about to find my shoes, which I had left outside. One of the brothers on watch, I don't know who, sat beside the tent with a flashlight. With the aid of his light, I put on my shoes, walked away from the tent, and when I squatted the light turned off (the moment it became dark, the Milky Way lit up the sky), and when he heard the sound of my footsteps again, the light came back on to guide my way back to the tent.

What a fiasco—the cold air had sapped my body of all its warmth. Nestled under the covers, tucked in on all sides, a sweet, soothing warmness enveloped me once more. But the thought of someone standing watch outside left me with a heavy heart.

AT 3:00 A.M., I was nudged awake. The temperature was at its lowest point of the day. Kama used the hot tea she had stored in a thermos before going to sleep to pour everyone a bowl. She then brought out the bag of mutton on the bone that Apa had prepared for us before we left. Even though the frozen meat crunched in our mouths as we washed it down with our tepid tea, it was still delicious.

Oh yes, for the trip, Kama had made the extravagant decision of bringing packs of instant noodles. Sadly, the tea bowls were too small to soak them in. So she tore open one side of the packaging and poured hot water directly into it. Everyone sat, tightly pinching the tops of their bags in anticipation. It was so cold that the water quickly cooled. Pieces of solid grease floated on top of the noodles, which were still dry. Even so, everyone slurped them down with relish.

Though the noodles were likely terrible, they were nonetheless appealing in the frozen wilderness. I was looking forward to a bag of my own, but, somehow, I had given them the impression that I didn't eat instant noodles. All I could do was drool at the aroma. At least my sacrifice allowed the two men to eat a little extra, which was good. They had been working the hardest.

I didn't understand why we had to wake up so early. It wasn't as if we did anything but drink tea for an hour and a half! And there wasn't much to talk about. Most of the time, we just sat there nursing our bowls in silence. I couldn't tell if it was because they found it enjoyable or because they were too tired to move. Indeed, even though I had slept, comfortable and warm, the night watchmen had had a much rougher time and needed some hot tea to recover.

After our teatime in the dark came to a close, we got to disassembling the tent, packing the supplies, and loading the camel (a few hours was all the pack camel had had to wander before it was trussed up again). I was responsible for using the flashlight to light up everyone's tasks and occasionally lent a hand propping open a sack. Everyone worked patiently and methodically.

At 6:00 a.m., as the sky began to glow, we were ready to go. After a final head count of the cattle and sheep, everyone mounted their horses and we set off. When I glanced back, the ground was as clean as when we had arrived; we had left no trace of our passage.

By the light of dawn, the team advanced southwest in silence. Little by little, the sky turned red. Its color deepened as it spread, swelling into a cascade, setting the eastern sky ablaze from south to north. At 6:30, the sun ascended steadily up a sea of red clouds. Sunbeams swept the land, stretching our shadows out toward the horizon.

With the slow passage of time, our shadows gradually returned to us. They inched behind us, then crossed over to our northeast. Like that, another day passed.

It was a day not unlike the one before, about eight hours of riding. But the land we passed was even emptier and more monotonous. Cuma had once taught me that if no one was around to help me down from my horse, I should look for a depression in the ground and park the horse in the ditch. That way I could step onto the rim where the distance to the ground was not so great. But finding a ditch on land that is flat enough to gallop across was as unlikely as finding a mountain.

When the surroundings started to look like the salt flat of the day before, I couldn't help but feel like I was hallucinating: Did we just make a big circle in the desert? But of course, we had only been going southwest.

YESTERDAY'S LI JUAN was only responsible for leading the camels. She sat comfortably on her horse's back and followed the team. Seeing that I was still in good spirits, Kama decided to assign me a new task today: fetch the wandering camels. As a result, on the second day, I ended up miserably tired. By the time we reached camp, my legs were aching and stiff, my buttocks were too sore to sit on a saddle. As for the intractable camels—I dare not put my rage in words here.

Starting at midday, our camel team entered a stretch of hills where the road meandered. In theory, we were already in the desert, where yellow sand stretched as far as the eye could see. Except, given the extraordinary snowstorms last year, spring burgeoned from an abundance of water. The pasture grew so lush that the area before us was more like a furry desert. Never mind the cattle and sheep, even the mice lived lavishly. The sheer number of holes in the sand stood as testament to their long and prosperous lives. No matter how cautiously the horses walked, they couldn't avoid occasionally stepping in the holes. With each stumble, the rider was met with a violent jolt.

At 2:30 in the afternoon, the camels stopped in a narrow valley between two hills. The ground was littered with broken twigs—evidence that it was an especially well-trodden camp spot. Nearby, saxaul shrubs grew on a ridge. Wonderful! Half the kindling brought by the camels had been used up the day before. I was almost worried that we might run out.

We had more than enough firewood, but there were only five matches left. In a panic, I asked Kama, "Are you sure there are no more?" Filled with skepticism, I watched her light the matches. When there were only three matches left, I snatched them from her to try for myself. Down to the last match, we exchanged looks of horror. Neither of us wanted to touch that final match. But, of course, it failed too. As fast as the flame licked into life, it fizzled out in a mighty gust of wind.

This was when Kama rummaged through a sack and fished out . . . a lighter. She could have mentioned it earlier! I nearly had a heart attack.

As with the day before, we started the *oshak* stove and put up the tent before the herd arrived. But here the snow was much thinner and I had to walk quite a ways before I managed to find a hilltop with enough snow to fill a bucket. But that Kama, after a small loop, she came back with a whole sack full of snow! It was like sorcery.

The melted snow was packed with sand and dirt, but after settling, the water was clear enough. When the young men came charging into the camp that evening, they were so thirsty that they leaped from their horses, scooped bowls full of cold water, and guzzled down. How could they swallow such icy water, I marveled. But by the time I had herded the cattle back to camp, I too was so thirsty that I gulped down the water even more fiercely than they had.

Herding cattle in the sand was full of challenges. As I ran, I stumbled over a mouse hole (poor little mouse, digging the hole can't have been easy either . . .). What's more, in the past I'd herded livestock by shouting and throwing stones at them. But in the desert, even stones the size of a thumbnail were hard to come across. The next best thing was tossing dry horse manure at them. But manure was too light and didn't scare the cattle at all.

OTHERWISE, IT WAS JUST like the day before. The fading light provided a sense of urgency. It wasn't until dark that we could finish the day's work. Inside the tent, we huddled, drank lukewarm tea, and chomped on icy meat shards. Under the flashlight, we puffed thick white breaths in silence.

Suddenly, Shinshybek said, "This is *ter-mos*," as he pointed to a thermos. He added, "This is *chyny*," as he presented me the bowl in his hand.

It was a little unexpected. Even though I already knew both of those words in Kazakh, I still repeated them back to him as best I could. He smiled, triumphant. Then he proceeded to teach me the name of every last utensil in our little tent.

I was told that, at first, they didn't think I could make it to the end of the journey, and even complained about Cuma's decision to take me along. They thought that I would be a nuisance, nothing more—if I tried to quit halfway or cried about wanting to go home, or if I fell ill, or fell off a horse . . . it would have ruined their trip!

So, I wondered, were they assured yet?

Earlier that morning, when the cattle and camels were still walking together, the brothers had assigned me a few simple tasks. For example, to keep the flock on course by flanking them from one side, or to intercept a break-away camel. I don't know about them, but I thought I had done a good job. As they say, "Even the littlest toad has some kick in its legs," so in spite of my size, I hoped I was good for something!

Like yesterday, it wasn't until deep in the night that Kama laid out the bedding and went to sleep with me. The men wrapped themselves in their blankets and sat in the darkness to keep watch, exchanging a few words every now and then. During the sleepiest of hours, they took turns dozing off.

Despite the sunny weather, it still felt cold during the day, especially when the wind picked up in the afternoon. But when I checked the thermometer, twenty-six degrees was all it read! And at the very coldest point of the night, it wasn't even as low as minus four. At first, I suspected there was something wrong with the thermometer. But then I thought about it some more: perhaps the temperature wasn't so cold after all, but prolonged exposure distorted my perceptions.

THE THIRD DAY BEGAN at 3:00 a.m. as usual with an hour-long breakfast tea. In the murky dark, we pulled down the tent, packed up the sacks, and loaded the lead camel up with heavy gear. Under the starry sky, we set out toward Orion, half sunk beneath the horizon. A crescent moon hung on the eastern sky.

Again, our progress followed that of the slow, majestic sunrise. Before the sun emerges, the whole world is a dream, the only real thing is the moon. After the sun emerges, the whole world is real, only the moon fades into a dream.

The camel team and sheep flock advanced quietly side by side, apparently now accustomed to the pace, as if they'd accepted this as their fate, entirely unaware that this was their last day of travel. The two groups broke apart much earlier than before. The camels set foot onto the true desert at half past eight in the morning, while the sheep stayed back. They were intent on eating their fill.

It really was the "true desert." Looking east, a sand dune. Looking west, a sand dune. As far as the eye could see were towering waves of immaculate golden sand dunes where not a single blade of grass grew. Unlike the white expanse of the previous days, the earth was only dotted with thin scatterings of snow. The air was warmer too.

For around an hour at midday, I led the camels by myself while Kama was off chasing after one of the team that had wandered far from the rest. Before she left, she said, "Follow the road! Just follow the road forward!" Scanning the vast world before me, I was intimidated. But to reassure her, I promised to do just that.

Compared to the roads on the scrubland, the desert trail was a blur. Worse, we had entered other people's pastures so the trail was crisscrossed with all sorts of cattle tracks that made my head spin. At first, I tried to look for the most densely trodden trail and pulled the reins left and right to steer us along that course. Later, I gave up, slackened the reins, and let my horse find its own way. Of course, the horse knew better than me all along. After a long stretch of dry grass, we came upon a clearly defined road.

Alone with a team of camels, I moved timidly through the desert. The earth was bare, the sky was like the dome of a yurt. A single cloud hung at the center of the sky. It was shaped like a stairway. There wasn't a soul in sight, emptiness in all four directions. It didn't feel melancholy or exuberant; rather I experienced a tranquilizing ennui. Over the past thousand years, how many herders had walked this same land alone, feeling the same as I felt?

The six-month-long winter and the infertile land imposed a nomadic "life-style" onto the Kazakh people's ancestors. Year after year, survival demanded obedience to nature's rhythm. From the depth of the Altai Mountains to the open expanse north of the Heavenly Mountains, the herders covered nearly six hundred miles every year. Those that migrated the most frequently did so on average every four days. The Cuma family's winter pasture wasn't far from their summer pasture, so they traveled little by comparison. Still, I calculated that on average they had to pack up their home every twenty days—such is their unforgiving life; such are their lonely, implacable hearts.

DURING THOSE FIRST three days, as soon as afternoon rolled around, I would begin asking Kama over and over, "Have we arrived?" in Mandarin.

At first, she didn't know what *daole*—"arrived"—meant, and I had no way of explaining it. Then, the more I asked, and because I announced, "Arrived!" whenever we got to the site where we would set up camp, she figured it out. From then on, whenever I asked, she replied with either "Not arrived" or "Arrived, we have." The former meaning it was still early. The latter meaning soon.

It was half past noon when Kama took a sharp turn directly south off the straight southwesterly road—I knew at once that we had almost arrived! My heart leaped for joy. I asked her the same old question and she simply smiled. But this new road seemed to go on forever. Each time we followed it across an expanse of open desert and found ourselves on top of a dune, we were greeted by another expanse of interminable desert, in the middle of which the trail continued to stretch . . . promising more exhaustion ahead.

That day's journey was the longest, the most tiring. Seeing how well I had handled myself the day before, Kama basically put me in charge of the whole camel team.

The flock and the camels waiting in the morning mist to set off

Horseback riding is a rough sport. If by "riding," you mean sitting still on the back of a horse, then anyone can "ride." But if you also have to chase down cattle and sheep, crack your whip, yank on the reins, spur the horse, and shout at the top of your lungs . . . well then. After a whole day of riding, your bones will be ready to shatter. You'll feel like you have just taken a beating.

When at last, in anger and frustration, I had rounded up all the deviating camels back to the main pack, I ascended a sand dune and my jaw dropped. On the other side was a patch of black dirt! Kama was dismounting! She turned to shout, "Arrived, Li Juan! Today has arrived! Tomorrow, no walk! Tomorrow of tomorrow, no walk!"

Then, "Mother and father will drive here!"

I looked at my watch: it was 3:30 in the afternoon.

Then came the snow and a strong wind. After unloading the supplies from the lead camel, before we even had a chance to get organized, we sat on top of the packs and nibbled on dry *nan* in the wind and snow, basking in the joy of "stopping." There was still a lot to do, managing the livestock, setting up shelter, preparing dinner . . . but we had arrived! It felt like an arrival that could have lasted forever.

3.

The Importance of
Sheep Manure

WHEN SOMETHING IS HARD, locals say it's like chewing *kurt*. *Kurt* is a hard cheese made by straining boiled yogurt. Especially when it's made from aged yogurt, the stuff is harder than a rock! Even with the strongest of teeth, you'll struggle to even make a dent in it. To eat this kind of cheese, you have to roast it on the stove until it's soft, or soak it in scalding tea until it becomes chewy. A single lump of Kama's *kurt* can last three or four rounds of tea over the span of two days. When a round of tea is finished, you can store the cheese in your pocket to be soaked again with the next round. Kama had endless patience for this process, because it was fun.

At any rate, eating *kurt* is an ordeal. But whenever I got hungry while herding the team southward, I chewed on *kurt*. Once, as I waited for the camels to get back on track, I was so famished I managed to eat an entire big lump of the thing. It was like I was possessed by some supernatural force. The point I want to make here is: cleaning up a sheep pen is like chewing *kurt*.

We arrived on the third day. Yellow sand stretched across the vast, monotonous winter pasture, dotted with white patches of snow. But the dip in the sand dunes in which we lived was pitch-black. The sheep had lived in this spot for many winters, their manure accumulating year after year. The repetition of the manure being broken down and replenished was what had turned the depression black.

Inside the sheep pen, there was a layer of especially thick and hard manure. Cuma said that every month, it would rise by half a foot, and so it needed to be cleaned out several times over the course of the winter. The first cleaning, upon arrival, and the final cleaning, before departure, were the most important and most laborious. The first cleaning meant digging out a layer of mostly dry manure. The final cleaning happened during the warmth of spring, when a thick layer of soft, wet manure is dug up and spread around the sheep pen to dry for the following winter. Once dried, this manure is black and pure and just the right size. There is no better fuel for the winter.

The lowest layer of manure is close to the earth. Mixed with sand and soil, it becomes hard and clumpy. After a whole summer exposed to the sun and air, it can be dug up in slabs as straight as concrete. These manure slabs can't be used as fuel, but they are the desert's most important building material. The Chinese national anthem goes, "Use our flesh and blood to build a new Great Wall." For the sheep, it's "Use our poop to build a shelter from the wind and cold." A sheep pen built from manure slabs is both neat and sturdy. What else could you use to build it with anyway? In the desert, there are no trees, soil, or rocks, only tufts of brittle grass jutting out of soft sand.

Even the place where we humans eat and live—our burrow—requires sheep manure. A burrow is a six-foot-deep pit. In the sandy desert, its four walls would easily collapse if not for the manure slabs. A few logs are laid on top of the manure-lined pit, some dry grass is spread on top, then smear some manure crumble on top of that and you have a "roof." Finally, dig a sloping passage to enter the sealed cave. Of course, the passage walls must be tiled with manure slabs as well.

Even the wide platform on which we slept was built with manure slabs. Basically, we lived in sheep manure.

"Living in sheep manure" might sound unappealing, but in reality, it's great. Not only is sheep manure the sole building material available in the desert, it is also incomparable—in the dead of winter, only animal feces can magically, continuously radiate heat. This was never more apparent to me than on the coldest nights when we herded the sheep into their pen. The northern winds howled. It was so cold, I could barely open my eyes and the pain was like I had just been punched in the face. But the very moment I came near the thick manure wall, the cold vanished and a feeling of warmth washed over me.

ON THE EVENING of our first day at camp, a snowstorm raged. Cuma, who arrived by car, was drunk as usual. Amid the pandemonium, it was impossible to organize our things. Soon it was nighttime. Exhausted, everyone fell asleep in their clothes on the manure slab bed that hadn't been made yet. Our heads rested against the manure wall. Every time one of us rolled over, bits of manure stuck to our faces and necks. If you had the habit of sleeping with your mouth open, then you were in big trouble! But even with your mouth closed, the next morning, well . . .

Fortunately, after a good night's rest, everyone woke up in high spirits, ready to make up for lost time. A collapsed manure wall was rebuilt. Inside the burrow, the bare walls were covered with *tus-kiiz* and embroidered *syrmak* (patterned cotton wall hangings and patterned felt rugs or tapestries, respectively; it was a pain getting nails to stay in those "walls," they just wouldn't stay put). By the afternoon, the burrow was unrecognizable from the day before—it was as good as new, beautiful even. The manure slabs were all covered up like background actors on a stage, hidden well behind the curtain.

It wasn't only us humans who had the sheep to thank for our manure homes—even the cattle were in their debt. Their burrow was built from sheep manure slabs as well. In the winter, cow dung doesn't have much use. Because it's so wet, cow manure becomes icy and hard in the winter; it wasn't until we moved to the drier and warmer spring pasture that we replaced sheep manure with cow dung for fuel.

Our top priority when we arrived at the winter pasture was to set up the burrow, because people need sleep. The second priority was to clean out the sheep pen, because sheep need to sleep too. As for the cattle, well, they could wait. After all, there weren't as many of them.

Previously, the sheep pen was only used by Cuma's family. Now, with Shinshybek's family sharing the pasture, there were suddenly two hundred extra sheep, so the pen needed expanding. On the first day, we tried to cut corners. We cut the pen's three-foot-wide wall by half into a foot and a half. In other words, we scooped out a ring from the center. Next, we tore down some partition walls that had made a space reserved for the goats. But when the sheep returned in the evening, there were still a hundred-some-odd that couldn't fit inside. The next day, we duly removed the entire west-facing wall, adding a hundred and thirty or so square feet to the pen.

Cuma used a pickax to break apart the solid manure floor, and while Shinshybek and his younger brother, Kurmash, used pointed shovels to dig up slabs of manure, Kama used a square shovel to toss the resulting debris over the wall. From there, Shinshybek's wife, Sayna, and I used our hands to pass the larger slabs over to Sister-in-law, who in turn erected a new wall with them. With the new wall built, the leftover manure had to be removed from the pen, which the other women and I hoisted out in woven polyester sacks, one sack at a time. The job took a whole day. How tired we were! And not to mention the manure dust that filled the air, choking up our noses and mouths. Everyone coughed incessantly. Our necks were caked with manure. In this pit's cleaning session, we removed at least a foot and a half of the manure floor.

There was no time to herd the sheep, so the flock was left to wander about nearby. We worked without rest until the afternoon, but the job was still far from complete. My lower back was hurting more and more. Once when I stooped to lift a heavy slab, I barely managed to stand back up. But I was too embarrassed to let it show, so I pushed myself, even as my movements grew ever more sluggish. Fortunately, I wasn't the only one. By noon, we had all slowed down. When the wind picked up in the afternoon, Kurmash was the first to give in, slumping on his shovel in utter stillness. Not long after, Shinshybek joined in this slumping posture. Cuma worked for a bit longer in silence before suddenly shouting, "Allah!" as he dropped the heavy pickax and plopped bottom-first to the ground. First he took out a towel to wipe his face, then he pulled out his can of yellow Mohe tobacco and papers to roll a cigarette. I thought, it's time, I can finally complain about my back now. But before I had time to open my mouth, Sister-in-law pulled out a long strip of something—painkillers wrapped in plastic. She offered each of us two of them as if she was passing out candy. Like jelly beans, we chewed and swallowed them. Another bout of silence. I was silent too. Thank goodness I hadn't opened my mouth. . . .

THAT NIGHT, WITHOUT CONSULTING anyone, Kama boiled two pots of water to wash her hair, which was immediately met with her parents' disapproval. Cuma said angrily, "There's more work to do tomorrow, your hair will get dirty again. Don't waste water!" Kama pouted, but there was nothing she could say. It was true; in the desert, water is precious.

After another full day of work, we were finally finished. As soon as we set our tools down, Kama and I changed into clean pants (they were so dirty they had hardened) and boiled a little extra water to wash our faces and arms.

But as soon as we had cleaned ourselves up, we received nightmarish news: the flock still couldn't fit in the pen, so the following day we'd need to expand the pen by another hundred square feet. . . .

Just because you've washed your face and changed into clean clothes doesn't mean you can avoid work—we had no choice but to change back into our dirty pants.

On the third day, everyone threw themselves into the work and we finished in time for afternoon tea. We were all exhausted. At noon, when we had sat down to eat boiled mutton on the bone, no one had said a word.

Though the work was hard, I took comfort in the fact that the meals had all been excellent. There was meat to eat every day! And wheat porridge stewed in a meat broth to slurp, with yogurt paste mixed in . . . and potato and cabbage stewed with dried meat, the meat having been first seared in sheep fat . . . and *plov* (pilaf) steamed with chunks of meat. More importantly, the tea those days was spiced with black pepper and cloves. Oh my—the aroma!

As for the sheep pen, this time the size was just right. The sheep were crammed in shoulder to shoulder, so close together that they couldn't even turn around. I imagined that on those long, cold nights, it must have felt warm to be pressed close like that. But herding the flock into the pen became a challenge. To get the last dozen or so in, you had to shove their butts as hard as you could to squeeze them all in.

Cleaning out the sheep pen made of manure bricks

Still, work on the pen was not over. To prevent snowstorms from covering up the manure bricks surrounding the walls, which would have made them difficult to access, Sister-in-law and I spent another afternoon erecting a wide portico out of manure along the outer walls under which we could store a winter's-worth supply of black bricks.

A problem arose from having removed the manure floor from the sheep pen, which was that their "mattress" had become too thin. The air close to the ground was so cold and wet that the frailest of the sheep would struggle to survive the winter. It was up to Kama, Kurmash, and me to spend the next two sunny, breezy days filling up dozens of sacks with wind-dried bits of manure from near the burrow to give the pen a bit of padding. But that still wasn't the end. Every day thereafter, when the flock had gone out to pasture, the people who remained at home would dig up the wet manure from the part of the pen shaded by the wall, then break up the manure, spread it under the sun to dry, and at night flatten it back down. Every few days, a few more sacks of dried manure would be added to the floor of the pen.

4.

Winter Pasture

O N T H E F I R S T D A Y of our journey south, the camels and livestock traveled for a long time through endless hills. It wasn't until midday, after
ascending a final peak, that the world before us opened up to a plain that was
flat enough to gallop through. The earth was pale and boundless, but the sky
was as dark as metal—heavy, lustrous, and hard. Nothing else existed between
heaven and earth. There was another world across from our world, one beyond
the curtain at the world's edge, a seemingly impenetrable world. Yet, slowly
and silently we crossed into it.

In the middle of this expanse, I could fully feel the roundness of the
earth—the earth curved down in all directions as our team of camels inched
along the crest of the sphere.

After about two hours, a metal fence appeared in our sights. It went from
east to west, cutting across everything. We continued, and eventually we were
near enough to see that where the dirt road met the iron fence, there was an
opening. Passing through, we continued farther southwest. After a long time,
we saw the other side of the metal fence—still running east to west as far as
the eyes could see.

Why would anyone undertake such an enormous effort to fence in empty
land in a desolate, rocky desert?

According to Cuma, it was an effort to turn the scrubland into Kanas (Altai County's most famous prairie national park). They didn't want our sheep grazing there anymore; only the wild horses can eat there, so the grass can grow back. Otherwise, when the tourists come from inland, they will say, "I heard Xinjiang is a beautiful place, but there's nothing here besides the desert!"— without grasses and wild horses, there would be nothing to film, nothing to photograph, nothing at all worth looking at. That would be embarrassing! So it has to be protected.

I assumed this was an impromptu explanation some grassroots cadre had offered to the nomads during a propaganda meeting. The real reason likely had to do with the "Grassland Restoration" policy implemented a few years ago to prevent overgrazing. The land was to be partitioned and rotated into use. The metal fence was to remain for five years. So far, it had been there for three.

OUR NEIGHBORS WERE a family of four, husband, wife, a young man, and a baby. Shinshybek was the man of the house. After arriving at the burrow, I asked Cuma what the wife's name was, but Cuma said he didn't know. So I asked what the boy's name was, and he didn't know either. Then I asked about their ages, and he still didn't know. I was perplexed: "Aren't they your neighbors?" I later found out that this was their first year they were neighbors, so they didn't actually know each other.

Until that winter, only Cuma's family had used this pasture of thousands of hectares. Then, Shinshybek's family's land was fenced off because of the restoration policy. For the loss of their pasture, they were compensated with a subsidy. Using the subsidy, they were able to rent pasture land so that they could continue to graze their sheep. That winter, Shinshybek paid Cuma's family four thousand yuan to use their pasture. Given last year's heavy snow, the grass was especially lush. As a result, Cuma's family was happy to rent it out.

After some further probing, I learned that these neighbors owned over two hundred sheep and more than thirty large livestock (mostly camels). In other words, each animal was paying less than twenty yuan for a whole winter's worth of food! They were the model of thrift.

Not long after settling into my new life, on a foggy moonlit night, two travelers who had lost their way arrived, bearing bad news. Apparently, they were headed for a pasture to the north but had gotten lost. They claimed to have been driving a car, but it couldn't have been much of a car, as they were dressed for horseback. One had on a pair of oversized rawhide pants, and the younger man wore a heavy fleece vest with fancy sapphire-colored embroidery. The pair were in a hurry to get back on the road. After sharing the news and asking for directions, they left without even a drink of tea. When the guests left, Cuma flew into a rage. He began arguing loudly with Sister-in-law, and harangued her nonstop as if it was all her fault. Sister-in-law continued to spin yarn on her spindle in silence.

As it turns out, the pasture didn't only belong to Cuma's family after all. Originally, it had been shared by three families. But many years ago, one of the families moved to Kazakhstan. Not long after, the other family changed trades and went into business. In the years since, Cuma's family continued to make use of these thousands of hectares, alone, without bothering about ownership. But as soon as they had rented the pasture to Shinshybek, the family who had gone into business decided to solicit their share. They believed they had a right to half of Shinshybek's rent, so they had petitioned the county authority. Cuma yelled, "He never even comes here, how can he blame me? Never mind the county authority, even if he went straight to the Central Committee, I would still be in the right!" But I really didn't think he was.

After two days of discussion, the Cumas had prepared their arguments and waited for the other family to come reason with them. But the other family weren't fools; why would they bother to come all this way just to argue? Naturally, the government mediator wasn't going to come either. The government is poor, where would they get the money to reimburse the cost of fuel?

So it was that nothing more came of the matter, and everyone heaved a sigh of relief. But I still felt troubled by the precariousness of the life of herders and their pastures.

IN FABLES, THE FINEST pastures are the ones where "milk flows like a river and skylarks build nests to warm their eggs atop the sheep's woolly backs"—a promise of peace and plenty. The reality, however, is more one of desolation, loneliness, and helplessness. In reality, year after year, everyone must submit to nature's will, oscillating endlessly between south and north. In spring, the herders follow the melting of the snow northward, and come autumn, they are driven slowly back to the south. They are forever departing, forever saying goodbye. In spring, lambs are delivered; in summer, they are fattened; in autumn, they breed; in winter, they are pregnant again. The lifetime of a sheep is but a year in the lifetime of a herder, but what about the lifetime of a herder? In this homeland stretching over six hundred miles, in every secret wrinkle on the earth's surface, every nook and cranny in which shelter can be sought . . . youth, wealth, love, and hope, everything is swallowed up.

Much later, a trader came to buy horses from us. He declared that in two years—at best—families of nomadic herders would be a thing of the past. Next year, when these southbound flocks return north to the Ulungur plains, he said, they will never make another journey south again.

I was shocked. "So soon?"

My reaction angered him. He put down his bowl of tea and turned to look at me solemnly. "Have we Kazakhs not suffered enough for you yet?"

I kept quiet. What I'd meant was, even though this age-old traditional way of life is indeed drawing to a close, wouldn't such an abrupt end be traumatizing and disorienting to these people's souls?

After a long while, I couldn't help but ask again, "Are you sure? Who said this? Are there official documents?"

He said, "Of course, there are documents, but not for our eyes. In any case, it's what everyone says."

Cuma yelled out the name of a national leader and barked, "He said it! He called me yesterday on the phone!"

Everyone laughed, and we changed the topic.

I still wanted to ask, "Do you look forward to settling down?" But I realized it was a stupid question. Of course, settling down is good! Who doesn't yearn to lead a stable life of comfort and ease?

In the end, this wilderness will be left behind. The herders will no longer be its keepers. The cattle and sheep will no longer tread its every surface. The grass seeds that drift onto the earth in autumn will no longer feel the force of stomping hooves that bury them deep into the soil. The masses of manure that fertilized their growth will no longer fall on them. This land will remain forever open, majestically alone in its vastness. The wilderness will be left behind.

While to the north, along the banks of the Ulungur, vast tracts of badlands will be cultivated into farmland. Crops will greedily suck on the solitary river. Chemical fertilizers will engorge luxuriant grasses with fats and juices, more than enough to nourish the livestock over the long and cold winters. What better option is there?

WHENEVER CUMA GOT DRUNK, he yelled at me to get out. Had I been the willful type, I would have kicked the door open and left. But after kicking the door open, where would I go? Outside, in every direction, there is only sand and snow. No matter which direction I chose, I would have to walk for a week and still not find a road. Besides, I would have to lug a bag bigger than I was, not to mention the wolves. There was no choice but silent resignation.

When I first arrived to the winter pasture, while the weather was still good, at the end of each day's work I would go on a long walk by myself. Using the black patch around the burrow as a landmark, I set out for several miles in every direction. Crossing stretches of open desert plain, whenever I climbed up a sand dune to gaze out at the landscape, all I saw was another stretch of open plain and another endless ridge of sand—from where I stood, how I wished to see people and homes and chimney smoke! But there was nothing, not even the shadow of a figure on horseback. The sky folded into the earth seamlessly, blue, singular, unchanging. When the light of dusk swept across the plains, the grasses shimmered. The most beautiful among them was a slender white grass. In the waning light, the luminescent stalks stood tall. Their darkness was perceptible only in their shadows, shadows that stretched long and thin eastward like schools of fish swimming mightily in formation over the earth.

I walked for a long time in the deafening silence. When I glanced back, the sheep flock suddenly appeared less than forty feet behind me (when we first arrived, no one tended to them and they wandered freely nearby), heads bowed, chewing on cud. So quiet. I remembered only a moment ago there was nothing behind me. Where did they come from? Why did they approach so quietly and patiently? How could they possibly hope to rely on a flimsy coward like me?

WAS THERE ANYONE or anything in this wild, undependable land that one could rely on? On the second day, after we had settled in, we stuck a shovel into the crest of a nearby sand dune and hung an old coat on it. From afar it looked like a real person standing there—it was meant to scare off wolves. A herder looking for his lost camels had stopped by and offered us a reminder: a few days ago, two wolves attacked his sheep in broad daylight, devouring four of them.

From then on, the dummy became our landmark. No matter how far off we wandered, the sight of the thing standing firm was enough to calm our nerves. When your nerves get the better of you, the whole world turns into a disorienting mirage. This was especially true on cloudy days.

Speaking only a morsel of Mandarin, Cuma says "forgot" instead of "lost." He would say, "This afternoon, I 'forgot' again. Where were the sheep, where was I, here, there, I didn't know!"

I tried asking him for the name of the area where we were living, but such a simple question was beyond Cuma's conception. As such, I still don't know where in this vast landscape I spent an entire winter. All I can say is that it is around a hundred miles southwest of Akehara—three days by horseback—bordering pastures owned by the town of Dopa, where the land rises toward the east and drops toward the west. According to my preliminary findings, there were just over twenty families in the area (separated by a one-day trip by horse), with very few households exceeding four members. There were a total of about ten pastures, each ranging from thirteen hundred to two thousand hectares in size. A rough calculation would imply less than half a person per hundred square hectares. (Later, I checked the official data from the Animal Husbandry Bureau. The population density was even less: all the winter pastures in Koktokay County combined averaged less than one-fourth of a person per hundred square hectares.)

Upon departure, our guests would put down their bowls, open the door, and step into the cold. When the door closed behind them, we could hear them singing. I could relate. Three steps out the burrow door and I couldn't help but burst into song either! When all you can hear is the faint sound of your own breath, when nothing can fill the void of the enormity before you, all you can do is sing. To sing is to expand your presence; to occupy the vast silence with your voice.

KAMA ALWAYS WORE the same pair of cheap, crude red rhinestone earrings, which seemed rather tacky to me at first. But it wasn't long before my perception of them changed. In this desolate land, their color and their sparkle were as glamorous as the sun and the moon! On her finger, she wore a silver ring inlaid with a pink tourmaline stone. This was the real thing, no doubt, and expensive. It endowed her every gesture with beauty and grace.

I had noticed that many elderly Kazakh women's wizened and twisted hands, after a life of toil, were crowded with large, dazzling gemstone rings. Such ostentatious ornaments added dignity into their drab existence, marking every moment of pride and glory in their humble lives. These were the wilds after all—vast, monotonous, lonely, harsh—here, even the smallest of trinkets couldn't but shine brilliantly and intensely.

One day, Kama found an imitation gold ring buried in the pocket of some old jacket. By that point it had been crushed into a mangled clump. Cuma pried it apart, slipped it over the end of a steel rod, and rolled it until it returned to its former shape. As a sign of friendship, Kama gave it to me. I was overjoyed because it looked just like a real gold ring. In the past, I would never have worn a fake ring on my finger. But now, deep in the wilderness, on this vacant patch of our planet, as a member of this humble, even wretched family, owning only the most basic of daily necessities, this ring became my sole indulgence and an important source of comfort. It was a reminder that I am a woman and that I possess hope and passion. Whenever I herded the calves deep into unknown terrain, I couldn't help but touch the ring finger on my left hand with my right hand . . . as if the ring was my body's one antenna, its one point of entry, the place where my body began. Under the blue sky, the ring was ever so bright and so profound.

IN EARLY DECEMBER, every couple of days, teams of colorfully festooned camels and sheep would migrate past our pasture heading south. Kama and I stood on top of the highest sand dune and followed them with our gaze, silently counting the livestock in their herds and calculating their wealth. There was no reason behind it and we had nothing to say about it. They marched on, proud and alone, the most stubborn things across the land.

One day, after morning tea, Kama called me outside. Another team was moving slowly southward across the lands to our west. "Look, no horses," Kama pointed out. Upon a closer look, sure enough there was a lone person on foot, leading the camels and herding the sheep at the same time. Scanning the land, there wasn't another person in sight. Compared to the teams that had passed us on previous days, all of which included motorcycles and resplendent, decked-out horses, this was a pitiful sight. Kama concluded that there were no horses because last night, when this lone man's family had set up camp, the horses ran off; the man was alone because his family was elsewhere looking for the horses.

Whatever the case, it was heartbreaking to see. Out in the wilderness, all kinds of setbacks must be endured; every type of disaster must be allowed.

5.

Our Underground Home

ONE DAY, WHEN SISTER-IN-LAW and I went to gather snow from the dune ridge at the western edge of the plain, we came across a huge burrow with an opening the size of a soccer ball. It was even bigger than the marmot holes one might find in the summer pastures. This meant that the occupant of the burrow must have been at least as big as a marmot, right? What could it have been? All I could think of were wild mice and rabbits . . . but a mouse hole is, at most, the size of an egg, and a rabbit's only slightly bigger than a fist.

The entrance to the burrow was shaped like an *n* with smooth interior walls. I stuck my head in to take a look and noticed a second chamber—a two-room apartment! In the sand outside the hole, Sister-in-law noticed footprints that must have been left by the creature who lived there—they were as big as Ping-Pong balls.

That evening, after returning from herding the flock, Cuma heard my description of the burrow and declared with certainty, "A fox hole!"

So foxes lived underground too.

This made me think of wolves. In the wild, surely wolves needed somewhere to hide from the wind and cold, right? Did they also live in underground dens?

"Of course," Cuma replied.

I tried to picture a haughty wolf digging a hole . . . hard to imagine.

Without shovels and blueprints, animal housing development seemed mysterious and solitary.

I asked, "Do they only live underground?"

"Don't we only live underground?" Cuma retorted.

I thought: that's right! On this ever-shifting landscape, there is no bold vegetation, no solid stones, only endless sand, flat and exposed. Where else was there to find shelter? Burrowing into the ground is the only option. The earth is the safest sanctuary.

But what about the birds? Land-bound animals have four feet, the front two for scooping out dirt, the back two for pushing it away—a burrow will form one way or another. But birds only have two scrawny talons that aren't even webbed. . . .

Perhaps only plants can live aboveground here. But even they have to send their roots deep down to cling on to the earth.

Indeed, only in the wilderness can a person truly experience the meaning of the word "gravity." Earth is simply the largest magnet there is. The living world comprises a single membrane around it, like a skin pulled taught across its surface, afraid of even the smallest separation. Here, even birds spend most of their time scurrying around on the ground on their two measly feet. And when they fly, they glide low and close to the earth. In the wildlands, I hardly ever saw the shape of a bird in the sky, no matter how convinced I was by their lively chorus that I must be near a forest.

But come to think of it, the dog slept on the ground—it curled up all winter long beside the chimney on top of our burrow. The roof radiated heat for his bed. Although pieces of the ceiling would plummet below whenever he moved and the crumbs of manure and dry grass occasionally landed in our tea bowls, no one ever thought to chase him away. In fact, the dog was never even admonished.

OUR HOME WAS BURIED six feet underground and measured less than two hundred square feet. There was a door facing southeast, and a window was cut out facing west covered with a plastic sheet—the lighting wasn't bad. The four walls were stacked neatly with manure slabs. The stove was made using a large portion of an oil barrel, with enough capacity to heat up most of the room. Even so, the face towel I hung a few feet away from the stove was frozen solid. Toothbrushes were always frozen to the cup because of the water that trickled to the bottom. You had to break it off with force every time you wanted to brush your teeth.

Cooking utensils were kept on the right-hand side when you walked in through the door, and every piece of paper waste this household produced—a tattered paper bag; two crinkly, colorful newspapers in Chinese; a sketchbook left by the oldest daughter, Sharifa, who majored in fine art; directions included in packaged food—all had been meticulously flattened by Kama, then used to paper over the sad-looking bare sections of kitchen wall. They hung next to delicately embroidered *ayak-kap* ("pouches") containing salt, tea, needles and thread, and other odds and ends.

As you come down the passage and through the door, there is a step about a foot high. Across from the door is the sleeping platform, which is as long as the room is wide. The three low walls surrounding the back of the bedroom are each a little over six feet wide and are covered with an array of old *syrmak* and *tus-kiiz* wall hangings boasting eclectic, colorful designs. This is the main space in which we carry out our daily lives, where we host guests and rest. The soft and beautiful tapestries that hang against the three walls made the room feel especially cozy. This was all Kama's handiwork. Cuma and Sister-in-law didn't contribute one bit. It is work for a young girl, and by doing it, she is given respect and approval.

Kama had an eye for details. With passion and joy, she poured her heart into beautifying our home. Even an empty plastic soy sauce bottle couldn't be discarded. Once she took off the top part, it became a chopstick holder. And even something as simple as a chopstick holder could not escape Kama's tireless improvement—with a pair of scissors, she cut frills into the edge.

To be frank, the first time I laid eyes on this house, I didn't hold out much hope.

It was the last day of our migration south. Just before we arrived, I had spent five or six hours locked in a struggle of wits and courage with a handful of runaway camels. Flames were shooting out of my eyes and my voice was hoarse from all the yelling. Kama steered the camel team farther and farther into the distance before disappearing behind a sand dune—like she had innumerable times before. I set off as fast as I could to catch up, oblivious that we had finally arrived. I had just coaxed three camels back onto track from the east and was en route to block another two to the west when I noticed that one of the camels up ahead was glancing back suspiciously, as if looking for an opportunity to slip away. I was spent. My knees, hips, and inner thighs were in excruciating pain from the bumpy ride, but I still held on tight and whipped my horse into a gallop, cursing at the top of my lungs. By the time I had finally driven the last two camels up to the top of a dune ridge, I could see that the camel team below had come to a stop. Kama had dismounted. She stood there coiling up the reins. . . . I was so happy I could have cried. No more chasing down camels, no more early mornings to hit the road; no more camping in the wilderness. We had arrived!

Below me there were a number of structures like engravings in the black-ened sand: a manure-walled sheep pen from last year and three squat, dilapi-dated burrows (one of them for the cattle). This was to be our home for the rest of our winter.

Nimbly, I slipped off my horse all by myself (before, because of my bulky clothing, I had to be helped down) and walked toward one of the burrows, horse in tow. One of the door frames and the window were all topsy-turvy; another rotten door had split open; and the walls of a narrow passage had caved in to block the entrance. The manure wall by the door of the other bur-row had half crumbled too. It was dark inside. The window had collapsed and the step at the entrance was flooded with sand. It was a grim sight. How can you call this a home? Even my horse was disappointed, taking a quick look and then turning its face away.

But in only two days, everything had changed. The men effortlessly repaired all the damage like they were playing with toys. They placed new plastic sheets on the palm-sized window, instantly bringing light into the room. Cracks in the door were patched with scraps of felt, and gaps along the door frame were filled in. Cuma and Sister-in-law drove a few camels to someplace far north and used them to bring back sacks of dirt (there was no dirt where we lived, only sand), mixed it into mud, and used it to plaster and smoothen the base of the stove. Cuma performed this type of work with precision. With all his flaws, this man held himself to a high standard when it came to being the lord of his own castle.

Quilted felt *syrmak* were laid out and *tus-kiiz* were hung. Kama draped quilted covers over all visible household items—blankets, clothes, a small iron trunk, a battery pack, a speaker (the kind of MP3 player you stick a memory card into) . . . until everything assumed a feminine and cozy appearance.

One day, when Cuma came home after working on the cattle burrow, he brought with him a dirty plastic clock the size of a palm and said he'd found it on the ground (ten years ago, the cattle burrow used to be another family's burrow). He patiently wiped it clean and asked me for a used battery. With the battery in place, the thing ticked! Pleased with himself, he said, "It's the cattle's clock! If they don't want it, we'll take it!" And so, we called it the "cattle clock." After that, it found its perch, along with the rest of the things in the room, on top of the speaker. In short, both in appearance and functionality, our burrow was becoming more and more like home.

Even the horses took a liking to our burrow, crowding around the doorway as soon as they came back from pasture. They knew that the people who walked out that door were wealthy—they had magical pockets filled with unbelievably delicious corn.

THE OWNER OF THE neighboring burrow hadn't been on pasture for many years. Having been empty for many winters, that burrow was so dilapidated that it was nearly a lost cause. But it was the will of the men to return the burrow to its former purpose, to stand steadily upon the earth and provide a warm and tidy space to shelter.

No matter what limitations life imposes on us—for example, having to make a home in a hole in the ground—it still cannot be lived thoughtlessly. Shinshybek's wife, Sayna, made a point of bringing along her nine-year-old daughter's diploma which awarded her the "Prize for Progress in the New Year." After tidying up their burrow, she carefully pasted the diploma in the most prominent spot—below the hanging clock on the left-hand wall inside the entrance. This way, every guest would know that in this household, there was a remarkable daughter. Even if company was in pitifully short supply out in the wild.

The Shinshybek family's wood door had four crooked Chinese characters written on it: "Thanks a bunch!" The signature below was in Chinese too, in a smaller font: "Shaymardan Ziya." Who was Shaymardan? Who was he thanking? It felt like a farewell note, left for anyone who might be traveling through this desert, happened upon this burrow settlement, and left it undamaged.

Was the child Shaymardan all grown up now? His family had left their flock far behind. He had left the winter burrow far behind, forever abandoning this once-cherished home deep in the desert. His busy and crowded childhood; his robust, invigorating adolescence; his inkblots of joy and sorrow . . . gone without a trace, with the exception of these two lines of characters written in uncertain brushstrokes still filled with hope.

At the peak of a sand dune to the east stood a steel tripod several feet tall. Cuma said it had been left there last summer by a team of engineers prospecting for oil, likely as a marker that there's oil beneath the ground in that spot. These workers crossed a vast desert to this remote location only to take a sample and leave a tripod. Did they take a peek inside the burrows before leaving? Were they amazed or saddened? Whatever the case, they did no harm to the feeble structures.

The burrows ducked their heads low, afraid to move. Curled up in a winter crevice, they seemed meager and shabby, but in fact, they were strong and generous. They were not just homes for humans but also a haven for all the little insects. Even on the coldest of days, flies, dung beetles, and spiders kept us company. And the secret corners were the domain of creepy-crawlies and gnats. How many of the winter's lucky survivors had this warm cavern harbored?

During the winter, we took in frail, sickly sheep and newborn calves, passing one cold, long night after the next in the burrow. They were quiet and calm as if they were even more at home there than we were. The cat found them particularly exciting, always putting on a show of climbing up the central supporting post. The sheep and calf sat in quiet admiration. But if the cat seized the opportunity to sneak up close to them, they instantly turned on it, leaping to their feet, their tiny horns ready. Then, the cat would retreat, hiding behind a shoe (which only hid half its head), silently observing, preparing an ambush.

Once, my cell phone fell out of my backpack, which was hanging on the wall, and the calf chewed on it quietly for the rest of the night. The phone had been turned off, but the calf managed to turn it on by chewing on it. Cuma said, "Little calf misses mama, he wants to give her a call."

Every morning in the burrow, we all clung greedily to our warm beds. Sister-in-law had already lit the stove and boiled the tea. Time and again, she attempted to rouse Cuma and their daughter, but no one heeded her. Eventually she sighed and crawled under Cuma's covers. Kama, who was sleeping at the other end of the platform, squeezed in with her parents too. With the two of them crowding him so, Cuma had no choice but to get up. As he dressed, he grumbled, "Bad little girl" and "Bad old woman."

Come evening, even when it was already late, we were reluctant to sleep. By the dusky yellow light of a solar-powered bulb, Kama embroidered, Cuma read old Kazakh-language newspapers aloud, Sister-in-law spun wool, I read and took notes, and the cat pounced here and there practicing its hunting moves. The kettle had been whistling for a long while when Cuma sighed, "Let's drink some tea." Sister-in-law put down her handiwork, laid out tablecloth and bowls, and everyone gathered in a circle to sip in silence. The light grew dimmer and dimmer. Suddenly, Cuma screamed while pointing to my feet. I looked down—to pour the tea more easily, I had put the milk bowl by my feet instead of on the tablecloth. In my carelessness, the pink kitten, Plum Blossom, had snuck over and was lapping up the contents of the bowl with relish. I screeched as I swiped at the cat, much to everyone's amusement. The last of the milk was ruined by the kitty, what a shame! But no one seemed to mind. They kept ladling the milk into their tea as usual. Indeed, how could that little pink mouth be considered dirty? He was still just a kitten after all.

Our tea drunk and newspapers read, Cuma pondered for a moment before retrieving his iron box from the nightstand. Then, for the hundred and first time, he made an inventory of his little treasures. Inside the iron box was everything of value the family owned: superglue, a spare light bulb, nuts and bolts of different sizes, as well as a stack of wrinkled papers, forms, notes, debt receipts, and the like. I grabbed a sheet to take a look. It turned out to be a prepaid phone plan receipt. What use is that? Rummaging some more, I discovered a plastic bag sealed with several tight knots on top. When I finally managed to untie it, I found a packet of Mohe tobacco! Cuma rejoiced, grabbing it and hugging it tightly. He barked, "Mine! It's mine!" And so, it was a fruitful inventory check after all.

CLOUDY DAYS WERE my favorite because they were usually warm and there was a chance that we might see some snowfall. Snowfall would relieve the drought so we wouldn't have to walk so far to collect snow. But more importantly, on cloudy days there wasn't much sun to charge up the solar-powered battery. If we ran out of electricity, we could go straight to sleep. . . .

The nights dragged on longer and longer. No matter how long you had already been sleeping, daylight was still a long ways away. Anyone who went to the toilet in the middle of the night took a moment to clean out the stove and refill it with a few bricks of dry manure. It was too cold. On cloudy, snowy days, Cuma's arthritis kept him awake all night. He was always getting up to take an aspirin and roll a cigarette, coughing his lungs out. Sister-in-law ground her teeth for long periods at a time and moaned in her dreams—even in her dreams, she was never far from sickness and pain. Kama slept pressed up against me, kicking me now and again. The pink kitten searched for any possible opening in hopes of squeezing under my covers . . . all night. He woke me again and again in the still, dark night, but I wasn't bothered by it. The burrow was safe and tranquil.

BEING A DECOROUS HOUSEHOLD, every part of daily life must be lived with dignity. Even if it was just to go herd the sheep, Cuma took the time to make sure his boots sparkled. And on days when Sister-in-law suddenly handed him a clean change of clothes, he would sing until the sheep came home.

Because we burned manure all day, which produced smoke and ash, a thick layer of soot accumulated on the roof beams. When a careless animal stepped on the roof, ash would come raining down everywhere. As a result, warm days were devoted to sweeping. We all pitched in. First we moved everything that could be lifted outside and covered what couldn't with plastic tarps and polyester sacks. Kama, dressed in dirty clothes and with a towel around her hair, swept all the beams. Then, Sister-in-law picked up the felt rugs and beat them against the snowy ground outside until they were clean. Finally, we returned everything to its rightful place, and felt instantly clean.

Originally the floors of the burrow had been made of sand. After Cuma coated it with a layer of mud, the floor became much more solid. But after a while, the mud became rutted with use. The problem was especially severe at the base of the walls, where without the reinforcement of the mud, sand cascaded down like a waterfall. Cuma patched the mud whenever he found the time. Before the winter's end, all three sacks of dirt were used up.

And whenever Kama had a free moment, she picked up a small broom and swept the ground outside the burrow's entrance. Although sweeping simply meant erasing the hectic footprints in the sand, replacing them with smooth and orderly lines—still, it was necessary!

Weeks into our stay, when the vet came to administer vaccines, Sister-in-law asked him to deliver a bag of food too delicious to eat ourselves to their spring and fall encampment. Living at the encampment at the time were Apa, Kama (who had gone back), and the Cumas' other three kids, who were home for winter break. I found it odd because transportation was so much easier there. Whatever they fancied eating, they could have bought for themselves! Whereas out here, there was nothing to buy even if you had money . . . after all, we were deep in the desert, so shouldn't they have been sending us food?

But after some thinking, I realized—this was the real home! Even though we didn't have a sturdy house, or nice things, or the conveniences of modern life, the cattle, horses, and camels were all here. All of their wealth and hope was here. This was the foundation of their existence. The encampment on the banks of the Ulungur River, on the other hand, was only a fickle, distant satellite that had to rely on this place to subsist.

Interestingly, when the vet arrived, he brought a big bag of *baursak* (deep-fried dough) from the encampment. When he left the burrow, he took a big bag of freshly fried *baursak* back to the encampment . . . why bother?

WHEN WE WERE BRINGING the herds south, Kama and I, along with the camels, always arrived at the camp first and hurried to set up tent and boil tea before the arrival of the main herds. When it was all ready, Kama would always tidy up the temporary camp. But what was there to do really? As far as I could tell, it was humble beyond words, but when I came back from a short stroll, our tent looked like something else—all the blankets were neatly stacked (I had assumed that since the blankets were to be used soon, there was no reason to stack them . . .), and just like in a real home, all the utensils were placed to the right-hand side upon entering the tent, in accordance with custom. She even spread a plastic bag under the bowls and chopsticks. It was the cleanest of all the plastic bags, folded squarely and meticulously. A real "home," even if we would only be staying there for a mere six hours. But when the men herding the sheep flock and large livestock arrived and saw this tidy "home," how their weary hearts must have felt warm and happy!

Our earthen burrow at dusk

6.

Winter Slaughter

AFTER WE HAD SETTLED into the burrow and completed our first major undertaking of fixing up the sheep pen, the next task was the winter slaughter.

Cuma said, "This winter we will slaughter three sheep and our neighbors will slaughter a two-year-old mare." He went on, "Slaughtering a horse is more or less like slaughtering three or four sheep!"

For every herder family, the winter slaughter is a crucial part of preparing for the winter. Through the long winter, all spring, and half the summer that follows, this fragrant meat is the greatest consolation in a life of scarcity. Many of the Kazakh families who have settled in cities still maintain this tradition. At the end of fall, they buy livestock and slaughter it to prepare for the winter. In those months, the green belts of grass that surround urban apartment blocks are riddled with slaughtered sheep hanging on public exercise machines, their skin removed, their carcasses butchered, offal cleaned out, and hair burned off their heads and hooves using blowtorches. . . .

There is no better time of year to slaughter livestock. First of all, every day is colder than the previous one, which is ideal for hygienic storage; second, the sheep, recently returned from the summer pastures, have not yet lost their fat;

and lastly—at any rate this is my guess—heading into a winter of scarcity, it reduces the numbers of mouths to feed.

Although witnessing the end of a life is inevitably a difficult experience for me personally, I nevertheless decided to prepare myself. But when the moment came for the slaughter to begin, Kama dragged me off to help her carry a sack of snow! So exasperating . . . and the sack was so full that I could barely stand up. Three steps, then a break, five steps, then a longer break. By the time I'd lugged the sack of snow over the sand dunes and was nearly home, I saw in the distance that the horse had already fallen! I threw down the sack and ran to see. But by the time I got there, the blood had already been drained. The horse's eyes remained open, silent and still; its body was likewise motionless.

Thankfully, I caught the next day's slaughter.

There were plenty of sheep, and when it came to choosing one, there didn't seem to be much of a difference—to my mind, one was as good as the next. The flock was noticeably more anxious and alert than usual, as if they knew that this time, it wasn't going to be as simple as getting sprayed with "Lice Eliminator." The unlucky one had already been caught, but it still kept jumping and squirming, bleating out heartrending screams. Cuma grabbed onto the wool on either side of its neck and dragged it to the open space outside the burrow where he told me to bring over the kettle we used for washing our hands. Then, he pried open its mouth and told me to pour some water in. He explained, the sheep hadn't "eaten" yet today, "It shouldn't die on an empty stomach, or else its soul would feel mistreated." But a mouthful of water—isn't that only a symbolic gesture? It all sounded a bit too convenient.

Next came the *bata* (prayer). The *bata* happened in a rush, less than half a sentence and it was over, and the knife was out—again, no more than a gesture. I didn't even bother to ask what the prayer meant. When Cuma would lead us in *bata* before sitting down to eat meat, he was equally terse and expedient, a couple of syllables and it was done.

Did the sheep hear? Did it understand? Its butcher had watched it grow up. Its butcher had used his own hands to pick it up from its placenta on the spring pasture floor, gently nestled it in the warm felt sack he had prepared, and after carefully strapping it to the saddle, brought it home. . . . Its butcher had led it across hills and plains in search of the lushest, most succulent grasses, and when it wandered astray, he braved the rain to find it. . . . Time and time again, he gave it delouser and tended to its inflamed wounds. . . . In the cold season, he had led it to the warm southern plains. . . . Did the sheep remember any of it? Could its butcher have felt a shred of hatred or meanness in those happier times? Perhaps that is the way of all life: in the end, to each his own, so long as your conscience is clear.

A Kazakh writer that I like, sister Yerkex Hurmanbek, once said, "You shouldn't die for your sins, we aren't born to go hungry."

ON THE FIRST DAY of winter slaughter, as soon as the horse was killed, the preparation of its meat began. Its blood drained, the men started flaying the skin from the hooves upward. When they reached the horse's abdomen, Kurmash clenched his fist and punched the underside of the belly repeatedly until the skin separated from the fat covering the meat. He laid the hide out on the ground, and the carcass was pushed onto it to be dismembered. While Shinshybek and Kurmash cleaned out the organ meats, the two women took the intestines and stomach away to wash. Cuma and Sister-in-law carried large slabs of leg meat into a yurt where they hung it from the frame to be cut up. Inside the burrow, Kama was preparing lunch for everyone, dicing up a big slab of fresh meat. As for me, I tried my best to help wherever I could.

I had no problem acting as the assistant, but they were always giving me the bloodiest tasks! Hold the flayed shanks, pull out the organs, pluck ribs out from under the skin, carry slabs of meat. The organs of a freshly slaughtered animal are steaming hot, still warm with life, they twitch in your hands, not to mention the squirting blood. . . . I was grossed out, but I couldn't refuse.

Thankfully, the neighbors' baby, Karlygash, woke up and started bawling, so they told me to take care of her. But I soon realized that the bloody slaughter work was preferable! There's nothing more tiring than watching a child—the moment you play, she laughs; the moment you stop, she cries. I had to jump up and down like a monkey to keep her calm. I wondered how Sayna did it. Clearly I was doing it wrong—it shouldn't be this strenuous.

A little over six months old, Baby Karlygash was already a good girl. She seemed to have understood what the day was all about. No matter how much she bawled, the moment someone entered the room, she would cease her tears and start laughing and clapping. When the adults were unusually busy, it meant that for lunch and dinner there would be feast and celebration.

JUST LIKE THAT, by lunchtime, a horse that had been running free in the light of dawn was a heap of meat and bones. We spent the whole morning carefully covering each individual piece of meat and bone with black salt to be air dried. Fat from the ribs and all the other bits of loose fat found between the skin and meat were stuffed into the intestines to be hung up.

After all the hard work, lunch was laid out on the Shinshybeks' family table with Kama's stir-fried meat, as well as *baursak*, *kurt*, and a plate of dried apricots.

I never ate horsemeat, perhaps because horses are too hot tempered? Their meat might be too—unlike sheep, chickens, and the like, docile and weak willed. But that day, I made an exception. It wasn't because I was hungrier than usual, but after all that prayer and slaughter, I felt I could eat with a clear conscience. The plate before me became simply food. It was the final gift of power the horse left to us, to give us the energy to endure the long winter.

That evening, to thank us for our help in slaughtering the horse, Sayna brought us a basin full of meat chunks, offal, and rib sausages.

When she left, Cuma turned to me, pleased, and said, "Horsemeat, that's the good stuff! Better than lamb! Real strong!"

I asked why.

He said, "Because horses are stronger than sheep!"

Strange logic . . .

Later, Sister-in-law minced the horsemeat and used it to make something resembling dumplings. So delicious! She boiled up a huge pot, enough that we had leftovers to warm up and eat for breakfast the next morning. Even though being soaked in water for a whole night made the dumpling skin too soft, they were still so good. I never eat leftovers, but even I ate a big bowl of dumplings in the morning.

THE FOLLOWING DAY was when we butchered sheep. Shinshybek and his family came over to help. And me, I was still the babysitter. . . . When the job was done, we gave them a big basin of lamb and offal as a thank-you. Then, in the evening, we made a huge pot of lamb and wheat porridge to share with Shinshybek and his family. We ate to our heart's content, and drank one cup of cold water after another.

The meal finished, Kama went around with the kettle in one hand and a basin in the other so that everyone could wash their hands. Kurmash didn't wash his hands but asked Kama to bring down the leather harness hanging beside the door. Slowly, he ran the thin leather straps along the spaces between his fingers until every drop of grease was soaked up. Beads of oil from his hands were instantly absorbed by the leather. I was fascinated, so I gave it a try too. The men laughed out loud, but then everyone started to do it. What a wonderful way to maintain leather.

"Why is it that inlanders [migrant workers from south of the Great Wall] working at the same mine [mining is one of our county's core industries] can save money but the Kazakh fellas can never save a single penny?" Cuma declared. "It's because the Kazakhs can't live without meat. Without meat, they have no energy. As for the inlanders, they can eat nothing but steamed bread and porridge all day!" he exclaimed admiringly.

When the lamb, bones, and offal had all been processed, all that remained were the three heads that had been tossed to one corner of the bed pallet. Cheek by cheek, three sets of eyes stared into the distance. No matter how panicked the sheep had appeared before their deaths, now their expressions were peaceful and calm. As we busied ourselves with other things, hurrying in and out of the burrow, we often passed by and sometimes brushed up against the severed heads when we sat down. While chatting with Kama, I often found myself stroking their furry foreheads without ever thinking, "This is a corpse." When I was feeling in a particularly good mood, I even lifted a dead sheep's ear and asked it loudly, "All good in there?"

Several days later, when Sister-in-law had a spare moment, she found sticks with which to skewer the sheep heads through their throats. After lighting a manure fire in the clearing outside, she burned off the fur from the heads. Only then did they close their eyes.

As for the large basin full of blood, it froze into a block of ice that we dumped in the snow nearby. This was the dog's only snack, and he licked it all through the winter. It wasn't until February, when the weather warmed up, that the dog had finally licked it clean.

7.

The Only Water

B EFORE I LEFT, my mother said to me with envy, "This winter you'll be drinking the very best water there is!" I thought it must be true. After all, the burrow was in a desert, where the only source of water was snow. What could be better than snowmelt, which is distilled water fallen from the sky? By contrast, Akehara village is situated on the banks of the Ulungur in the scrublands. The well water in the village is very hard. It's only gotten saltier and more bitter over the years. If you cook with it, there's no need to add salt. And all our clothes come out of the wash stained with thick rings of mineral scum.

In reality, while desert water doesn't taste bad—you might even say it's sweet and refreshing; it certainly does not taste salty or peculiar—but in terms of clarity . . . in the past, seeing water like that would have made me feel faint.

Last year's snowstorms were a disaster, but this year, it was record drought. There was decent snowfall at the end of November, but then it stayed dry until the end of December. On a few late nights, we did get a rare flurry that turned the earth white. But the following morning, when I went outside full of hope, all I saw was the same old black burrow settlement because the snow was always followed by strong winds. I envied the herders to the east. Our snow must have been blown over to them.

Luckily, once the winds died down, snow had accumulated in the ditches along the sand dunes and at the bases of tufts of grass. Unfortunately, collecting snow like this for half an hour only produced enough water to wash one pair of socks. Because the snow had been blown over the desert by the wind, it had collected dirt, hay, and bits of manure, all clumped together. When the snow melted, it was turbid, depositing over an inch of sand in the pot (no wonder it was so heavy!), a number of sheep droppings I refused to count, as well as objects as large as horse dung that, even when fully settled at the bottom of the pot, still left the water suspiciously orange—maybe my socks *were* cleaner.

On the other hand, my socks were stinky, while the water was odorless, so it must be cleaner than my socks. Drink up!

To be fair, we weren't exactly careful about collecting snow. If we had been as meticulous as watchmakers, there's no doubt that our snow would have been a little purer. But at the same time, it would have taken over a week to fill a sack.

I used a shallow plate to shovel small clumps of hard, wind-blown snow into the woven sack. Kama used a ladle. Ever practical, Sister-in-law simply used a broom to sweep the snow into a pile before filling her sack. Kama worked twice as fast as I did, and Sister-in-law was ten times faster.

Cuma never did things like collect snow, which made him rather picky. Every day, after bringing home the sheep, the first thing he did was to peek into the big tin pot. If there were only a few sheep droppings and not a single piece of horse dung, he would observe, happily, "This pot of water must have been brought to us by Li Juan." Correct!

After three days of scavenging for snow like this, I decided I wouldn't take another shower all winter. A week later, I decided I wouldn't wash my clothes either.

The sacks we used for collecting snow had once contained fifty-five pounds of mixed animal feed. Once filled and compacted, they each carried thirty-three pounds of snow. The weight was bad enough, but the distance made it much worse. And each day, we had to travel farther than the last! Snow from the nearby sand dunes had already been collected long ago. Each trip required at least five rest stops, and by the time I got home, I was so exhausted I was seeing stars. Yet, each day required at least two trips to collect enough snow to make water to last a family a single day.

For our family of four, most of the water was used for making tea. Other than myself, everyone else drank massive amounts of tea. Six rounds a day was the minimum, and each round emptied a whole large thermos at least. The rest of the water was used for cooking. We only ate one meal a day, which was a proper dinner in the evening, consisting of noodle soup, hand-pulled ramen, and the like (at other hours, we ate dry *nan* soaked in tea). The remaining water was used to wash the bowls (one bowl of water could clean a whole stack). And the very last of the water was used to wash our hands and faces—pouring water straight from the kettle was the most economical method, using up less than half a basin for all four of us.

Even the little water we washed the bowls with was saved to soak pieces of dry *nan* for the dog or as a nutritional boost for the pregnant cow. When we first set up camp, the mud Cuma used to patch up the base of the stove, ceiling, and door frame was mixed using water we had already used to wash our hands.

IN THE MIDDLE OF DECEMBER, Kama had to leave. Her grandma was ill, so she returned to the banks of the Ulungur to care for her. As a tidy, self-respecting young woman, she refused to emerge from the wild with a dirty face and messy hair. She had to wash her hair. So that evening, after milking the cattle, Sister-in-law ventured out into the twilight in search of snow and returned with a big sack in the dark. Her little girl had enough to wash her hair, and some of her clothes as well.

Even though I had already determined I would never wash my hair again, watching Kama wash hers still left me green with envy. After that three-day journey through the wind and the three days spent working on the sheep pen, my hair had become a dirty clump. More than ugly, it was uncomfortable. So the day after Kama washed her hair, I forced myself to make three trips collecting snow. But when the time came to actually use it, I could only bring myself to use half a basin . . . although I had carried it all on my own, I would still have felt ashamed to use too much of it.

I washed my hair Kama's way, using only a half-full basin to wash and rinse. When I was done, my head was still full of shampoo. The water that dripped from my bangs stung my eyes. Kama believed that when the hair gets to a certain level of filthiness, you had to opt for the strongest of cleaning agents. So, for the first wash, she used laundry detergent, and only for the second wash did she use shampoo. The shampoo had been given to her by her sister Sharifa. She used it sparingly.

Laundry detergent seemed a bit much. . . .

Still, how black that half basin of water had become. As a woman, I felt ashamed. But I consoled myself: Better than not washing it at all, right? And although my hair was still full of harsh chemicals from cheap shampoo, my head felt at least two ounces lighter.

Kama would use the water from washing her hair to wash her clothes. I didn't do that because I worried it would make my clothes even dirtier.

In a grave tone, Cuma announced that he and Sister-in-law waited until April to bathe. I was speechless. Only later did I learn that it was a joke. How could it have been possible? You'd die from itching.

I resisted the urge to bathe precisely because I was worried about the itch; think about it: all lathered up with only a bowl of water to rinse off. A bath like that could only make you itchier. As a result, whenever I itched, I scratched. And if it was somewhere I couldn't reach, I simply leaned into a post and wriggled. Cuma laughed himself into tears as he said, "Li Juan is just like cattle."

Fortunately, I learned that after the itching got to a certain point, it gradually started to go away.

NO MATTER HOW DIRTY or scarce it was, at least we had water. The pastures thirty kilometers north of us didn't have any water at all, not even the foulest of liquids! In the middle of December, on one of Cuma's days off, he went north to help a relative dig a burrow. It was two hours by horse, which is plenty far. Still, it was the same region—so why was it so different? Cuma said there was practically no snow there.

The reason, it turned out, was because it was too flat. When the wind blew, there was nowhere for the snow to collect. The herders there had no choice but to rent a car and drive farther north to the Ulungur River, where blocks of ice could be excavated and brought back. A fifty-five-pound sack of ice fetched twenty yuan . . . the herders could barely scrape by, but what about the livestock? The poor animals had to make do with the minuscule bits of snow stuck to the base of the grasses they ate (and impossible to collect manually). To ingest just a bit of snow, they had to swallow a mouthful of sand.

Cuma said he had never seen drought like that.

When he returned from helping his relative, Cuma also brought eight sacks of ice from the Ulungur River. On the coldest or busiest days, we didn't go out to collect snow, but melted the ice instead. Even though Sister-in-law and I (Kama had left by this point) did our best collecting snow every day, and we all used water sparingly, we still managed to use up all the ice. It was already the end of December and it had still not snowed.

Herding sheep was hard on Cuma. On several occasions, while bringing home the sheep, he stopped at the top of a sand dune just north of the burrow, unable to move. When he got off his horse, landing butt first on the sand, he started slapping and punching his outstretched legs. They must have been frozen numb. There was nothing I could say to comfort him, only, "It's all right, one more day and you can rest. It will be Shinshybek's turn to herd the sheep." He sighed, "Rest for what? Sitting at home is no good, nothing to do, just drink tea all day, and we're nearly out of water. . . ." It was heart-wrenching to hear.

One morning, Cuma went to patrol the pasture's western reaches on horseback. When he returned, he told us that the snow by the dune ridges was thicker and asked Sister-in-law and me to head there once we had finished the household chores, to fill up as many sacks as we could. On his day of rest, he'd drive the camels over to retrieve the sacks.

At midday, the two of us set out with six huge polyester sacks under our arms. After walking nearly two miles across a flat expanse, we gradually entered an area with sand dunes. Sure enough, on the wind-facing side of the dunes were patches of perfect, porcelain-smooth snow as deep as five centimeters. I was thrilled; the sheer number of snow sacks we could fill! If only we could share a few with our neighbors to the north.

Bracing against the cold, howling wind, we shoveled for two hours without pause. The sacks were filled until they were full and hard. We fastened them shut with metal wires and piled them together. As we walked away, I turned to see them still huddled together as if afraid of something. So conspicuous against an empty background . . . might some curious beast come at night and ram them over or kick them down?

Two days later, at the crack of dawn, husband and wife, along with a camel, went there to haul snow. It was amazing to me. A place so far away in the vast wildlands where everything looked the same. Without a road or any markers, how was Sister-in-law planning to find those snow sacks? But they did. This haul of snow lasted us more than three days. Even though it was a bounty, the time and energy involved was still too high a price to pay. Had it not been for our desperation, we would not have resorted to such measures.

THE NEED FOR SNOW led me to observe the clouds. On warm days, when weird-looking clouds appeared in the sky, I'd run to ask Cuma, "Does that mean it will snow?" He would only throw me a glance, unwilling to humor me with a response.

But if they weren't the harbingers of snow, then why did those clouds look so weird? Sometimes, clouds occupied half the sky in long arrays, radiating from the north, truly magnificent. Other times, they were like a pot of sticky rice balls bubbling up from the north. By dusk, they would begin to cluster against an emptying sky, growing massive and haughty. In the end, they would gather into a few wide rivers that ran in parallel, flowing from east to west, disappearing into the sunset.

During boisterous sunsets clustered like mountains, nebulous nights etched with the moon's halo, and those dawns dim and gloomy . . . it must have been hiding, ruminating, brooding, equivocating—a whole month and still no snow! On foggy days, an odd flurry of hexagonal white flakes fluttered our way. At times, the starlit night sky cast off a nonchalant spattering. But those mere sprinkles took flight with the lightest of winds, how stingy.

It wasn't until one dark morning when uneven clouds blotted the entire sky. I climbed a sand dune to the northeast and saw a wave of golden light stretching along the horizon from north to south, crashing toward us, blocking out the sun. I returned to announce with excitement, "It will snow for sure!"

This time, Cuma confirmed it. But then he added, "It won't be much."

Indeed, at ten o'clock that evening, dense snowfall whirled into our camp.

Indeed, it was short-lived, unable to stick.

After bringing home the sheep the next day, Cuma told us that it had snowed heavily six miles to the west, enough to cover your ankles!

I asked, "Oh no, that couldn't have been it, could it? There'll be more this evening, right?"

He laughed, "No, the snow's moved on."

I thought he meant it had gone elsewhere, so I asked in exasperation, "Where to?"

He said, "To Urumqi, to see the doctor." Which was a joke. But it was clear that he was in high spirits.

Still, it was a good start. The sky had finally offered us an opening. From then on, the days remained warm and misty. The promise of snow seemed to hang thick in the air. Finally, at the end of December, before the real cold front came, it snowed three times in quick succession! The earth was buried beneath four inches of the stuff.

As soon as the sky cleared, I ran out to haul snow with glee, bringing back three sacks in under half an hour.

Cuma exclaimed, "Wow! Li Juan is certainly in a good mood!"

How could I not be? There was snow everywhere! A few steps out the door and I could start collecting it, no need to walk one or even several miles. Even more remarkable than its abundance was its purity; the water that melted from it had never been clearer. It was fluffy, soft, and light as a feather. Carrying a full sack home was child's play! In the past, a sack that size would have left me dizzy by the time I got home.

After the sky cleared, it was bright and dazzling beyond words, as if it had been emptied of everything, giving every last flake over to the earth. The sky was no longer so heavy, no longer so burdened.

AND SO IT WAS, with the coldest days approaching, we said farewell to drought. Looking back, our month of drought was manageable, especially when considering our neighbors to the north.

To me, what felt most rewarding was the contrast between the difficulty of hauling half a sack of snow at the beginning to the feeling at the end, when I was transporting snow in leaps and bounds. That's the kind of progress you could describe with a sentence that might begin with "Before you know it!"

Realizing that we didn't need the remaining ice, I melted it all. The three of us closed the door and bathed ourselves in turn. Sister-in-law washed all the tablecloths and towels. Then the next day, she washed all the bedding and pillowcases. And the day after that, all our coats and sweaters. How extravagant!

By the way, Sister-in-law's homemade sheep-fat soap was rather extravagant as well—the size of a basin, a thick, round cake of it! When she used it, she chucked the whole thing into the basin and simply rubbed clothes against it. She didn't find it cumbersome, nor did she think to cut it into smaller pieces before using it.

THERE WAS SNOW, finally, but for a while, it seemed to never stop. It was all right during the daytime when light sprinklings fluttered in and out, but come night, the plastic sheet over the window began pitter-pattering. It was the sound of hail.

When there was no snow, everyone was extremely worried. Now that there was snow, it wasn't long before we started fretting again. Cuma looked up at the sky and said to me, "Last year was like this too, snow for two days, rest for one. . . ." Unfortunately for herders and the herds, the previous year had been a rare disaster.

But as it turned out, he didn't need to worry. After a few large snowstorms during the cold front, the rest of the season stayed bright and clear. It had turned out to be a good year!

A FEW MORE THINGS about snow:

Every few days, whenever snow was carpeting the ground, Sister-in-law would carry the felt *kiiz*, *syrmak*, and *tekemet* that covered the bed outside and beat them against the fresh snow, one at a time. Once cleaned, she laid them back on the bed. Alas, everyone went to bed with their boots on and Cuma's cigarettes were always ashing on the bed. So it didn't last.

The biggest challenge on snowy days was cleaning out the sheep pen. Before the flock was led back in the evening, we had to shovel out the snow (if only we had a big bamboo broom!), then pad it with a layer of dry manure. If the pen had been cleaned but the sheep wouldn't return for a while, several large plastic tarps had to be laid down to stop the snow from covering the pen again. Once the sheep were finally filing in, the tarps had to be yanked back out along with the snow. Sheep sleep crouching on their bellies, and if their stomachs get cold, there's a risk of diarrhea.

Whenever snow covered the solar panel, we quickly ran out of electricity so we went to sleep early, which I liked.

I feared running out of snow so much that whenever the weather got warm, I began to fuss, "If it stays warm like this, we'll run out of water!" To which Cuma only laughed.

On clear days without snow, the flock was unbearably hungry and thirsty.

8.

Cold

WINTER ARRIVED. The sheep and goats grew new coats, the horses donned shaggy bell-bottoms, and the camels were given new felt blankets that Sister-in-law made for them (besides the pack camels, who remained in the buff). The cattle, it seemed, kept their same old short hair. As a result, the cattle were given the special treat of sleeping inside a burrow like us humans, while the horses, sheep, and camels all spent their nights beneath the stars. The most that could be done for the sheep was to raise the manure walls surrounding their pen a bit higher—but how much cold could that really keep out? It was more for keeping the wolves out, I imagine.

The arrival of winter united us against the cold. Every day we stuffed ourselves at mealtime and scooped endless manure bricks into the stove (sheep manure is a weak fuel that burns up quickly). Early each morning, once the flock had been led out, those of us who were staying home would dig up the damp manure from the sheep pen and spread it out to dry. Then we filled it back up with dry manure. Next, we cleaned the cattle burrow, tossing the wet dung and frozen pee-soaked muck out through the high window before laying down dried manure. Shinshybek and his family went the extra mile—they brought the camels into the burrow settlement every night to check that their clothes hadn't been lost or torn during the day.

As the end of December neared, the days only got colder. Sheep walked around with mounds of snow on their backs and the horses were covered in frost, with long icicles hanging from the corners of their mouths. The cattle and camels grew white beards and eyebrows that made them look like wise old men. And anyone who went out on horseback returned with frozen eyelashes and eyebrows, their scarf and hat brim coated in white.

It was during those days that the Kazakh-language radio station forecast announced a cold front in the first week of January, when the temperature in the winter pasture south of the Ulungur would drop to minus forty-three degrees Fahrenheit. They warned the herders not to lead livestock too far from camp. We started readying ourselves. With what little soil we had left, Cuma managed to mix enough mud to plaster over the heavily frosted walls, filling in any leaky corners. Our neighbors covered their cattle burrow with a plastic tarp, at last—until then it had no roof. It had been bothering me. Whenever their cattle came back to a cold home, they would simply cram into our cattle burrow, refusing to leave no matter what.

We even braved the heavy snow to scrape up a dozen or so sacks of dry manure from around the sheep pen to pad the floor, making the thickest "mattress" yet.

Sister-in-law brought back a bucket of dry manure to lay down a pad as thick as a bed, for our sickly sheep "patients."

When she milked the cows, she used a broom to sweep the snow off their backs.

The four hand scoops of corn we had added to the horses' diet was increased to five scoops.

During morning tea, Sister-in-law placed a few cypress twigs on the top of the stove. She explained that the scent they emitted could prevent colds.

FINALLY, THE COLDEST OF DAYS arrived. In the morning and at night, the column of mercury on the thermometer hovered at around minus thirty-one (which was the lowest notch on the meter). I wondered how much lower the actual temperature would drop on the coldest nights, if the mercury would eventually be sucked back into the little ball at the bottom. But even if I had managed to wake up during the darkest hours, I would not have had the courage to leave the warmth of my bed to check. . . . Curled up under my blanket, the thought of their dog, Panda Dog, sleeping out on the roof was heartbreaking.

Sometimes, at nine in the morning, the temperature rose to minus eleven degrees Fahrenheit, but at ten, it dropped by two degrees. One day, it was minus twenty-two at noon. So cold on such a sunny day! How odd.

Perhaps the most unfortunate were those among us who were constipated . . . that meant frostbitten butts!

Calves were so cold that they came home early. They bounded straight for their burrow without bothering to even drink their mother's milk—their one and only proper meal of the day.

On a minus-thirty-one-degree morning, no matter how much steaming-hot, pepper-spiced tea I drank, my feet were still freezing. Sitting barely three feet from the blazing fire, my breaths were white clouds. Moving two feet closer, still white clouds. Closer, a foot away, still white. I kept inching closer when Cuma said, "What are you trying to do? Eat the stove?"

Outside, taking pictures of the wild landscape, I noticed some dust on the lens, so I blew on it out of habit. The humidity instantly froze on the glass, forming a layer of white frost. The more I wiped, the blurrier the lens became.

I finally understood why the elders say, "Icy winds pierce eyeballs." It was icy! It was piercing! Glancing up into the wind for mere seconds, I was covered in tears, my eyes in excruciating pain. My tears then vaporized in the cold, turning into steam that blurred my glasses, which in turn quickly froze, leaving me instantly blind. The wind wasn't even a strong wind, barely more than a gentle breeze. It was that cold.

And another thing I discovered: when it's really cold, you can't whistle. Stiff lips, perhaps?

Our home, despite its substantial repairs, still leaked wind from every crevice. Snow left in a pot overnight refused to melt one drop.

During dinner, I ignored every attempt urging me to drink tea—in fear of having to visit the toilet at night. . . .

ON ONE OF THOSE COLD DAYS, when Cuma returned home with the sheep and was shedding his thick, frosty layers of clothing and yanking off his enormous boots, he sneered, "This is brilliant! Just great! The colder it is, the happier I'll be. Minus forty just doesn't cut it, I'm waiting for minus sixty!" I asked him if anything was the matter and he replied, "The quicker my feet drop off, the sooner I can stop worrying about them freezing!"

I asked, "Why don't you buy felt overboots?" The neighbors had a pair that the two brothers took turns wearing. With boots and calves wrapped tightly in those bulky things, the entire foot looked warm and protected.

Cuma mumbled, "Had 'em last year, not this year."

Last year, the snow had been a disaster. I asked, "Did you ruin them last year?"

But all he said was, "I forgot them when I was over at my father-in-law's."

Cuma typically rode back quite late. At five, with the sun long sunk behind the mountains, the flock was still nowhere to be seen. It was fast approaching six before we even heard them approaching in the dark. As the sheep finally came into view, I'd run down the sand dune to greet them. As I drew near, Cuma would give his horse a kick and gallop home, leaving me to slowly herd the sheep back by myself.

But on the coldest day, Cuma didn't even wait for me to appear before abandoning the sheep and galloping home. When he reached the northeast dune, which marked the final hundred or so meters, he dropped from his horse and flopped to the ground as if he couldn't make it one more step. Sister-in-law walked over to tell him to rest inside. He muttered, "Wait a moment," before slowly sitting up, lifting up his legs, and tapping them against one another. They were numb, perhaps even frostbitten.

As I herded the sheep, my cheeks were so cold, they hurt like they'd been slapped a dozen times, and the back of my head felt like it had been beaten with a stick. Every day, after putting the sheep away and returning to our warm burrow, taking off my bulky coat and pulling off my hat and scarf was like shedding a shell of ice.

After five bowlfuls of tea, Cuma finally said, "Tomorrow, I'm riding to Urumqi!"

"What for?"

"To buy overboots!"

EARLIER IN THE WINTER, Kama had been the one who stayed in bed the longest every morning. Now it was Cuma. When Sister-in-law snatched his blanket from him, he clung to it, whimpering, "Today is one day, tomorrow there will be another! Old woman! There's tomorrow too!" He had an agreement with Shinshybek: each of them would take the herd for five days and then switch. All Sister-in-law could do was rub his back and console him, but he could not keep the blanket.

Before setting out each morning, Cuma spent a long time getting his gear on, especially his boots. Despite being two sizes larger than he would normally need, they still weren't big enough for him to wear both wool and felt socks.

Wearing both would cut off his blood circulation, making his feet even colder. After weighing the pros and cons of wool versus felt, he eventually settled on felt. Though the felt socks were uncomfortably stiff, they were more insulating. Then, he wrapped a length of camel hair around each ankle and went about cramming all this into each boot. Once dressed, he sat down with considerable difficulty to drink three bowls of hot tea before setting off.

"Off he goes to get some exercise!" I announced.

With a sudden seriousness, he stood up straight and began shouting slogans: "Streng-then body! Pro-tect country!!"

Then, whip in hand, he marched out the door.

THE BROTHERS NEXT DOOR always came out of their burrow looking like thieves. From the felt overboots to the hats and gaiters, the only part exposed was their eyes. Cuma, by comparison, was scantily clad—in an old fur coat and two camel-hair sweaters. Before long, Apa had the vet deliver two lengths of raw sheep hide to us from the Ulungur encampment. I spent half a day sewing them into a pair of sheepskin pants. After that, Cuma's life was much improved.

But the sheepskin pants were made from the hides of two different sheep, one leg from an older sheep with a thin hide and the other from a young sheep with thick hide. He decided to wear the young sheep hide on his right leg, which had a chronic pain, leaving his left leg to bear the brunt of the cold. Following my recommendation, he cut a leg from an old pair of long johns and sewed it inside the thin sheep hide leg as a lining.

Protected by his new invincible sheepskin pants, his mood soared. After accusing his neighbors of always leaving him to retrieve wandering camels and clean out the sheep pens, which he said was unfair, he cheerfully set out to clean out the sheep pen and retrieve wandering camels.

Cuma said that before he had his sheepskin pants, he had to tear branches off saxaul shrubs every other hour and light a fire to warm his feet. Once, even though he was only half an hour from home, he still had to stop and light a fire before he could continue. He went on to say that the use of these wonderful burrows was a relatively recent advancement. The Kazakh herders used to spend their winters in yurts! When he was young, everyone sat around a large fire at the center of the yurt, which warmed their faces but left their backs shivering. Outside the yurt, it was winter everywhere. And as hard as it is to imagine, the Kazakh children were so poor back then that they could only wrap themselves in a sheep hide to get through the winter, with no pants or coats.

Hearing this, I volunteered, "Which direction are you taking the sheep today? I'll bring you hot tea in a thermos!"

He replied, "*Koychy!*" No need!

But coming home that evening, the first thing out of Cuma's mouth was, "Didn't you say you'd bring me tea? I was waiting all day. . . ."

BEFORE SETTING OUT FOR the winter burrow, my biggest concern had been the cold. There had been a rumor that this winter was to be a "thousand years' freeze," so nearly all my efforts were geared toward being prepared to keep out the cold. I wore more clothes than anyone else, which invited mockery from my companions.

When I was preparing my clothes, I desperately tried to sew together three pieces of clothes into one. That way, I would have two fewer layers to bring. Following this strategy, the clothes I brought looked nothing like something anyone would wear. In my mother's words, they looked "like something the Monkey King would wear." But since my presence in the winter pasture was an aberration anyway, a bizarre outfit was only to be expected.

I took apart a sheepskin vest and sewed the leather into a cotton coat. I then cut the sleeves off the coat to give my arms more room, resulting in a long cotton vest with a sheepskin lining. But it turned out to be too slim. My good friend Chunr gave me her son's down anorak that he had grown out of. Kids' clothing tends to be roomy and warm, easy to move around in, but the anorak was too short. I also prepared a pair of camel-wool long johns that were so wide that I could fit both of my legs into one side. But they were too long—when I put them on, they bunched up from my feet to my thighs. At least they would give when I walked, and climbing onto a horse would be easier too (in reality, they weren't flexible enough and I still needed a hand to mount). On top of the long johns, I wore my mother's pants. Inside and out, my clothes bulged in all directions. I imagined that having bulk would make me look taller, but in reality, I looked even shorter. So to hide the mess, I wore a coat on top of everything that covered me from my feet to my neck. Even the emperor's robe couldn't do more than that.

I had a nice fur hat, but it was too thin. Getting creative, I sewed three not-so-nice yarn hats inside it, making it an inch thick. It was warm, kept me completely insulated from the wind, but now it was too tight, squeezing my head until it hurt . . . so I cut one side open and patched it with a triangular swatch of cashmere, which finally made it comfortable, but it looked rather odd.

I had also brought a sleeping bag, which was supposed to be able to withstand temperatures down to five degrees Fahrenheit. Baloney. In fact, it couldn't even handle fifty-nine degrees. Even crawling into it fully dressed—coat, hat, gloves on and wearing boots, it still didn't live up to this claim. But at least it was windproof. Worst-case scenario, wrap a few pounds of wool blanket around it. Because I insisted on sleeping in a sleeping bag in spite of the hassle, Cuma decided to call me "gunnysack girl." He kept saying, if a bear comes at night, how will you run?

Even though from top to bottom, day and night, inside and out, I was a farce, I never caught a cold. I saw this as ultimate proof that reason was on my side. I was fine with the way I looked, so no one had the gall to say anything about it to my face. It was only when we went out together that they worried about me, about the embarrassment I was.

NO MATTER WHAT, with every new cold day the previous cold day became "a thing of the past." For most of our lives, the four seasons cycle predictably—coldness isn't a bolt from the blue, or an inexplicable natural disaster, or a permanent darkness. It is the destiny of every orbiting planet, the accepted

Early morning, before the flock headed out to pasture,
the goats jumped out of their pen.

rule of every living thing. Birds fly away. Larvae sleep deep in the earth. Those who remain on the earth's surface, without exception, prepare thick coats and grow fat. Have I not been larding on about my layers and layers too? Coldness is unbearable, but coldness is a matter of course, so coldness must be dealt with.

Cuma said that the most unbearable days of the winter always start around the end of December until the middle of January—there is no avoiding it. After that, as the days lengthen, it will gradually warm up, inevitably. It's true, everything eventually passes. The fact that people feel "happiness" isn't because life is comfortable, but because life is hopeful.

One evening in early February, as I was collecting snow on a dune ridge to the north, I looked up and saw the sun hanging high above the desert. Previously, around the same hour, the sun had been half sunken beneath the horizon. And its angle of descent had shifted noticeably to the north. A constant wind was blowing across the land. I faced the wind to determine its direction. East, it was coming from the east!

On the seventeenth of February, my journal noted the following: clear sky, very warm. When Kama came back, we went to collect snow together, not wearing our hats, only jackets. When we paused to rest, she said gleefully, "It's like summer! It's just like summer!"—as if she had already forgotten about the winter only a few days ago.

9.

The Sheep's Winter

EVERY MORNING, WHEN Cuma set out with the herd, he would stop his horse next to the dummy on the sand dune to the north and stare off into the distance. After a long time, he would reach for his Mohe tobacco, slowly roll a cigarette, then slowly smoke it. Sometimes, he would climb down from his horse, lay on his side next to the dummy, and continue to stare at some faraway place. Who knows what he was thinking about in those moments of stillness. What would send him into such silent, far-off bouts of contemplation.

Herding is hard work. He set off around ten in the morning, driving the flock across the desert with no food and no water. He circled around until the sky verged on black before bringing the sheep back home.

I asked Cuma, "What do you do when you're out there herding?"

He replied, "I herd."

Sorry I asked.

The wildlands are vast and empty—what else was he supposed to do? Of course he sat on his horse and followed the sheep around! Cuma became emotional: "Like a fool! I'm just like a fool! Wherever the sheep go, I follow! Seven hours, seven hours a day!"

Which was why, before he set out every morning, he spent a long time dawdling at the doorway . . . the loneliness that awaited him, you'd have to experience it to know.

I asked, "When the weather's warmer, will you let me herd them for a day?"

He retorted, "If you were to herd, the sheep would never get enough to eat!"

"How come?"

"If it were you, the sheep would be home before two o'clock."

On a darkest of snowy nights, when there are no moon or stars, heaven and earth are indistinguishable. I stood beside the dummy on the dune ridge and waved a flashlight to the east, offering a beacon to the herder returning in the dark so that he would not get lost, making circles in the gloomy night. Had there been a thick fog, even the flashlight would not have helped. Cuma said, "In that case, the whole family would have to go on a search."

I asked, "What if the people doing the searching can't find their way back either?"

He said, "If that person is Li Juan, then it's too bad. Sitting at home all day, never herding a sheep, what's the use of coming back anyway?"

As non-herding people, Sister-in-law, Kama, and I cleaned the cattle burrow and sheep pen every day, hauled snow, made *nan*, embroidered . . . but even if we worked from morning to evening, it still wouldn't have been nearly as tiring as herding.

I asked Cuma, "Where you go to herd, do you pass by any homes?"

"No," he replied, before saying to Sister-in-law in Kazakh, "She thinks when I herd, I can just pop in at people's houses and have some tea!" They all laughed.

I suggested he take a thermos of tea with him the next time he went out. He could fasten it to the back of the saddle. Or take a *kazan* pot and *sajayaq* (tripod) along with tea pellets and salt, so whenever he got cold, he could collect snow and make tea.

That's when he told me the story of the "Han shepherd." Once, at the Red Flag Dam (a dozen or so miles downriver from Akehara), there was a Han, herding for the first time. He had with him steamed bread, pickled vegetables, and water. He ate the salty pickled vegetables with steamed bread for lunch, and then, when he took the lid off the bottle, the water was frozen and not a drop would come out. He even tried to melt it by wrapping the bottle in layers of clothes. . . . After delivering the punch line, Cuma cackled.

It wasn't particularly funny, but picturing the Han's chagrin, his pathetic, adorable effort . . . I ended up laughing anyway.

Cuma's point was this: if you want to make it in the wildlands and survive its winters, any fear of pain or hardship will be met with derision.

THE HERDER'S WINTER is harsh and lonely, and equally, the sheep's is long and grueling. Every day, from December to March or April of the following year, the flock must leave their pen precisely at first light to wander the wildlands, scouring for withered grass. After they leave, the damp and warm sheep pen steams with white mist. During the day, while the sheep are out, bits of frozen snow float about. The sky is always overcast, the sun always gloomy.

At dusk, when the sheep should be on their way home, Sister-in-law and I clamber through the heavy snow to gaze east from the top of a sand dune. The world is a dim blur. Muffled calls reach us as if in a dream. After some time passes, camels emerge into view, galloping toward our burrow settlement. As darkness deepens, the snow picks up. The plastic tarp that once protected the sheep pen from snow has long become the roof on Shinshybek's cattle burrow, leaving snow to accumulate in the pen . . . but the sheep are still nowhere to be seen. From the burrow comes the sound of crying; Baby Karlygash has woken alone. But Shinshybek's family is out herding cattle, tying down camels, too busy to attend to her. Finally, at half past five, Sister-in-law is the first to spot something and calls for me to follow her east. As I walk, I find myself thinking, good thing it's snowing, if we get lost, surely we'll be able to follow our footprints back, right? But on second thought: with this much falling snow, won't our footprints get covered up? . . . The night is bigger than the land itself. To be swallowed by such "bigness" is much more horrifying than to be literally swallowed by anything "ferocious." But then I see the sheep—they were really there, not so far away, undulating through the dark, all covered in thick blankets of snow. What had they experienced that day? To be so quiet.

BEFORE SETTING OUT EACH DAY, Cuma would squeeze his way through the crammed sheep pen to check for signs of illness. If he found one with pus-filled yellow sores around its mouth, he would scratch off the crust with his fingernail to expose the bloody flesh beneath. Then he would call me over to pour saltwater over the wound, always turning a perfectly good mouth into a bloody, dripping mess that stuck out of the flock like a sore thumb. On such a cold day—it made me nervous, like it was something that wasn't right, but I was powerless to stop him. He had been herding sheep all his life after all, so it must have been something you could only understand with experience.

On the coldest days, Cuma would walk around with a kettle in his hand, looking for something. Every now and then, he'd grab a sheep, straddle it, pry its mouth open, and sprinkle water in it. I asked what he was doing. He replied, "Brushing its teeth." You wouldn't believe the things he says, you should see for yourself. I watched carefully until I learned that he was feeding the sheep pills. Only then did he admit that he was curing the sheep's "cold." When I asked how he knew which sheep had a cold, he said, "Runny nose, sneezing." Of course, his words should be taken with a pinch of salt, but my own observations were no better either.

As for when to apply the delouser . . . I couldn't figure that one out at all. I noticed that he rubbed the stuff mostly across their backs, but sometimes on their bellies as well. Maybe he determined the location of the bugs according to where the wool was messier? Where a sheep itched, they'd rub against the pen wall. Ah, on such a cold day, sheep's wool was like a thick, warm blanket. The lice must have been living in comfort, with a warm home and plenty to eat.

For an outsider like me, a sheep's existence seemed fragile and full of misery. Disaster lurked around every corner: the endless treks, the cold, the hunger, the pain of disease . . . but after all these thousands of years, they still managed to survive. Most of the time, what we observed were flocks wandering optimistically over the earth. So let us speak no more of their misery—it is only life's inevitability.

Besides, a sheep's fate so seamlessly dovetails with the rest of nature—how they resemble plants! They sprout in spring, grow lush in summer, set seed in autumn, and harbor that seed all winter long, pregnant, waiting. . . . While chasing the flock through the wildlands, I often thought about how most of them were with child, how most were calm, content mothers. Suddenly I felt the winter's significance running deep and far.

ONE DAY, AFTER BRINGING the sheep back, Cuma didn't immediately drop from his horse to hurry home. Instead, he reined his horse to one side and watched us herd the flock into the pen. Then, he pointed to a brown lamb with parted bangs that was sluggishly following behind the rest, and said, "That one, it's struggling, take it home and have a look." So Sister-in-law and I grabbed two legs each, flipped the lamb on its belly, and carried it into our burrow.

The lamb with the parted bangs looked frail; its ribs jutted out beneath the flesh. Cuma said that earlier in the day it was so weak, it was wobbling. But after examining it with a flashlight, we found no external injury, so perhaps it was just too weak. We decided to keep it "under observation" for a time. Like that, our burrow acquired a new member.

We set up a nest near the head of the bed and dug up a sack of dry manure to give it a "mattress." Every day, it was given a patient's meal—kernels of corn. Even so, it couldn't adjust to this new life. After returning each evening, the patient did all it could to resist our invitation inside. Sister-in-law and I struggled for three days carrying it inside. On the fourth day, Sister-in-law furiously seized the sheep's middle and swung it over her shoulder, gripping its front hooves in her right hand and its hind hooves in her left, hoisting it inside. By the fifth day, she simply grabbed one hind leg in each hand and pushed it inside like a wheelbarrow.

Sheep are weak, but they're no less stubborn than a cow or camel. The lamb with parted bangs not only refused to follow us into the burrow, it rejected the hot stove and corn, preferring instead to curl up in a corner looking lonely and stressed. It didn't eat or drink, lying beneath the window until morning, chin perched on the edge of the bed, eyes wide and unmoving. Its body tensed up at the slightest noise, ready to defend itself. But how could we just leave it alone? Every day, Cuma and Sister-in-law had to fight to shove half a bowl of corn into its mouth. A few times we even fed it our own food—cracked wheat. Husband and wife teamed up, one person would pry the lamb's mouth open while the other shoved corn down its throat. Then they clamped its lips shut so it couldn't spit anything back out. But somehow, it was able to do just that, spitting up however much we fed it, wasting a large amount of food. Sister-in-law was so angry, she slapped it in the face. Cuma, just as angry, declared, "Might as well be dead! Good riddance!" And, "That's one day of food we won't be eating!" (half a bowl of cracked wheat can yield a whole pot of porridge).

Sister-in-law tried feeding it salt, but the sheep still refused, sending granules across the manure floor. We were truly at a loss. What sheep doesn't eat salt?

Even though it was breaking our hearts, we still didn't give up on the lamb. Every night, when the sheep returned, we patiently searched for it beneath the stars for a long, long time (finding one sheep in a flock of three hundred near-identical others was a miracle as far as I'm concerned . . .). When it was cloudy, we had to use a flashlight. At that time, a cold front was passing over us. It was so cold.

I suggested that we put a marker on its body somewhere, maybe spray-paint some lines on its back, something that would make it stand out in the crowd. But they didn't take my suggestion. It wasn't until the following day, when heavy snow coated the sheep in blankets of white that I understood why. . . .

So I suggested tying a piece of red cloth or some sort of colorful fabric around its neck. Sister-in-law considered it for a long time before she agreed. She rummaged through the yurt beside the burrow for a long time before finding a red neckerchief her children used when they were little. Wearing the neckerchief, the lamb immediately acquired a sort of gravitas. It had become a glorious Young Pioneer.

A week later, our Young Pioneer had finally gotten used to this weird, warm space and began exploring its every corner, sniffing and ramming everything it came across. Later, it even mustered the courage to sniff my hand and nibble my toes, but it still refused to eat the fanciest of feeds, corn. How ridiculous! If any other sheep was given even the smallest kernels of corn, I guarantee that it would've been smiling ear to ear.

I asked, "Could its throat be swollen? Maybe it can't swallow?"

Cuma barked, "I saw it eat grass today!"

Incredulous, I tore off a leaf of napa cabbage to give to the sheep. After a sniff, it swallowed it whole.

Now, I was angry: "Corn's too hard for you then!"

But how could we feed it cabbage? We only had half a head left, and we only used a few leaves a day to boil with the family's evening dinner. So we forced the sheep to eat the tough corn.

Finally, on the tenth day, our Young Pioneer finally seemed to have fig-ured it out. It finally understood that we weren't trying to hurt it. It finally realized how good corn is! And after it took its first bite, it began chomping like a hungry wolf. We were delighted. After eating its fill, it ran over to the tin pot at the other side of the stove to drink some water. That was our water for cooking! But no one said anything; we just made sure it didn't drink too much. Drinking too much water with a belly full of dried cereal can make you burst. After it had had enough to drink, we tied it to a post. The next day we let it drink some more. From then on, the lamb's standard of living had greatly improved—there was no need to crunch snow anymore.

Having adjusted to domestic life, the Young Pioneer no longer needed to be pushed or dragged. It only needed a few pats on the back before it began trotting straight for the burrow with its warm stove and corn kernels.

Once inside, it hopped down the step and casually traipsed over to the bedside. The pink cat would come to welcome it with a kiss. Then it went over to the right-hand corner of the room to drink the clean water we'd left for it. It felt right at home! If we didn't tie it to the post by the time it was done wandering about the room, it would have jumped onto the bed and stomped around.

On quiet, cozy nights, as we ate and chatted, it stood a couple of feet away, peeing—*pssh pssh pssh*. It was a peaceful coexistence not without its small joys.

But right as Red Neckerchief settled into this new life, becoming dependent on it even, Cuma decided that it was time for the Young Pioneer to be discharged from the hospital. He said, "Look, all cured!"

During one of Cuma's days of rest, he and Sister-in-law built a small pen in the corner of the main pen. They covered the top with a plastic tarp and hung felt curtains around it, making it much warmer than the outside pen.

I asked, "Who will be living here?"

Without looking up, he said, "Li Juan will."

I had such patience. "It's for the pregnant sheep, yes?"

Head still down: "Yes."

And yet, that evening, when I went to look—what? It was clearly for the goats!

After observing for a good while, I noticed that while some of the goats were fighting to get in; others stayed out as if their life depended on it.

So I said to him, "I bet it's for this year's kids!"

But he replied, "Big ones, little ones, they can all use it."

Question: "So, it's for the unhealthy goats?"

Answer: "Sick ones, healthy ones, they can all use it."

In the end, I never did figure out which of the sheep or goats would be staying in the shelter. The Young Pioneer, however, who had its "burrow residency status" revoked, was staying there for certain. Upon its discharge, Sister-in-law sewed a small corn mask for it. The corn mask was a small cotton bag tied with string. The bag is filled with corn and placed on the lamb's mouth, the rope tied behind its ears. This way, when it ate its special meal, no other sheep could steal from it. Cuma assigned me a new task: when the sheep return, put the mask on Young Pioneer and wait for it to finish eating before putting it in the pen.

He announced to everyone, "All right, from now on, this will be Li Juan's only responsibility!"

I complained, "But that's a difficult job."

He asked why. I said, "It takes a long time to find the sheep, a long time to put the mask on, a long time to wait for it to eat the corn, then take the mask off, then run it into the shelter—all in the freezing cold!"

He laughed as he translated my words for Sister-in-law, gesticulating and embellishing. Then he added, "This winter, Li Juan will herd one sheep!"

In reality, there was no need to search for Young Pioneer. As soon as I dangled the corn mask in front of the flock, the red neckerchief emerged, rushing toward me, nibbling my hand, ramming my waist, harassing me incessantly.

But all good times come to an end. One day, Cuma said, "Don't give it any more corn! Look at how high it hops, it's completely cured!"

I didn't care and continued to give it the special treatment . . . after all it was a lamb that almost didn't make it through the long winter! It nearly died, so it deserved endless comforting.

EVER SINCE THE SHELTER was created, herding sheep into the pen became strenuous work. Once they were inside, we had to pick out the sick sheep one by one and enforce social welfare upon them. Fortunately, a few days of the good life was all it took before the sick began making their own way into the shelter. But a couple of dummies, their brains apparently frozen, forced Cuma and Sister-in-law to look for them in the dark with flashlights and manually drag the ingrates where they belonged.

On those coldest nights, the clear black sky was only lit with a gradually waxing new moon and a light they called "Chulpan" (even though it was the planet Venus). Using our flashlight, we searched for the last few sick sheep that slipped through. We searched again and again, silent and patient. Despite the howling wind, squeezing among a flock of sheep left us feeling warm and at ease. When all the patients had been gathered, we drew the curtain around their corner, closed off the main pen's exit, carefully sealed the cracks with pieces of felt to prevent the sheep sleeping near the exit from catching a cold, and left. Soon, the sheep crouched down, one by one, and drifted off to sleep. The night is long. Keep warm and wait for the light.

TOWARD THE END OF JANUARY, Cuma started to carry a felt bag with him to pasture for the expecting ewes—it was to wrap up the newborn lambs. Even though the best lambing season wasn't until the warmer months of April and May, there were always a few disobedient little ones who arrived early.

These lambs enjoyed the same special treatment as the Young Pioneer, starting their lives in the burrow.

In February, the days began to lengthen and the weather gradually warmed. It was time for the two families to clean out the sheep pen once more. They dug down a foot deep, using the manure to thicken the walls to more than three feet and increasing their height a fair bit too. This was to prepare for the impending windy season.

In mid-February, the "hospital wing" was torn down. When the flock returned in the evening, only the goats went into the main pen, while the sheep lay for the time being halfway up the sand dune to the east. It wasn't until the middle of the night, when the temperature reached its lowest, that the rest of the flock was herded inside. Cuma said as the days get warmer, the bellies of the pregnant sheep get bigger, the pen gets smaller, and being squeezed too close together will make them too hot. . . .

Whenever we discussed the future, Cuma would talk about the spring pasture. Our spring pasture ran beside the national highway through a place called Sanchakou. Setting out from the banks of the Ulungur River to the

Our Young Pioneer stepping outside, midrecovery,
to join the rest of the flock, searching for food

north, it was a three- to four-day walk (without newborn lambs, it would have only been two days). The flock would stay there for a little over a month. After the spring lambing was finished, they'd continue north toward Kiwutu and proceed into the summer pasture from there.

Kama gleefully listed off all the good things about Sanchakou: no need to stay in a burrow or a yurt, we would sleep in a brick house instead! And there's cell-phone signal by the road! . . . And how Kiwutu was great too, good cell signal, and warm enough to wear a T-shirt . . . and how great the summer pasture was, the water was good, the grass was good—even Apa would be living with them there . . . all which set my imagination ablaze, giving me the urge to follow them one season after the next! But Cuma had to be a jerk about it, always talking about how I only herded one sheep all winter long. . . .

Masters of the Wilds

10.

Kama *Suluv*

N INETEEN-YEAR-OLD KAMA IS about five foot five inches tall, willowy and graceful. Her skin is pale, eyebrows fair, and she has pretty, rosy cheeks. Her hair, though perhaps thinner than she'd like, flows silky and glimmers with the same subtle golden hue as her eyelashes. Her sage-colored pupils are set into a clear ring of black. Kama may have a baby face, but if you just glance at her, she is not without mature beauty. Given a closer look, the first signs of aging are already visible on her forehead and around the corners of her eyes. The hardship of life on the pastures takes its toll.

Weirdly, despite her daily manual labor, Kama's hands are white, slender, and unblemished. Except for her fingernails, which are seriously gnarled, with deep grooves cutting into their tips, likely a symptom of years of vitamin deficiency. To conceal this blemish, she uses hair dye to color her nails a bright tangerine.

I once decided to call Kama "Kama *suluv*"—"Kama the beauty." She bashfully refused my compliment and then called me "Li Juan *suluv*."

Nearsighted as I am, even with glasses, things that are distant remain a blur. I was always complaining, "My eyes don't work." So, the second time I called out "Kama *suluv*," she shot back, "Your eyes aren't working."

THIS YEAR, WITH THE ADDITION of Shinshybek and his family to the pasture, the two families took turns, so the work of herding sheep became less onerous. Once the coldest days were past, Kama *suluv* took over the herding from her father. The previous year, the family had relied on this girl to do all the herding. The harsh winter and their lack of neighbors meant that Cuma, the head of the household, had other more important work to do. Because of last year's rare blizzard and record low temperatures, half the family's livestock froze to death, and they lost their only mount. Cuma spent a long time trying to find the horse, leaving only Kama and Sister-in-law at home. Every day, Kama herded on foot, while Sister-in-law did housework and watched the cattle and camels. Apparently, the snow last year was so heavy that it buried everything. The path that was cleared by the camels in the morning was completely filled in by the wind and snow in the afternoon. The hardship . . . one could only imagine.

Herder girls are a rare sight on the pastures. There's a Kazakh proverb that says, "A girl is a guest in her family." She is only born there and grows up there, but she will eventually marry and become a member of another family. Therefore, she must be treated kindly and given respect, like a guest. That said, even without such a custom, wouldn't the parents feel guilty? Making your daughter work like a boy . . .

Cuma said that come next summer, they would not be sending Kama out to herd, no matter what. They planned to help her with an investment so that she could open a convenience store in Shaikyn Bulaq. They even included me in this plan. Kama would be in charge of selling and I would be in charge of supplying. The two hardworking partners would sell things at the lowest prices, certain to incur the wrath of all the other shopkeepers. Cuma had a special kind of antipathy toward continually rising prices.

In my opinion, running a store is a hectic, busy line of work, not to mention the thin profit margins. Kama was better off opening a little eatery. She could make anything taste delicious; business would be booming for sure. I evaluated all three of Akehara's eateries and concluded none could hold a candle to Kama's cooking.

Cuma said, "I already thought of that, but there are too many Kazakh drunks! A girl running an eatery all on her own is too risky."

I agreed, "That's true," and thought to myself, "You're one to speak, you're a drunk yourself!"

KAMA HAD DROPPED OUT of school during the first year of middle school and had been running with the herd for the five years since. But even after five years, she could still recite from memory long passages from her Chinese class: "Spring is here, the swallows fly back from the south . . . spring rain pitter-patters . . . the grass is green," and more complicated poems, like "Pitch-Black Eyes" and "Big Blue Ocean." She knew the morning exercise routine, which she always did to the music of *Kara Jorga*, the "Black Horse Trot"; and she made me hold her feet while she did sit-ups; and she liked push-ups, standing long jumps, the triple jump, and in general practicing the many things you only ever learned in school.

When it came to her time in school, Kama had a lot to say. She told me they called her Chinese teacher "Little Teacher," and when I asked why she wasn't called "Big Teacher" (I assumed it was the surname *Xiao*, homonym of "little"), she explained that this "Little Teacher" was from the Grain Team (a Han work brigade stationed near Akehara village) and used to sell vegetables. The vegetables probably didn't sell well, so she decided to try teaching. As Kama fondly recalled, "'Little Teacher' was wonderful, she always complimented me!" I concurred, "Of course she did. You are a good student who loves to learn and works hard," which made her even more blue.

She said, "I've been herding sheep for five years, while my big sister has been drawing for five years."

When Kama was fourteen, Sharifa, her sixteen-year-old sister, wanted to study art in the Normal School in Ili. Sharifa was the pride of this humble family. Ever since she was little, she'd been able to replicate any drawing she saw. She had quite a reputation in her family and among the clan folks. No one could bear to crush Sharifa's dreams. But the only boy in the family, Zhada, wasn't ten yet, and the third sister, Nurgün, was still a child. There was no one else who could do the work. So, it fell to Kama to drop out of school and follow her father onto the pastures.

This made Kama rather sad, but she never complained. She loved her sisters and brother. Mention any of them and she'll have countless good things to say about them—Sharifa was great at art and dance; Sayragül excelled at singing and learning; Zhada was the smartest, he could even repair motorcycles. And lastly, she sighed, "I'm not good at anything, so I herd sheep. . . ."

I didn't know how to comfort her, so I just repeated over and over, "Now, now . . . that's nonsense, such nonsense!"

The truth is, Kama was far brighter than the average girl her age. Had she stayed in school, she would have excelled.

Kama told me that when the local youth gathered at the Kara Jorga Ballroom in Akehara, they took turns singing in front of a mic. Deep down, she really wanted to sing too, but she didn't dare, even when everyone was egging her on. Shyness and insecurity—just imagine, the girl barely spends one month a year among other people in Akehara. The rest of her days, it's all deserts and plains, flora and fauna; the only companions of her youth are cattle and sheep. Though many women herd, it was rare for girls as young as Kama to work the winter pasture.

At home, Kama was a happy, relaxed, and playful young woman. Every morning she'd wriggle into her parents' warm bed to snuggle, nothing like a nineteen-year-old. Yet her parents seemed to enjoy her childish side and doted on her endlessly. Except for when it came time for work—then the couple was all business and refused to spare her feelings even one bit. Whenever I saw Kama bringing back the horses at dawn, her face blue from the cold, I felt pity. But her parents found it perfectly natural and simply shouted at her, "C'mon, tea's ready." I couldn't understand how parents could be so heartless! But the more I thought about it the more I realized: feelings are really only useful for enjoying the happy moments in life. Otherwise, it's better to use them sparingly.

Young Kama was diligent and attentive. Neighbor Sayna often asked for her help tidying up her house. A request like that was never an order, and it wasn't to take advantage of her, but rather a recognition of her abilities, a way of praising her.

When drinking tea at the neighbor's, Kama felt like a host in her own home, cutting *nan* and pouring tea for everyone. She never sat still in her seat like a stranger.

NOW THAT SHINSHYBEK and his family were sharing the workload, Kama wouldn't be as busy, so she laid out the following plans: embroider two decorative white scarves following a pattern (even though she was copying a pattern, she ended up with much neater and prettier scarves) to hang over the *tus-kiiz*, add embroidery to two new *syrmak*, sew a set of black velveteen saddle decorations for her horse (she was a big girl now and needed to look elegant while riding), complete a cross-stitch pattern with over forty different colors, and make a small felt cushion. Having achieved all her objectives, she still had time on her hands, but she had run out of projects. She groaned, "I'm out of things to embroider, what do I do now?"

Kama's hands were nimble. A lot of girls learn to be nimble through prac-tice and experience, but not Kama. There were so many tasks that she could master on her very first try. The designs of her band-weavings were rich with variations. Patterns transformed through such a complex logic that it was almost dizzying to look at. They were nothing like next-door Sayna's designs: three lines, a circle, three lines, a square.

On the *syrmak* over our bed, the sections that were sewn by Kama were clearly better than those done by Sister-in-law. The needlework was stunningly precise.

Perhaps it is because dexterous people are more inspired; Kama wanted all her embroideries to be original, refusing to do something that had already been done. Before drawing up a pattern, she'd come up with several different designs in her sketchbook and even ask me for my opinion.

I pointed at one design and exclaimed, "That radish is brilliant! It's blooming."

She roared, "*Koychy!* That's an apple!"

I quickly pointed to a different design. "The cabbage is nice."

By now she was on the brink of tears. "That's a tree—an apple tree. . . ."

In any case, my point was: whether a radish or a cabbage, they all had ele-gant forms and graceful curves. Were she to study art like Sharifa, there's no question she would have succeeded as well.

I once saw one of Kama's round *syrmak* back at the encampment in Ulun-gur. The perimeter was done according to traditional patterns, but in the cen-ter, there was an adorable teddy bear wearing a red bow tie! Still a child after all, she said she had copied the design from her younger sister's T-shirt.

So when Sayna set out to make a new rug, she asked Kama to use her tal-ents and help design the pattern. Kama asked me, "What's something no one else has sewn before?"

I thought for a while, then declared, "The Gate of Heavenly Peace."

"*Koychy!*" She burst out laughing.

IN BRIEF, KAMA *SULUV* was pretty, clever, and capable, but somehow, she still didn't have a boyfriend. If I broached the subject with her, she would panic and say "*Koychy*" nonstop. She was only two years away from being of marrying age, but in her mind she was still a little girl.

When we stopped to rest on the way home, carrying sacks of snow, Kama began grumbling about all the clothes she was wearing: the jacket used to belong to her little brother, the sweater was borrowed from her mother, the thermal pants belonged to her father, the jeans were hand-me-downs from her sister, even the socks were Grandma's . . . all things considered, only the gloves and shoes were truly hers.

I said, "It doesn't matter. Once you're married, everything will be yours, your man included."

Kama grabbed a handful of snow and chucked it at me.

One evening a few days later, after completing work on the cattle burrow, while waiting for the sheep to return, the two of us sat quietly in the dark. It was cold out; we planned to wait until the sheep were a little nearer before going out to meet them. In the dark, neither of us felt much like speaking. Then Kama started to sing.

Her voice wasn't clear, but it was moving, crooning a melody winding and melancholy. I listened quietly. Light from the stove danced across her face as her body melted into darkness. Such youth and beauty, but no one was there but me to see it.

Later that evening, braving the cold wind, we herded the sheep beneath a starry sky, one of us at each end of the flock. I couldn't say for sure what it was, but Kama didn't stop singing the whole way. Though her song was mellow, I had a feeling there was something stirring beneath the surface. Sure enough, as we neared the bottom of a sand dune, she said, "Two days ago, the herder looking for his camel shared the news that Kacipa from Shah's family is starting school in Altai." Kama was jealous and wanted to go to school too. Frankly, the news of Kacipa going to school surprised me. I knew Kacipa well—she too had dropped out of school and herded sheep for many years (not quite battling at the frontlines like Kama though). In the past, she whined day and night, saying she wanted to go back to school, but her family always refused. Who would have thought that after years of perseverance, her dream was finally coming true. Heavens, that fearless and unruly super-shepherdess . . . I couldn't imagine what she'd learn from school!

I didn't know what to tell Kama. One girl was realizing her dream, while the other was feeling hopeless. Kama was a pillar of her traditional household. Without her, they wouldn't be able to live as they do, at least not these last couple of years.

Then, on her own, Kama brought up the topic of marriage, explaining how there weren't many suitors (probably out of fear of Cuma, the drunken father-in-law), and of them, none were without their own problems, so nothing could be settled for the time being. She went on to say that many of her former class-mates were already engaged and some were even married. She spoke with a sense of despair, adding, "If I don't marry, I'll be an old lady, and no one wants to marry an old lady. If I do marry, I'll be just like Mom, day in and day out doing housework, cattle work, sheep work . . . from now until when I'm old."

She talked a lot that day, about how she wanted to work in a town somewhere, maybe learn a trade. She thought five hundred yuan a month would have been enough, as long as it could get her out of the wilderness. . . .

Who knew that this cheerful, resilient girl harbored such a humble, desperate dream.

I WONDERED IF THIS was what drove Kama to so assiduously study Chinese with me—she was determined to learn not only to speak but to write too. She borrowed my Kazakh exercise book to copy out the vocabulary list and phrasebook in the back. She wrote out the pinyin next to each character, studying as if she were really in school. But the content itself was not at all practical, with phrases like "Courtesy must always be a two-way street" and "Life is finite, time is infinite" . . . what in the world was the editor thinking?

I also sought to learn better Kazakh from Kama, but she always ended up going on and on, to which I had to say, "Enough, enough already, I'll need a week to learn all that!"

She smiled. "For me, it would only take a day."

She was right. Words that she learned at night, she had memorized the next day, acing her spelling quiz! I had to increase the difficulty, taking points off for writing even just a stroke out of place. As a result, she only got ninety-five points. Angrily, she crossed out the ninety-five and demanded that I change it to a hundred. I took the pen and wrote "85." Her eyes bulged. Panicking, she relented, "All right, all right, ninety-five it is. . . ." She was completely serious.

As a result of our mutual language lessons, our tongues often crisscrossed to comic effect. The best gaff of mine was: "Add some more black?" while her most memorable blunder was: "*Por adam, por* donkey." The former meant, "Add some more sheep manure [to the stove]?" The latter was, "One person, one donkey."

IN THEORY, AS THE ONLY child of theirs who lived with them, Kama should have been the Cumas' least cause for worry. And yet, she worried them the most. Cuma rarely got riled up about anything. When he did, it invariably had something to do with Kama. For example, one day he spent an hour ranting about "excessive drinking among Kazakh boys these days." This came up because someone had suggested a potential spouse for Kama. The boy was great in every respect—except it was said that he loved to drink. Another time, Cuma was bemoaning the uselessness of education, citing over a dozen examples in one breath, simply because Kama had revealed her envy of Kacipa and her wish to go to a technical school in Altai herself.

In fact, Kama was a sensible and mature young woman. For years, she had made so many sacrifices for her family that both her parents felt plenty of guilt. The reason they rebuffed her wishes and refused to let her attend school went far beyond "losing an extra pair of hands," or anything selfish like that. I believed that as her father, Cuma wanted to keep this daughter by his side, secure a stable marriage for her, and ensure that she lived a stable life. He feared change. He wanted to stay in control of his child's fate, forever protecting her, taking care of her, keeping her from hardship—as far as he was concerned, the only way to avoid misery was by sticking to the old ways.

Even though once upon a time, his eldest daughter Sharifa had been Cuma's biggest source of pride, now, when he talked about his children, Cuma would say, "Aside from Sharifa, the rest of the kids are good kids, carefree." When I pried, he explained, "Sharifa has been away, going to school for five years, that's five years without her parents at her side, who knows how she's changed."

I met Sharifa when she was still young, before she went to Ili for school. She had spent the whole winter sewing a quilt with an intricate landscape. At the time, she was worried about running out of scraps of yarn, while I happened to have a bunch left from my embroidery, so I offered them all to her. She was so delighted that she wrapped herself around my arm like a twisted dough snack, begging me to take her to my house to get them. Back then, she was just like Kama, carefree, witty, and playful. Now that she was far from home, she dated frivolously and didn't save a penny of her paycheck. At family gatherings, she was conceited and aloof, perhaps even a bit distant.

But no matter what, Kama was growing up too. Sooner or later she would have to leave her parents and the home that she had been so reliant upon. She had at most two more years at home, listening to her parents, helping out the family. But what would happen after two years? When Kama leaves (for work or marriage), who will herd the sheep? By then, the two youngest children will have graduated middle school. I asked Cuma if they could continue their education or whether they would be called home to work.

The question caused Cuma to ponder for a long time. By the time I'd given up on an answer, he exclaimed, "Guess we'll see what the babies want! If they don't want to go to school, then they'll receive a share of the property and join in the work. If they want to keep going, then they'll keep going. If there's no one left to herd, then we'll sell the sheep, keep twenty or so cows, and go back to Akehara to farm. If other people can get by farming, why can't I?" Not long ago, he'd been laughing at farmers for being so poor that they couldn't eat meat more than a few times a year.

Although Cuma claimed to be ready for both eventualities, I knew that he was already crystal clear what his children's decisions would be. Their youngest daughter had worked hard in school, having determined that education would be her way out of this life. And their son was in love with machinery, and was determined to become a mechanic.

So in the end, the fate of the family rested solely on Kama's shoulders. . . .

EVERY DAY I WROTE a little in my notebook. When Kama asked me what I was writing, I replied, "Kama's story." She said, "*Koychy*, that many stories?"

As time went on, she became inspired and decided to write something herself. Once, before taking the sheep out, she asked to borrow a pencil and a sheet

The trappings Kama embroidered over the course of the
winter would adorn her mount in the future.

of paper from me. When she returned that evening, she filled the sheet with pretty Arabic script. At dinner, she read it aloud to her family. Her parents put down their tea bowls and listened keenly. When she was done, they both said, "Great." They even took the page and read it over and over in silence. I asked, "What's it say?" Cuma said, "A letter to Li Juan." I was astonished and demanded that he translate for me. But the man only translated one sentence: "The state of Li Juan's work with our family."

Only one month after we had settled in the wilderness, Kama had to return to the spring and autumn encampment on the banks of the Ulungur River. Apa was sick and had been admitted to a hospital. There was no one else to watch the cows and goats. That left only the three of us at the burrow, which made me feel lonely just thinking about it. Kama, on the other hand, was thrilled. Could it have something to do with the Black Horse Trot Ballroom she was always daydreaming about? A world of young people, the prospect of love, the chance of finding a job, the possibility of life changing . . . I wondered if this winter, our big girl Kama *suluv* might finally gather the courage to stand up and sing for the world.

After Kama left, we all felt lonely. In early January, she sent us a letter by way of the vet. This time around, Cuma earnestly translated the whole thing for me. It began with: "Dear Papa and Mama, and Li Juan, out there in the winter burrow, how are you? How is your health?" That was enough to bring tears to our eyes.

11.

Cuma

CUMA WAS A NOTORIOUS drunkard-*cum*-rascal. So when I decided to stay with his family for the winter, many people were shocked. Yet those who really knew him agreed that, aside from his drinking and his shenanigans, he had a lot of qualities that were worthy of admiration and even respect. He was a meticulous, dependable worker with a quick wit and charisma. People enjoyed his company. Whenever he opened his mouth in a crowd, everyone quieted down and listened to what he had to say. And how he loved to talk. When it came to bragging, he'd outdo himself, lining up his words like a string of pearls. Any joke that he told would circulate for a long time after. As a result, he had acquired a certain prestige among the herders.

Their world was something like this—a big sky and a big earth, in which they dwelt alone and far apart; where the days were quiet and dull, life hard and lonely, deprived of contact with the outside world; and where most people were resigned to a life of quiescence. So the presence of a character like Cuma offered people a sense of joy and relief! He could always unpack everything in the frankest of terms, saying what had been on everyone's mind and—with a few well-chosen words—effortlessly untangle the most intractable matters of the heart. Of course, among the nomadic folk, there were the even more empathetic, eloquent Kazakh musicians, the *aqyns*, who were naturally revered by them, to the point of deification.

In short, little did it matter that Cuma the raving drunk was tyrannical and mean—people didn't hold it against him, and were ready to forgive this foible of his.

Cuma was approaching fifty, had graying hair, stood tall at five foot nine, and weighed a hefty two hundred forty-two pounds. The earth shook when he walked. Although he was ostensibly old enough to be a grandfather, since I was over thirty myself, I ended up calling him "Big Brother."

Cuma and my family have known each other for many years, so by this point we are old friends. Every time he shopped at our store, my mother would strong-arm him into buying only the goods with broken packaging. There was no love lost between him and my mother, but he had no choice but to keep shopping at our store. We were the only ones who allowed him to keep an open tab.

Cuma could speak a mouthful of Mandarin. Even if it was rather muddled, it was nonetheless expressive. For example, instead of "sand dune," he would say "tall sand," and instead of "a long journey," he would say "a lot of desert!"

One day, after reading the supplement in a Kazakh newspaper, he pondered for a moment, then explained to me, thoughtfully, "This piece of paper says that here, where we herd sheep, was once used for moving this"—pointing to an embroidered fabric on the wall—"a road for bringing the fine, shiny string we draw it with!"

It took me a moment, but then I got it: oh, he means the Silk Road! It was true, Altai was on the northern route of the ancient Silk Road.

He didn't know the Chinese word for *sew*, so he replaced it with "draw." After all, Sharifa, his eldest daughter, was studying drawing. I imagine that in Kazakh, the two verbs must be the same.

Cuma was a quick learner. At first, the only swear words he knew in Mandarin were the "three-word classics." But ever since his argument with my mother, who screamed at him that he was "not even human," he finally learned a new phrase. When a cow was disobedient, he cursed, "Not even human." When a camel was mischievous, he cried, "So not even human!"

Because he was always making up stories about the country's leaders, saying, "Back when we were herding together, he did this or that," I would tease, "You counterrevolutionary!" Delighted, he adopted this new phrase as well. While ushering the sheep into their pen at night, he shouted as he corralled them, "You, a counterrevolutionary! You, also a counterrevolutionary!"

I EVENTUALLY FIGURED out why Cuma spoke Mandarin so well. As a child, he lived in a production brigade on the outskirts of the county. His neighbors were Hui Chinese Muslims, so he was able to pick up on some Mandarin. Later, when the Akehara People's Commune was looking for someone to drive horse-drawn carts, his father took the gig and relocated his whole family. When all the people's communes were disbanded, his family gradually became nomadic. Cuma once said, had he stayed in the town, he would have continued with school, found work, and would have become a city dweller by now, but instead, he became a herder . . . a disappointing turn of events. It left him with a sentimental sort of pride.

Yet, he was always cheery. At the crack of dawn, while everyone was busy running around, he had nothing to do. He tried to strike up conversations but no one paid him any attention. That was when he took down a mirror and told jokes to himself, putting on all sorts of voices. The more the family ignored him, the more he upped the ante, wearing a stern face and mimicking the tone and tempo of a CCTV newscaster as he recited a long list of leaders' names. I couldn't help but play along: "What, you know them?"

He boasted, "Of course! We used to herd together. . . ." He noted that a few of the leaders "were drunks too. . . ."

We couldn't hold back our laughter anymore, and gave a collective "*Koychy!*"

IT WASN'T JUST THAT Cuma couldn't control his jesting; he couldn't keep his hands still either. When he wasn't herding sheep, he spent the whole day rummaging through things, fixing this and that. In a single day, he managed to do all the following: help his wife patch up all her broken shoes and polish them until they shined, add a supporting pillar to a twenty-plus-year-old beam, repair the solar panel, plaster leaky doors and windows, mend the stove, fix a sieve, repair Kama's crochet needle, fix his own sunglasses (herding for a long time in the snow without sunglasses leads to snow blindness), fix my glasses (I left them on the bed once and then sat on them, snapping the arms—it couldn't be helped, I wasn't wearing my glasses, so I couldn't see), fix a handsaw, fix a knife, and, finally, lay a warped steel bar over the pickax and whack it straight, then whack it some more until it turned into a new pair of charcoal tongs! Sadly, they were a little short. He said, "Then let shorty here use them!" How rude—he was referring to me.

Only after finishing all these chores did he bother to reveal that his stomach had been hurting all day and asked Sister-in-law to prepare him a hot-water bottle so he could go to bed early and get some rest.

Granted, the guy knew how to make life comfortable and took care of his family like a good man, but there was something very annoying about him— while he worked on his own chores, everyone else had to act like his assistant. One minute I was sent to find shoe polish and a brush, the next moment Kama was asked to bring the hammer, and after that he ordered Sister-in-law to get up to fetch the hemp rope.

Sister-in-law refused: "I'm spinning thread!"

He snatched the spindle. "What's so impressive about that, you're just twisting a thread!" With that, he turned the spindle and started spinning for her.

She surrendered, slipping off the bed to fetch the rope. When she came back with the rope, her face went red—in the short time she was gone, he had managed to tangle the whole spool into a hopeless mess. . . .

Even this jack-of-all-trades had his moments of failure. Once he tried to mend a cracked plastic bucket. First, he set flame to a plastic bag and dripped the melted plastic onto the crack . . . nope. Next, he found a piece of hard plastic and used a red-hot poker to try to melt it onto the crack . . . that didn't work either. After hours of struggle, he lost it! He got some clear tape, wrapped it around the bucket a few times, then chucked the thing aside, never to think about it again.

Worse, whenever he was trying to do something, regardless of whether he failed or succeeded, nobody was allowed to express skepticism. For example, once he was attaching a new handle to a hacksaw, and I asked in passing, "Is that gonna work?"

He lost all confidence. Days after it had been fixed, he continued to grumble, "Who was it that said it wouldn't work? Who? Was it you? Take a look, does that look like it works or not?" And whenever he used the hacksaw, he wouldn't forget to comment, "See, what a beauty! Sure works good! Li Juan didn't think so at first!"

It was one thing fixing all the broken objects in the house, but what really amazed me was the day I saw him doing needlework! A bowl of tea at his side, he slowly mended his tattered sheepskin jacket. After that, he mended some gloves, then a pair of socks, all the while grumbling to himself, "My old woman doesn't care about me anymore, doesn't she love me anymore? . . . I have to do this myself, that myself, what if she stops cooking for me too. . . .

This old woman, should I keep her or should I not?" Sister-in-law shuttled in and out of the burrow, busy with work up to her neck, and paid him no mind.

Then he would mumble on about how it was such a pity with Li Juan, one of these days, she must be given a proper meal and asked if I preferred dumplings or hand-pulled noodles. I was surprised and asked Kama if it could be true. She said, "Sure, my dad can do anything! Milk the cows! And bake *nan* too!"

I was impressed: "He's practically a Han man!"

That was when Cuma told me that when he was little, his mother broke her hand, so as the oldest of his siblings, he took over all the housework.

As if afraid that I wouldn't believe him, he immediately offered a demonstration—scooping up Sister-in-law's half-sewn rug, he began threading the needle through the felt! He pointed out which of the flowers he'd cut and stitched, which ones were Kama's, and which were Sister-in-law's. . . . I couldn't believe it! With those hands as big and rough as palm-leaf fans.

Still sewing, he continued, "When Li Juan gets married, this old brute'll take this carpet he's drawn, roll it up, strap it to a horse saddle, and send it to her house!"

Quickly I said, "No thanks!"

"Why?"

"Your embroidery can't be all that good!"

Turns out, Cuma's embroidery wasn't bad at all! Granted, the stitches were a bit too close together, but just the way he held the needle was enough to prove that he knew what he was doing.

Later, I learned that he could even crochet a floral trim! And fix simple home electronics, working with tiny circuit boards. . . . Don't let that pair of big hands deceive you, they could manipulate tiny objects with impressive dexterity. He even used his fat finger to pick Baby Karlygash's nose! His hands may have looked clumsy, but really, they were patient and gentle.

Yes, Cuma adored Karlygash, he was always kissing the little one, offering more affection than she knew what to do with. He'd pinch her nose with chopsticks and pretend to pop it into his mouth, chewing it like it was the most delicious thing. When the little one watched him smack his lips, she rubbed her nose nervously, afraid that he had really eaten it.

Cuma loved to pick her up by her arms and dance with her, doing the Black Horse Trot. The quickness of the rhythm left her laughing out loud. He wrapped her up in his arms, lifted his shirt, and pretended to feed her "milk."

Karlygash stared at his big white belly and chest full of hair for a moment before bursting into tears.

BEFORE SETTING OUT for the winter burrow, my biggest worry had been whether Cuma would be drunk the whole time. Fortunately, there wasn't much booze around—he only brought three bottles. On the drive to the winter burrow, he had finished off a bottle in the passenger seat (poor driver . . .), and what remained was only enough to get him into trouble a couple of times. His antics generally involved a lot of yelling, keeping the rest of us from sleeping. Other than that, there was bowl throwing, which was both infuriating and frightening. Had the burrow been a little bigger, at least there would have been somewhere to hide, but the place was only so big. Luckily, of all the bowls he threw, none ever broke. Thank goodness the floor was made of sand, the walls plastered with manure, and the bed covered in thick felt.

The worst thing about Cuma wasn't even the drinking, it was the compulsive lying. He was always lying to me as a way to pass the time. One day, for example, he suddenly said that on top of the dunes far out west in the wilderness, there was cell-phone signal. So the following morning, of course, I ran out, diligently trekking several kilometers up all the highest sand dunes. . . .

He also told me that only men can cook sheep hooves, women can't. He spoke with such authority that I really thought it was some sort of tradition. Good thing I thought to ask him, "Why?"

He continued earnestly, "When women cook 'em, they get smaller; when men cook 'em, they get bigger. . . ." What did that have to do with anything!

Then, there was that night when he exclaimed, "The big black cow will be calving tonight! We all have to go help!" I couldn't sleep all night, afraid that I'd miss the little calf's birthing. It turned out, the cow didn't give birth until a month later. And when it did, there was no need for "help."

Because he was always like that, I could no longer believe anything that came out his mouth. No matter what he said, I had to verify with Sister-in-law or Kama first. What a chore.

The second most annoying thing about Cuma was whenever we were in an argument that he couldn't win, he'd mock my mother, imitating her crying and sniffling. Then he'd complain that our store was full of fake goods and accuse my mother of "ripping off even her friends." Clearly, that fired me up. Cuma had already burned his bridges with all the shopkeepers in Akehara, except us.

The third most annoying thing was when he bullied the kitten. I eventually learned that he really had nothing against the creature, it was just to annoy everyone else. If someone decided to show pity, then he'd hit him even harder. He threw the little kitten, who was barely four months old, mercilessly against the ground. I couldn't help but scream. Then I realized that other than me, everyone else pretended like nothing was happening. Silence, it turned out, was the only thing that could stop this behavior—the more you tried to stop him, the more of a kick he got out of it. Like a spoiled child! Infuriating.

For a time, I even thought the kitten might not live through the winter. But he was steadfast, pouncing around, practicing his mouse-catching skills whenever he had a chance. So young, but already learning to be independent.

In fact, on most days, Cuma loved the kitten more than anyone else. When meat was served, he ignored everyone's objections and cut chunk after chunk to feed the cat. At teatime, he often instructed Sister-in-law to pour a little milk into the cat's bowl, knowing full well how precious milk was in the winter . . . and one evening I even found the cat sleeping under Cuma's covers!

In short, idle Cuma, Cuma after all the boots were mended and polished, after all the dents in the pot lids had been beaten back into shape, was just awful. He not only drove us crazy, but it made him feel angry as well, harassing one thing one moment and provoking something else the next. Then he'd let out a heavy sigh: "Nothing to do, I can't do nothing!" And then succumb to a long sleep. But when he woke, he'd drink some tea, take an aspirin, and be right back to troublemaking.

Wide awake, full, sober, with nothing to do and no one to talk to, even Karlygash was taking a nap, his loneliness was magnified. Cuma slowly climbed up the sand dune to the north, stood at the highest point beneath the all-embracing light of day, and gazed at the movement of the flock in the distance. For a long time, he didn't move.

THOUGH THE BROTHERS next door were also herders, Cuma treated the sheep with much more care and consideration. He kept a close eye on each and every sheep. At the first sign of sickness, Cuma would immediately pull the sheep from the flock to diagnose it. Any sheep that was struggling would be whisked back to the burrow, where it was "hospitalized"; any parasites were immediately treated. When the temperature dropped, Cuma constructed a warmer, roofed pen for the cold goats. As for Shinshybek, it was already minus forty degrees Fahrenheit and their cattle burrow still lacked a roof!

Similarly, when Cuma herded, he stayed out on the pasture until the sky was pitch-black before heading home, so that the sheep could eat their fill. As for the neighbors, when the sun had barely set, their sheep were already lingering near the burrow settlement barely half a mile away.

Though Cuma was a lackadaisical troublemaker most of the time, when it came to work, he deserved respect. He was big and strong. When it came time for the neighborhood to cooperate on a big project, he was always the leading force. Everyone else circled around him, helping where they could. Before he declared it was time to rest, no one would dare to go home to drink tea. If any of the nearby families needed to dig a new burrow, they'd always ask for his help.

On one of Cuma's days of rest, after repairing the cleaver that broke while chopping a cow's head, reattaching the handles on the steamer, and mending a pair of boots, he was bored again, so he began sorting through years' worth of receipts. I leaned in to take a look and saw that they were all debts that people owed him. Some were written in Chinese, including one for helping someone herd twenty-five sheep one summer and one for leveling the foundation at a reservoir construction site in Akehara one fall, and in the same year he helped to hull sunflower seeds for a large oil producer—what an industrious man! Always going out of his way to earn money. Just as I was starting to get sentimental, I noticed one invoice that was a hundred and nineteen yuan short! I pointed it out straightaway. Cuma was thrilled; while thanking me for being a big help, he cursed the guy for being immoral, "He will even rip off a friend!"

Tall, stocky men like Cuma aren't suited to such intense labor, year after year. Only fifty years old, his ankle and knee joints were ailing. When the weather changed, he complained about joint pains. He took aspirin every day like it was a part of his meal; just the sight of it was distressing. Chronic migraines plagued him twice a week, often forcing him to get up at midnight to take another pill. When he slumped down without a word in front of Sister-in-law, she understood immediately and started to massage his neck. Apparently, his cervical spine also had problems.

It was worst on the days when he had to herd. When he returned in the evening, he was too tired even to climb into bed.

The only thing Sister-in-law could do was to make his dinner a little heartier. When she fried *baursak*, she improvised a humongous round cake, six times bigger than the others! She announced, "This one's for the old brute!"

When the old brute came home and plopped down exhausted in front of the dinner cloth, she ceremoniously presented it to him. For a moment, the old brute stared at the extra-large *baursak* in shock. When he came to, he grabbed it with both hands, turning it left and right like a steering wheel, while mumbling, *"Vrmmmmmm! Beep, beep!"* honking the horn nonstop—this old brute had always dreamed of owning car.

WHENEVER IT WAS CUMA'S turn to herd the sheep, I hoped that time would pass quickly so that his shift would end and he could get some rest. But when it really came time for him to rest, I once again hoped time would pass quickly so the guy could go back to herding sheep. Alas, when he wasn't herding, he was a nuisance. Not only did he bully the cat every day, he was constantly hassling the three of us, nitpicking, sticking his nose into everything. We couldn't even put noodles in a pot without him pointing and offering his own advice. He worried about absolutely everything—which is probably a common symptom that plagues intelligent people.

Intelligent and ambitious, capable and cocky. What joy was there for a person like that in a life like this? It was hard to say really, because while he was magnanimous with his feelings, he was also sensitive and prone to melancholy. At times, when I'd see him put on a happy face all of a sudden, my heart would wrench, overwhelmed with pity, but soon enough, I would be swept up in his joy as well.

While I was folding freshly laundered clothes during morning tea, he leaned over and snatched a jacket to wear. Sister-in-law, sharp-eyed and quick-handed, intercepted it and refused to let him put it on. It was a pristine, new piece of clothing, freshly washed, and it might get ruined by continuous use. Each held an end of it in a tug-of-war, neither side relenting.

Caught in a stalemate, Sister-in-law had no choice but to dig up an equally clean but older jacket for him. Reluctantly, Cuma released his grip on that spiffy-looking army-style jacket and begrudgingly slipped into the older jacket, whining, "Why won't you let me wear my good clothes? I'm bringing the sheep back early this afternoon! If you won't let me wear it tomorrow, the sheep'll be home at lunchtime! If anyone asks why I'm back so early, I'll tell 'em my old woman won't let me wear the nice clothes! Argh, how can I go out there like this, what will people think! They'll all say Cuma's old woman is a lazy broad. . . ." After putting on the jacket, it became clear that it was not only worn, it was too short, and too tight on him—hideous indeed.

One morning a few days later, however, Cuma got his wish and put on the new army-style jacket! Pleased, he said, "This is more like it; when I wear it, I feel like Chairman Mao!"

I said, "Herding sheep all day, who are you dressing up for?"

In a singsong voice, he replied, "For the sheep! For the goats! One look and they'll say, 'Wow, who's that? A new man is he?' Then they'll circle around me and never wander off ever again. They'll do anything I tell them to. They'll eat their food and come straight home, so good, so obedient!"

Sister-in-law and I laughed.

Later that day, I was herding the calves north when a quarter mile out, I heard a voice behind me. I turned to see Cuma on horseback, sporting a red neck gaiter and wearing his leather overcoat unbuttoned to reveal the new jacket beneath. He shouted at the top of his voice, "One, one, one-two-one! . . ." counting out a march for his horse. When he passed by me, he turned toward the calves and happily took over herding them deeper into the wilds, saving me a half-mile walk.

That evening, Cuma returned, blue in the face from a whole day in the freezing wilderness. Without a word, he quaffed bowl after bowl of tea. When he was full and warm at last, he took a long breath and asked me to bring him the mirror. He turned the mirror side to side, studying himself, before finally concluding, "Hmmh, still a looker! Why, he's still a young lad!"

My glasses, fixed by Cuma, on the ram's horn I was embroidering

12.

Sister-in-law

S ISTER-IN-LAW WAS RESERVED and, at times, too serious. But when
the mood struck, she'd wrap her arms around Cuma and "mwah" give him
a big kiss, leaving him in a daze.

Years of hard labor and ailments had left her with furrowed brows; she
always looked glum. And because of the chronic pain in her hips and legs,
she groaned whenever she bent over to pick something up. Don't be fooled by
the swiftness and efficiency with which she worked. The moment she finished
her work and returned to the bedroom, she was too tired even to squat down.
And if she did manage to squat, she wouldn't be able to stand back up. After
each day of work, she struggled onto the felt bedding and asked me to massage
her back and feet. But if at that moment, she heard the patch-faced bull calf
getting into the yurt, she leaped to her feet like a young man and charged
outside to do battle.

Whereas Cuma was tall and wide, Sister-in-law was tall and thin, which
made her appear frail and delicate. My mother's impression of her was that she
was always "down-to-earth." In the past, when Cuma went on his drunken
rampages, Sister-in-law simply took her frustration off to the side and waited it
out, at most offering a quiet "enough" when he was at his very worst.

Whenever we visited their home for tea, she acted the part of the traditional housewife, never initiating a conversation, always sitting at the end of the seating area, quietly offering food and drinks, a paragon of decorum. Whenever someone said something that set the whole room laughing, she'd quietly ask Cuma, "What is it?" as she could not understand Mandarin.

Sister-in-law rarely smiled. Her aloofness was enough to give you goose bumps. But when she did smile, she was radiant. Light beams shot out from between her brows as if she invented this "smiling" business.

AFTER KAMA LEFT, Cuma herded every day. And when he didn't, he was either out chasing horses and camels or fixing the pen. As a result, most of the time it was just me and Sister-in-law at home. We quietly did our own chores, communicating mostly with gestures. When the work was done, we sat down together for some tea. It was as quiet as if we were living hundreds of years ago. But this sort of silence felt natural, not at all awkward.

It wasn't like that at first. At first, our difficulty communicating led to all sorts of misunderstandings, which made me anxious. Of course, the more anxious I felt, the more ridiculous my mistakes became. My overreaction only caused her more stress.

As we slowly got to know each other, I began to realize that Sister-in-law was a straightforward, easygoing woman—I had been overreacting. All the things that I didn't know how to do, that I bungled, didn't worry her in the slightest.

Once while I was washing the bowls, I spilled a lot of milk. Panicked, I scrambled to clean up the mess. Cuma teased me, "Quick! Quick! Your Sister-in-law's coming! If she sees this, she'll beat you!" But Sister-in-law would never beat me. In fact, she spilled more milk and soy sauce than I did.

Whenever she spoke to me, she expressed shock: "Li Juan, cat!" The kitten would be asleep, belly up, all four paws sprawled out. When she exclaimed, "Li Juan, hole!" she'd found a large fox hole. At the time, we were trekking out west to collect snow from a sand dune. On the silent journey, her sudden outburst gave me the impression that all the while she must have been at complete peace.

Though Sister-in-law couldn't speak Mandarin, as Cuma's wife, she eventually picked up on everyday words like *cattle*, *sheep*, *horse*, *camel*, and so on, which was quite a few more than the wives of the other herders on the pastures. As our rapport developed, our communication soon became effortless.

When Sister-in-law said, "Cattle, house," I would run out to check if the patch-faced bull calf was near the yurt.

When Sister-in-law said, "Water, hot bottle," I would pour hot water into the thermos.

Short, simple, but effective. Cuma praised her: "Like a boss!"

And then there were those times when her ability to express herself went far beyond my expectations. When she wanted me to help coax a cow over to her calf, she said, "Li Juan, the black, the small, cattle's mother, bring!"

Sister-in-law's first task every morning was to let the cattle out and herd them away from the burrow. When the cattle were far enough, she then let the calves out and herded them away in the opposite direction. This way the mothers and offspring wouldn't run into each other during the day. What would it matter if they did? The consequence would be that the cattle wouldn't be in a rush to come home in the evening, and the calves would suck their moms dry, forcing us to drink our tea black, rather than with milk. . . .

From the moment I arrived, the responsibility of herding calves was delegated to me. Herding calves was a hassle. They weren't like the cattle that had been herded for many years, having long learned that the herder's intention was for them to walk straight ahead. Calves are stubborn by nature. You had to herd them at least a half mile out before they'd stop glancing longingly homeward.

In short, I was doing Sister-in-law a big favor. To show how thankful she was, she first hugged me, then led me by the hand to a high ground out west. There, she pointed to where the calves were to go and where the cattle were to go. I was pleased, full of confidence regarding our relationship going forward.

During the winter with the family, Sister-in-law taught me many things—spinning yarn, plying yarns together, quilting felt, band-weaving . . . not to mention all sorts of tricks and hacks for daily life. For example, when carrying sacks of snow, first put a clump of horse dung in the mouth of a sack, then grab the sack opening with the dung inside to prevent it from slipping. She also taught me how to clean a stove without the ash flying everywhere, and that when sewing with hand-spun yarn, you shouldn't tie a knot at the end of the yarn but instead pull the needle along with the old thread through the new thread and wrap it around a few times for a secure and even connection. . . . Of course, once I left this life behind, none of these skills would be of any use to me. But I am still grateful for having learned them. Suppose I were to devote more of my life to this path, and settle into it; perhaps these small lessons would eventually lead to even more bits of wisdom.

ON CLOUDY DAYS, the couple felt pain all over their bodies. Their lower backs, in particular, hurt so much that they struggled to sit up. I had prepared two heat patches for the winter. I stuck one onto each of them, hoping that it might help. As soon as the patches were on, they assured me that they would work. To make the most of the medicinal patches, they put themselves to work immediately, shouldering poles to yoke three sacks of flour and feed at a time, refusing to quit until they had transported a ton of winter supplies from a hiding place beneath the snow far to the north all the way back to the yurt.

I never found out if the heat patches actually worked, but Cuma wore his for three days straight before peeling it off. I was shocked: "Did it itch? Are there any side effects? The instructions say to wear it for eight hours at most!"

He pointed to Sister-in-law and laughed. "She only wore it for thirty minutes!" Then she lost it somewhere.

Sister-in-law worked with a nonchalant air. When she was finished with the broom, tongs, fire iron, or whatever else, she tossed it aside and that was that—she never bothered to return them to their proper place. Maybe that came as a result of having lived in nature for so long. In the end, I was the one who followed her all day long, picking up after her.

ONCE WHILE SHE WAS FRYING *baursak*, Sister-in-law screamed. I turned and saw that she had burned herself with a splash of boiling oil. Just as I was about to check if it was serious, she quickly composed herself and was right back to fishing the hotcakes out of the pan. I figured it was nothing serious, so I let it pass. Only when all the *baursak* were out of the oil did she move the boiling-hot pan aside, place it down, rock it to check if it was stable, then roll up her sleeve to pour cold water over the wound. It wasn't until then that I realized how serious the burn was! It had left an enormous blister that couldn't be touched for days.

Had she poured cold water on the wound immediately, the injury would have been less severe. What was she thinking? It was as if something as serious as a burn was an afterthought compared to burnt *baursak*! Or as if acknowledging pain was something that would lead to embarrassment! Either way, she showed a degree of fortitude and self-control that I couldn't wrap my head around.

SISTER-IN-LAW WAS FAR from being dull (though, she wasn't anywhere near as mischievous as Cuma either) and occasionally demonstrated a solid sense of humor.

When she played with Baby Karlygash, she'd say, "Karlygash, dance! Karlygash, smile! Karlygash, where's Sister? Karlygash, where's Apa?" It seemed to be the only game she knew. Even when the infant was swaddled and firmly planted in the rocking cradle, she still teased her with the same enthusiasm: "Karlygash, dance! Karlygash, smile! Karlygash, wheeere's Sister? Karlygash, wheeere's Apa?" Karlygash was absolutely helpless.

Karlygash was the focal point of the neighbors' lives, forever filling their home with happiness and laughter. By comparison, ours was much less exciting— we only had a cat. So Sister-in-law improvised and named the kitten "Karlygash" too. After that, whenever Sister-in-law had a moment to spare, she'd grab the pink cat's paws and force him to sing, dance, and look for Sister, not caring if the critter wanted to or not.

Before long, Cuma was bequeathed the nickname too. Early in the morning, Sister-in-law began to coo in a honeyed tone, "Karlygash? Hey! Karlygash! Wake up, look, Sister is already up!"

Cuma, went along with the joke. When Sister-in-law said, "Karlygash, dance!" he retracted his neck and arms and rocked back and forth.

When Sister-in-law said, "Karlygash, where's Sister?" he held his finger under his chin and shyly pointed toward me.

I wondered if Sayna, next door, knew about the "Karlygash" joke and what she thought about it.

COMPARED TO SAYNA, Sister-in-law was much sloppier looking. Sometimes Sister-in-law's headscarf was crooked, revealing a mess of hair beneath it. The two braids that had been likely braided years ago had loosened into two big cakes. Sayna's headscarf was always impeccably wrapped over her smoothly combed braids. Of course, Sister-in-law was also much busier than Sayna, especially once Kama left, spinning around all day like a top.

Normally, after the dough is kneaded, it must sit for a while. As she waited, she spent the time spinning thread. As a result, it wasn't unusual to find yarn in a bite of *nan* (once I even found a ball of newspaper). After having grilled one side of the *nan*, it was time to turn it over. In the time it took for the second side to cook, Sister-in-law could embroider a two-inch-long yellow ram horn. Halfway through laundry, while waiting for the water to heat (in a large tin pot outside the burrow), Sister-in-law could zip back inside to start boiling tea while tracing a pattern onto a piece of felt. Every fragment of every moment was made use of; even when she went to the neighbors' for tea and a chat, she never forgot to take her spindle or half-finished embroidery with her. After doing some work on the cattle burrow, she brainstormed as she rested—what else is there to do, all the yarn is spun, the freshly dyed felt is still drying, Li Juan has already collected two sacks of snow . . . another moment of contemplation before she sat up, ripped open two old pillows, and took out the stuffing—just wash the pillowcases then!

Cuma was often very childish and insensitive to Sister-in-law's needs. When dinner was just about out of the pot, he would run next door to chat. We waited and waited but he still wouldn't return, and we couldn't very well go there and get him. In the end, Sister-in-law had no choice but to send me over with a half bowl of fried flat noodles for him to share with the neighbors. Yet in this case, Cuma ended up throwing a tantrum, complaining about how he'd herded the sheep all day long, but when he got home, the food wasn't ready, he had to wait! So in protest, he went to scrounge food from the neighbors . . . but Sister-in-law had been working hard all day too. There was a sudden snow in the evening, so we had to clear the pen as quickly as we could before the sheep returned. It took a long time, and when we were done we were exhausted. Besides, didn't the neighbors make dinner later than us?

The couple sometimes quarreled. Cuma was always heated, using his loud voice and quick tongue to gain the upper hand. But Sister-in-law wasn't so easily perturbed. With soft words and a soft tone, she reasoned calmly, which in the end won her ultimate victory. When this kind of a victory presented itself, it always seemed like a win-win. Cuma's temper would cool, having nothing more to say. To me it was all very fascinating. . . .

Aside from the occasional fights, the two would also give each other the cold shoulder from time to time. Neither spoke, neither knew why, and neither knew how to end it. All evening, Cuma would ramble on at me about nothing in particular while Sister-in-law spun all the yarn in one sitting. The most unfortunate in these situations was the kitten, receiving a whack from whomever he passed, a truly confounding situation for the poor thing.

Next morning, at tea, the cold war persisted. After emptying his bowl, Cuma held it out for a refill. Sister-in-law didn't reach for it, so Cuma could only put it down on the dinner cloth. Sister-in-law took the bowl, refilled it, then placed it back on the dinner cloth, ignoring Cuma's outstretched hand.

Cuma was the first to lose his cool. He thought for a moment before suddenly shaking off his old jacket, jumping out of his seat to snatch the bag of clean clothes hanging on the wall, and pulling out that most precious item of his. Sister-in-law took the bait and also leaped to her feet and grabbed the jacket from him. Cuma clung firmly to the other end. The two tugged back and forth before suddenly, one let out a *pffft* and the two of them began chortling in concert. At that point, whether or not Cuma changed his clothes no longer mattered. The couple returned to the seating area and continued with tea, talking about one thing after another. My, they'd gone a long time without talking!

After a long, demanding day of work, the couple returned to the burrow. They stood there, exhausted, unsure of what to do next. Cuma wrapped his arms around Sister-in-law, hoping to give her a big surprise. Sister-in-law, in a rare moment of playfulness, wrapped her arms around him, giving him a big surprise instead. Then the two stood there in front of the stove, wrapped in each other's embrace, showing more loving affection than one could bear. I pulled out my camera and they immediately let go.

SISTER-IN-LAW WAS BORN into a farming family and spent her youth in Ciakutu, nearly twenty-four miles from Akehara. Once, I asked, "Ciakutu is so far from Akehara, how the heck did you meet?" That instantly made Cuma a chatterbox, going on and on. Apparently, when Cuma was a young lad, he had

Sister-in-law heading out to look for snow. She walked
farther and farther into the distance.

his sights set high, meeting all sorts of girls, none of whom could impress him. When he finally found one he liked, the parents couldn't come to an agreement, so before you knew it he had become an old bachelor. It wasn't until one fall, at a *toy* (feast) in Ciakutu, that he met Sister-in-law, after which he found himself going to Ciakutu every couple of days. . . . He giggled, "I looked left, looked right, and this gal was the best of the bunch! Slim, tall, pale . . ." One thing led to another and she was his, which still made him beam with pride. Sister-in-law was sitting off to one side nursing her bowl of tea. It wasn't clear if she had understood the story as she sat completely still.

Clearly, Cuma was satisfied with his marriage, admitting, "If life was bad, we'd be divorced already!" Next, he began to list all the couples in the village who divorced as soon as they married, as well as couples who were married for years before divorcing. "Ay, people nowadays, more temperamental than ever!" With that, he laid his head on Sister-in-law's bosom and pretended to sob. "A good old woman, gave me four babies, the old woman . . . waa waa . . ." Sister-in-law stroked his head while continuing to sip her tea, unperturbed.

Near the end of my time with the family, I picked a softly lit evening to take a proper portrait of the couple. When he saw the photo, Cuma commented in a serious voice, "I'm clearly over here, why is your Sister-in-law's head leaning that way? Maybe she doesn't like me anymore. . . ."

13.

The Neighbors

THE NEIGHBORS WEREN'T a tall family, though their horses were extra tall. Especially the white one—even a big fella like Cuma had trouble getting on. A little embarrassed, he offered an explanation: his clothes were too thick!

Compared to our family, the neighbors were clearly wealthier. They had more of everything: altogether more than two hundred goats and sheep, we only had about a hundred; twelve camels, big and small, we only had three; ten horses, we only had six . . . only our cattle outnumbered theirs, but their dairy production was far higher than ours.

Wealth allowed the neighboring couple an easygoing, self-assured, and dignified comportment. Yet, their day-to-day work was just as grueling as ours. When the lady of the house, Sayna, carried snow home, she was so squashed by the load that she was nearly invisible; we would only see a large sack slowly floating across the wilderness—why did she insist on carrying so much snow all at once? But of course, she had a baby that needed to be washed frequently, so their need for water was naturally great.

The man of the house, Shinshybek, was short and slim, with a dark face and bright eyes. He walked with a pair of chunky felt overboots, a pair of thick corduroy pants, and wore gloves wherever he went. One sign of his refinement was the "Red Snow Lotus" cigarettes he smoked for two yuan a pack, while Cuma only smoked "Mohe" rolling tobacco. Sitting together talking, each man smoked his own cigarettes, never offering any to the other.

No one spoiled seven-month-old Karlygash like her father, Shinshybek. As soon as he got home, regardless of how cold he was, he would jump onto the bed, hold his child in his arms, and plant endless kisses on her. When her face was thoroughly kissed, he would kiss her little butt; after kissing her fingers, he'd move on to her feet, which made the little one giggle to no end. Relaxing after bowls of tea, he'd lift her up to ride on his shoulders, letting her squeeze and pinch his nose, eyes, and mouth, before gradually drifting off to sleep.

Karlygash was an extraordinarily beautiful baby girl; just think, the breathtaking thing that is life! For Shinshybek and Sayna, a drab old pair, to possess such a shiny, delicate little beauty! The sight of the three cuddled together could only be called hope.

KARLYGASH WAS A TRULY charming child, not only pretty and healthy, but also quick to smile and to take to strangers. Whenever she heard anyone sing, she'd rock her head and swing her limbs. Even when Cuma was drunk and acting senselessly, he couldn't resist cuddling her, kissing her, and lovingly whispering to her, "Bad girl, naughty! Bad girl, naughty . . ." He was so taken by her cuteness that he didn't know what to do with himself. Strangely, even when it was a drunk in his element asking to hold their child, the parents still let him. . . .

Although she only had two teeth, Karlygash nevertheless managed to chew up all my books and notepads. A mere month later, she grew three more upper teeth, big and white, that could chomp even harder. When given a foot-long leg bone of a cow, she hugged it tight and chewed it fiercely.

As Karlygash's only plaything, Shinshybek's big leopard cat spent all day snuggling up against her, allowing her to tug its ears and nip its cheeks, its careworn face never flinching. Moreover, because it was Karlygash's only toy, before the little girl learned to say "*ma*" or "*ba*," she had already learned to meow. All day long, the big leopard cat would meow at her and she would meow back like it was some sort of productive exchange.

And why was Karlygash so happy all the time? She smiled at everyone she saw, and kept on smiling. Come to think of it, after spending most of the day strapped to her cradle in an upright position, swaddled head-to-toe with three layers on the inside and three layers on the outside, wrapped tighter than a *zongzi*, was it any wonder that as soon as she was freed, she'd celebrate as much as possible? I couldn't imagine what it would be like to be strapped in all night, unable to roll over! No wonder the little gal bawled in despair whenever she was getting strapped in again. But if you played with her when she cried, she'd instantly be gurgling with laughter again, having already forgotten the tragic moment.

AT THE END OF JANUARY, the drought passed. Collecting snow was no longer so tiring, which took the pressure off for the other household chores, so I began spending two hours a day helping Sayna sew and embroider *syrmak*. It made Sayna very happy. As thanks, she gave our family half a bowl of milk every day so that we could drink our tea with milk.

At first, seeing that her family had a single cow, I assumed there wouldn't be enough milk. After all, there were two men in the household, and men drink a lot of tea! Not to mention, they had a baby who needed pure milk to drink. But on the contrary, the tea in her household always contained more milk than ours, and they could still spare some for us every day. As it turned out, their cow was highly productive. Our two cows combined couldn't produce half a bowl of milk, while her one cow could fill half a bucket (an iron bucket with a seven-inch diameter)!

Why were our cows such a disgrace? Cuma said it was because his family had spent the summer herding other people's cattle, so for half the year, they had milked the other people's cows for all they were worth. Cuma's cows were therefore free to nurse their own calves, which allowed the calves to grow bigger and stronger. But without regular hand milking to stimulate them, the cow's dairy production gradually dropped. Hearing this, I couldn't help but think of my own two cows back home who were in someone else's care. Especially my poor little calf, only eight months old . . .

Cuma also said that the neighbors spared no expense, feeding their dairy cow nutrition boosts in the form of corn. While our cows went hunting all around the burrows every evening for dried dung to snack on, theirs didn't go anywhere; they just stuck close to the burrow door and waited.

SAYNA WAS SHORT AND ALWAYS wore a smile on her face. She was even-tempered, astute, and somewhat reticent. She was always spinning yarn, embroidering, and cleaning. Besides milking the cow, carrying snow, or collecting manure, we rarely saw her outside.

When it came to cleaning the sheep pen, herding livestock, and other forms of collective labor, she rarely participated, at most lending a hand to tie up a camel or two in the evening when everyone else was too busy. We all understood that this was because she had a child to look after.

The men spent most of their time outside herding sheep, looking for camels, and working on the cattle burrow and sheep pen. When Sayna and I sewed together, it was usually only the two of us. Her Mandarin wasn't even as good as Sister-in-law's, but she was happy to chat with me all the same. When I understood what she was saying, I tried my best to reply. When I didn't, I laughed and bumbled through. When she saw me laugh, she laughed back. Seeing that her laugh was heartier, I could only offer an even heartier laugh. When she saw that I was laughing even heartier, then . . . then the two of us kept laughing harder and harder until there was no way to put a stop to it. How exhausting.

But most of the time we concentrated on our own tasks without communication of any kind. Sometimes, as she embroidered, she'd start to sing. Soft and sweet, her voice was like a young girl's. I listened intently, not daring to look up, afraid that I'd interrupt the beautiful, delicate tune.

Once, when we all went to the neighbors' to drink tea, Cuma revealed that Sayna was the daughter of a blacksmith. Don't let her thin, short frame fool you, there was no smith work that was beyond her! He reminded me to pay special attention to her tin spoons and milk ladles. I studied them in my hand. They weren't exactly exquisite, but they were clearly thoughtfully crafted, with rings of decorative patterns modestly embellishing their surface.

Sayna was quite particular about the way she brewed tea, always adding pepper and cloves (our family only made this kind of tea on the coldest days), plenty of milk, and just the right amount of saltiness. Their *nan* was always fresh, unlike ours, which were rock-hard and turning sour. Her spreads always included *kurt*, raisins, and sometimes even a bowl of dried apricot soup at the center. In the bowl was a spoon, which everyone shared to drink the dried apricot soup.

THE NEIGHBORS' WINDOW FACED southwest; the afternoon sun cast a small square of light onto the bed platform. I spent almost every minute of every afternoon throughout January and February in this warm little square quietly working my needle, bit by bit expanding the colors and lines on the felt. When the patch of sunlight shifted, I shifted with it. By the time I reached the edge of the bed, I'd call it a day. The burrows were too dark; it was only possible to work properly where there was sunlight.

Beneath the window was a low platform made of manure bricks, covered with a green rug. On top of the platform was a tall stack of blankets draped with a shimmering muslin cloth. The big leopard cat often perched on top of the blankets, and through the hazy plastic sheet, stared entranced at the blurry sky outside. When the silhouette of a bird flitted across the sky, its body would recoil, ready to pounce.

Whenever livestock passed by, the roof shook and a tiny waterfall of sand cascaded in through the cracks around the window. If Karlygash was awake, she'd turn to stare at the stream of sand, mesmerized, enchanted, wanting time and again to climb up for a closer inspection. But for her, that was practically the edge of the universe.

Otherwise, she spent her time softly babbling to herself or tugging on the cat, trying to get it to stand up. The somnolent cat, like an empty, deflated hide, let the baby do as she pleased with it.

When we embroidered, we sat facing each other. Silently, we let our needles and threads fly. When Sayna felt tired, she put down her needle and picked up her little girl for a cuddle. Although Sayna appeared older than she was, she remained attractive, with a slender face, high cheekbones, rosy cheeks, big beautiful eyes, and a prominent chin. Her husband had handsome features too. The baby didn't look like either of them in particular. Hers was the unmarred beauty of a new life. Her curved profile was as refined and stylized as that of a cartoon character's. Kama explained that Karlygash means "swallow," as in the bird.

When Shinshybek and young Kurmash were in the burrow, the space remained just as quiet. Shinshybek was always sleeping, and Kurmash was always playing with his phone. Sayna sewed for a while, then did housework for a while. Karlygash played and slept, slept and ate, then ate and played again. Only the music from Kurmash's phone never ceased to sound from a corner on the left side of the burrow somewhere. That was where the standoffish young man spent every moment inside, never venturing to the world to the right side of the bed. To the right was the kitchen stove, Karlygash's cradle, the bag of yarn, and the pot of snow. That was the husband and wife's territory.

Three weeks after we reached this place in the wilderness, Kurmash left. There was no sign of him for half a month. The neighboring family became smaller, their day-to-day life busier, more demanding. Whenever Sayna had any small tasks like skeining yarn, she'd bring it to our burrow and ask me for help. And she often asked me to go over to babysit.

HAVING NEIGHBORS LIKE THESE was great. In addition to being able to divide the work, there was somewhere to visit and chat. If some little thing was missing, we could borrow from each other. When one family made delicious food, they'd share it with the other. No matter what, it was better than being a single family, alone in the vast territory. But as time went on, disagreements inevitably arose. When it came to the division of labor, everyone had their good reasons. On the whole though, there was camaraderie.

At first, when Sister-in-law would ask me to fetch Cuma back from the neighbors' for dinner, I knocked, opened the door, then stuck my head over the threshold to shout, "Brother, dinner!" Considering the job done, I returned home. Cuma came back right away and rebuked me: "With all those people there, how can you only call on me? If you're going to shout, then shout for everyone to come. When they hear you shouting for me alone, they'd feel unwelcome."

I asked, "But if I ask, would they really come eat?"

He said, "It doesn't matter if they come or not. You should still ask. We all live together, so we're one big family." It was a heartfelt complaint.

A little over a month later, when Sister-in-law sent me to fetch their son, Zhada, who had joined us by then, for dinner, Cuma made a point of emphasizing, "Just get Zhada . . ." which made it awkward for me, so I just stood outside our own doorway and shouted across the distance, "Zhada! Come out!" Only when he'd followed my voice outside and walked near me did I whisper, "Dinnertime . . ."

14.

Plum Blossom
and Panda Dog

T HE OTHER IMPORTANT MEMBERS of the Cuma household were
Plum Blossom and Panda Dog. When I carried twenty kilos of snow on
my back, lumbering up and down over the dunes, heart thumping, puffing
like an ox, only to look up and see that home was still no more than a speck in
the distance ... in moments like these, I felt envious of Plum Blossom and
Panda Dog. They must have been the happiest creatures in the world! While I
was struggling, Plum Blossom was likely testing out the most comfortable
position possible for sleeping, and Panda Dog likely also had zilch to do, besides
try hard to kill time, searching everywhere for imaginary foes. When I pictured
Plum Blossom sleeping beside the warm stove, a paw over his face one moment,
a paw over his ear the next, as if the whole world was disturbing his precious
nap, and Panda Dog dozing, curled up as tightly as she could with her head under
her belly, like a headless, tailless ball of fur ... I could only sigh—no work, no
burdens, to sleep whenever you're tired, what a blissful life that must be!

In reality, the wilderness does not tolerate helpless things, and the two pets
had their troubles too.

Plum Blossom was still too young to catch mice. As a loafer, he had a lowly
status in the home. Whenever Cuma was in a drunken rage, he was always
the primary target. It wasn't like the dog, who could run away whenever the

club was about to land. The burrow was only so big; where could the kitten go? It was so cold outside, so unfamiliar—he was only four months old, and its horizon hadn't expanded beyond his home. So, under this roof, he kept his head down. He lived his cat life with his tail between his legs, never daring to fight or even meow back. After a beating, he still had to bow down in supplication. Whenever he could, he practiced catching mice, sharpening his claws, working hard to grow into a useful cat.

Plum Blossom was once a yellow cat. One day, Cuma was out marking the camels, using red spray paint to write such and such county's such and such team on their felt blankets, even including his name and phone number. When he finished, he shook the can and noticed that there was plenty of paint left, so he gave the camels a red beard and a red tail. Then he shook the can again and there was still some paint left, which was unfortunate for the yellow kitten who was cautiously slinking around the yurt. . . . From that moment, the yellow cat became a pink Plum Blossom.

Furiously, I yelled at him, "How could you do that! If the paint gets in his eyes he'll go blind!"

Hearing this, Cuma didn't respond, he just sprayed, *ksss ksss*, gave the poor kitten two bright red cheeks. Angrily, I tried to grab the kitten from him, but he wouldn't let him go and quickly smudged the red paint all over his little ears and four paws. My mistake, Cuma isn't someone you can criticize.

Unsurprisingly, the kitten was distressed, yowling and pawing at his eyes. Little did he know, his paws were covered in poisonous paint too. When he rubbed his eyes, he screamed. So first, he learned to clean his paws, licking and licking until his mouth was bright red too. Then he tried to clean his face, and after a long struggle, he managed to smudge the red paint everywhere, making the situation even worse. Most likely bothered by the smell of the paint, he turned to lick his stomach, which meant more paint in his mouth. . . . I was livid! Cuma had gone too far! The kitten was so little, so fragile, that if the paint didn't poison him to death, the fumes would suffocate him.

That evening was mellow and relaxed; music played through the speaker, mother and daughter cooked dinner, and Cuma read the newspaper. Only I was exasperated, pouring water out of the kettle, trying to wash the kitten's paws and face. But how can you wash off paint? Not even soap made a difference.

Cuma pretended he was surprised by the kitten's new color, teasing, "Eh, what's this? I've never seen a cat like this before!" and he used a roll of newspaper to bop his head. "What happened? How'd you end up looking like this?"

The kitten's eyes must have really stung because he was squinting, unable to open them. Pointing at him, I blamed Cuma. "See, he's blind now! It can't open his eyes!"

So Cuma called out, *"Mushi mushi"* (the sound we made to tell the kitten there's meat), and Plum Blossom immediately turned to look at him with his big round eyes! The fool!

Cuma laughed. "See! See!" How frustrating.

In the days that followed, he kept picking up the cat and cooing, "Li Juan says you're blind. But tell me, are you blind?" Which was his passive-aggressive way of letting me know that I had made a fuss over nothing.

Perhaps he was right; perhaps these creatures were far more resilient and tenacious than I gave them credit for.

During our second week in the wilderness, I dropped some of the snow I was about to boil for water. Plum Blossom quickly ran over and thirstily licked up every last drop. Only then did it occur to me: no one had ever given him any water! Heavens, how had he even survived those two weeks?

Cuma said that if he was thirsty, he could have squeezed out through the crack in the door to eat the snow outside.

"How would he get back in?" I asked. The door opened outward, so squeezing out was no problem, but squeezing back in would require some creativity.

Cuma replied, "Dunno, but he could've."

One day, I saw with my own eyes how he got back in. First, he clawed at the door until it opened a crack. Then he quickly shoved his head in the crack, propping the door open with his mouth before wriggling his head until he forced his whole head inside. The rest was simpler, kittens being soft-bodied little animals. Ah, he was no fool.

Finding water to drink was essential, so fear of cold and dog notwithstanding, he still underwent this daily struggle. Growing up isn't easy.

Plum Blossom loved the scraping sound of a knife being sharpened. A sharpened knife always meant there was meat to be carved, and when meat was carved, he always got his share. Sometimes, when Cuma whet a knife for cutting cowhide, he would charge over there, full of hope. Cuma would scold, "You! Not even human!"

At first, I thought that Cuma didn't like the kitten, given that he beat him mercilessly whenever he'd had a drink. Seeing it made my skin crawl. But when there was meat, Cuma ignored all objections and cut slice after slice of meat for the kitten. It was no wonder that even after all the cruelty, Plum Blossom still adored him.

When Cuma fed the kitten meat, Sister-in-law would object, "*Koychy!*" When Sister-in-law fed the kitten meat, Kama would object, "Enough, enough!" When Kama fed the kitten meat, I objected, "It's already had plenty!" When I fed the kitten meat, Cuma would object, "It's eaten more than you have!" Anyhow, that was how the family tried to keep each other in check all the while spoiling Plum Blossom.

Sometimes Cuma would scold the kitten: "You sleep all day! You only know to eat meat! You don't even slaughter your own sheep, you always eat ours!"

I wondered, "His own sheep?"

Cuma said, "Aren't the mice his own sheep?!"

If the neighbors' big leopard cat was Karlygash's toy, then our Plum Blossom was Cuma's toy. One moment he lifted the kitten by its ears and as if weighing him declared, "Twenty-four pounds!" The next moment, he cupped the kitten's cheeks as he asked, "Why so angry? Did Li Juan hit you again?"

He was clearly the one doing all the bullying, pinching the creature till he squealed! But if I yelled at him to stop, he'd cradle the kitten in his arms and feign compassion. "Who just hit you? Tell me, don't be afraid. . . . Who was it, who? . . . Ah? Was it her?" He held the kitten's paw and pointed in my direction.

When he hit Plum Blossom, of course he fled. At which point, Cuma would begin sharpening the knife on the stove top. When the kitten heard the sound, he came back, only to be beaten all over again . . . the fool!

When he couldn't find the hammer, Cuma would blame it on the cat. "Since everyone else says they didn't take it, then it must have been you! Quick, hand it over!"

Even a kind and gentle person like me sometimes bullied Plum Blossom. Exhausted from lugging snow back home, I tossed the sack onto the bed without checking first. The sack crushed the kitten's leg—who had taught him to sleep all splayed out like that? At any rate, the injury was fairly serious; the kitten yowled on and on and had a limp for the rest of the day.

ALTHOUGH PLUM BLOSSOM'S situation was far from ideal, compared with Panda Dog, his life was blessed to the point of "decadence."

The dog was a fairly pure Tobet breed of Kazakh shepherd dog with a large head, big ears, stocky build, and a dense, curly coat. But her color came in patches of black and white like a Holstein dairy cow. The first time I saw the dog, I asked Cuma, "What's her name?" He made up a name on the spot: "Black-and-white dog!"

So I decided to call her Panda Dog.

Kazakh Tobets are stout and clumsy, with floppy ears that block their ear canals. To make them more alert to sounds at night, herders often cut off their ears when they're young. Our Panda Dog also only had a pair of ear stubs. The ear stubs usually stayed upright, but when the dog groveled, they fell to the sides, making her look bald, and even more timid than usual.

At first, I thought Panda Dog was living a good life. At least every evening she had food to eat—after finishing our dinner, Sister-in-law would take a few pieces of old *nan* from under the cloth napkin and put them into her bowl, then pour a little milk and starch water on top. Mama Jakybay and her family, whom I'd lived with before, never fed their dog anything. So, how did it survive? By sticking to a dog's unbreakable habit.... I have no idea why they hated dogs so much.

But Cuma's family wasn't like that. As soon as Cuma sat down on a sand dune, Panda Dog crouched close by his side. When Sister-in-law went out the door, Panda Dog stuck to her heels like glue. At most, they shouted at Panda Dog a little, but they never bothered her much.

The sheep had their pen, the cattle had their burrow, and the camels slept pressed up against the sheep pen walls. Only Panda Dog slept on the roof of the burrow, fully exposed to the wind. Even though, as I mentioned, the roof radiated heat, without any shelter, how comfortable could she have been? I considered digging a burrow for the dog, but was too lazy to actually do it. Besides, it seemed like she really didn't need one; she looked comfortable enough. This was especially true during the winter slaughter when we all took turns to feed her offal and odd bits of meat. The whole time, Panda Dog beamed with a joyful, wrinkle-faced smile.

Panda Dog's worst troubles came from the cattle. If Panda Dog wasn't around when Sister-in-law put food into the dog bowl, the cattle would run over to steal her food. If Panda Dog caught them in the act, her hairs raised immediately, and three steps away from them, she dipped her shoulders, hackles raised, stuck up her rear end, and barked ferociously. The fact was that no matter how much Panda Dog threatened them, if the cattle ignored the barking and growling, she was powerless. But cattle scare easily and they really did back off. Panda Dog then leaped onto what was rightfully hers and pitifully wolfed down whatever morsel remained. By then it was inevitably frozen solid.

For a time, because her meals had become too sumptuous, Panda Dog started to become a picky eater, leaving a few scraps in her bowl every day. As time went on, more and more food accumulated until it all became one frozen spiky ball. Then, for a while, the food became meager, so Panda Dog had no choice but to deal with the frozen ball. Pitifully, she gnawed and gnawed, and whenever she could, she gnawed some more until, after days of gnawing, the spiky ball was finally finished.

But those were Panda Dog's good days. After that came Panda Dog's bad days. . . .

Winter is the season of birth. The cows' bellies protruded, ready to calf. The sheep ballooned one after another with little lambs on the way. For a while now, we'd been preparing for these births. But no one imagined that the first babies to be born would be Panda Dog's! None of us could tell . . . no wonder she was so fat.

Cuma was the first to find out. That afternoon, he unexpectedly began digging a hole by the cattle burrow, explaining that it was a burrow for the dog. I thought this was just some of his nonsense and ignored him. The next morning, he asked me, "How many puppies do you want?"

I replied, "What puppies?"

He said, "Our puppies, four of them!"

I said, "You must have been dreaming again?"

Annoyed, he dragged me to look, and of course, in the newly dug burrow, four naked little pups were squeaking their frozen little tails off!

Panda Dog had given birth to the puppies the day before in a pile of snow, so Cuma dug the burrow and helped move the puppies inside. The weird thing was, normally, when dogs give birth, they become hostile even to family, snapping at anyone who comes near. And if you touched their pups, it'd be like poking a hornet's nest. But Panda Dog was so gentle! When I lifted a puppy out from under her belly, she didn't mind at all and even licked my hand, so trusting. . . . Perhaps she knew how harsh nature could be and that the pup would need the help of humans to survive the long, cold winter ahead.

As luck would have it, a cold front was sweeping in. A radio forecast warned that the nighttime temperatures would drop to minus forty-three degrees. Even at midday, the thermometer read below minus four!

Although the dog burrow was dug out of a pile of sheep manure, at best it would provide cover from the snow, but it would be useless against the wind and cold air. I had a feeling that the puppies wouldn't survive.

Those were some of the coldest days we experienced. On the way home with the sheep, my eyeballs hurt so bad, I didn't dare open my eyes wider than a squint.

For two days, Panda Dog neither ate nor drank. She curled up in a ball protecting her pups. The burrow was too small; a part of her body lay outside

(I hadn't realized at this point that the roof was half-collapsed). What a wretched life. Even worse, before she gave birth, Panda Dog's bowl had been full of frozen soup, so Sister-in-law hadn't fed her for several days as punishment, forcing her to eat the iced soup before she could get a refill. At the time, none of us knew she was an expectant mother!

Cuma told me to bring the frozen dog food inside and place it by the stove. After the better part of a day, it finally melted. The bowl was now full of liquid noodle soup and contained one measly chunk of *nan*. I was hesitant to put the defrosted meal outside again in case it refroze, so instead left it in the burrow. I forgot about it until the following evening when the puppies started yapping all of a sudden. Finally, Panda Dog had come looking for food! I went outside to confirm and sure enough she was anxiously sniffing around the area where the bowl used to be. I ran back in to retrieve the bowl, then back out again, but Panda Dog had already returned to her puppies' side. No matter how much I called, she wouldn't leave them again. So, I snuck over to place the bowl beside their burrow.

Sure enough, the next day, the food was frozen solid. She hadn't eaten a bite because she didn't want to leave her babies again, if even for one moment.

After that, whenever Panda Dog braved the world outside her burrow in the hope of finding food, I cringed, having nothing good to offer her. . . .

Sister-in-law soaked two Ping-Pong-ball-sized pieces of *nan* for her every day—it was far better treatment than what most families gave to their dogs, but was it really enough? I had raised dogs before and knew that they had bigger appetites than humans.

I'd heard that *kurt* was the best thing for staving off hunger, so I planned to steal some (*kurt* was too precious even for our dinner; it was only when Kama went out to herd that Sister-in-law produced two pieces from the securely tied bag). I stuck a piece straight into Panda Dog's mouth. The dog didn't even lift her head, she just swallowed it whole. Such a big chunk and the dog didn't even chew it!

Then I remembered that raw flour has a higher nutritional value than fermented or cooked flour. Rolling noodles that evening, I discreetly slipped a clump into my pocket. When I fed it to Panda Dog, she also swallowed the clump whole.

Sometimes, Sister-in-law gave me pieces of candy, which I saved for Panda Dog. They were calories after all.

Dogs need to eat bones. They need more calcium than any other animals. Every four or five days, we boiled lamb and there'd always be plenty of bones left over after the meal, but Sister-in-law was always careful to gather them all up—they could be sold back at the encampment. In this case, I didn't need to steal, I simply laid out my argument for why Panda Dog should be given some. Cuma agreed for me to take a few to the dog, but only a few. . . .

After that I started to steal Plum Blossom's food to give to Panda Dog. This is why I said Plum Blossom led a decadent life—the kitten never had to worry about food. Meat chunks, offal, *baursak*, milk-soaked *nan* . . . they were piled before him all day long.

For a kitten, meals like these were sheer excess. But for an adult dog, it was barely enough to get stuck in her teeth.

A FEW DAYS LATER, passing by the dog burrow, I stopped to watch Panda Dog as she crawled out bit by bit. Only then did I notice that the burrow had collapsed!

I panicked and ran over to investigate. As it turned out, there was no wood supporting the structure; Cuma had simply laid a manure slab over the hole, and at some point it had snapped at the center, collapsing inward. I felt around inside—luckily, no puppies had been crushed!

I tried repairing the burrow, but it was beyond my ability. Cuma had dug the dog burrow like a tunnel, horizontally into a large manure mound. Therefore, to fully reconstruct the hole, the several-foot-high pile of manure needed to be shifted, a mammoth project. Moreover, the puppies were still inside and I didn't dare make any big moves. If I botched the repair, there might have been nothing left.

Anyhow, after a difficult struggle, I managed to prop up the roof by four inches, enough for Panda Dog to slip in and out without too much trouble. But I was still worried.

I pleaded with Cuma to help with the repairs, and he replied angrily, "Do I have nothing else to do? Am I working for the dog now?"

I regularly added new manure slabs to the burrow and gave it a shove to check whether it was stable. At night, I covered the hole with a small plastic sheet (the only one left) to block the wind—if only as a symbolic gesture (it only covered half the opening)—and piled clumps of manure around to secure it. Out in the wilderness, it was even hard to find tattered old clothes or broken felt rugs. . . . I hated my powerlessness, unable to protect anything.

The others said, "Enough is enough! It's just a dog."

And Cuma said, "Do people have it any better?"

Four days later, something unimaginable happened. When I went to check on the puppies, I found two more! I counted them again and again; I was right—there were six! Before, there'd been two black ones and two spotted ones. Now there were two black ones and four spotted ones.

When I broke the news, no one believed me.

It must have birthed the first four puppies, then, realizing how dangerous the cold was, closed her birth canal. It waited out the most difficult days before giving birth to the last two.

It was an ordeal for me too, waking up at midnight, listening to the puppies squealing, worried whether the dog burrow had collapsed again. It was stressful beyond words, but I couldn't muster the courage to leave my quilt. What's more, had I gotten up from the bed in the dead of night for a dog, the others would have hated me. Fretting about this and that without actually doing anything about it, tying oneself up in knots—who doesn't hate that kind of person?

Cuma reassured me, "Don't worry, she's wearing a dog-skin jacket!"

But the puppies had no jackets! They were so thinly dressed.

Worst of all was that from the second week onward, Panda Dog no longer slept with the pups. Instead, she returned to the warmth of the burrow's roof to sleep alone. She likely wasn't producing enough milk and her empty teats were in pain from the suckling, so she was afraid to be near the pups.

The puppies whined all night from within their barely covered sheep manure mound—from the cold, or the hunger, or both. Every day, I slept restlessly. Even in my dreams, I kept thinking, who knows how many have already frozen to death when it's cold enough to freeze a droplet of water in an instant.

Yet, it all came back to these words: life is far more resilient and more tenacious than I give it credit for. All the puppies lived. And a week later, the weather became much warmer, even slipping into positive numbers on the odd midday. The puppies remained curled tightly together in a heap, growing up in the land of dreams. The ones that cried the loudest were always the two or three nearest the entrance, squealing as they tried to burrow deeper into the huddle. Once they reached the warm center of the burrow, they stopped crying, and it was time for those pushed to the outside to yelp and complain.

It was more than twenty days before the puppies could fully open their eyes, the lids parting ever so slowly. But every one of them was healthy and plump, a hefty handful. (Only I would hold a puppy in my hand. Everyone else thought it was disgusting, as if suckling pups were the filthiest things in the world, unfit to be touched. When Cuma's youngest, Zhada, wanted to look, he dragged a puppy out of the burrow with a stick, then poked it back in when he was done looking. . . .) Clearly, I was the squeamish one!

But their survival didn't stop me from worrying: almost a month old and soon to be weaned. What would they eat after that?

Once again, I was worried over nothing. After they were weaned, they were given away!

Which family's sheepdog had puppies on what day in what month—this was valuable information to know. Our Panda Dog was one of the central characters in the local gossip. A month after the puppies were born, a continuous stream of guests arrived asking for pups. Some even traveled from distant pastures nearly a day away on horseback. It was said that puppies born on the coldest days make for the best dogs, more robust and resilient than other pups.

After the people who came chose a pup, they stuffed at least ten to twenty yuan into Cuma's hand. This was a voluntary contribution; there was no bargaining involved.

Cuma said that they weren't actually selling the dogs. According to ancient tradition, if a person who wanted a dog didn't leave something for the previous owner, the dog they took would be equally irresponsible and refuse to guard the home or bark at intruders!

He said that in the past, people normally gave a shirt or some such, but now they just give money directly.

Four dogs were given away, leaving two behind. I wanted one of the spotted dogs, Cuma kept one of the black ones.

"Don't you already have a dog?" I asked.

"Who knows for how long?" he asked. Then, without skipping a beat, he took out his knife and swiftly sliced off the black puppy's ears. A dog's lot.

For how long? Isn't that true for everyone? Hence, the effort to make new life.

I COULDN'T TELL if Plum Blossom understood Panda Dog's plight. He was afraid of dogs. When they crossed paths outside, Plum Blossom recoiled, puffing up his pink blossoms and growling intimidatingly at the dog. The dog approached nonchalantly and stuck out her nose to sniff the kitten, then sniffed again—not food. Situation confirmed, Panda Dog continued on her way. Plum

Plum Blossom's blessed life in the earthen burrow

Blossom viewed this encounter as a personal victory, offering a few more roars before dashing back into the burrow.

As his courage grew, he began to show some goodwill. When the starved Panda Dog planted itself at the burrow's entrance, blocking people's way in and out in the hope they might take pity on it, Plum Blossom would join the roadblock. Except that, in order to maintain the same height and vantage point as Panda Dog, Plum Blossom crouched on one of the slim wooden posts. From there, he locked his eyes intensely with Panda Dog, and if she was close enough, he extended a paw to try to touch the dog.

Plum Blossom and Panda Dog were both incredibly well-behaved. There was no table in the burrow, so the tablecloth was laid across a wooden plank on the floor. When we all sat around to drink tea, the kitten stalked around the periphery, not daring to step beyond his domain. The edge of the tablecloth served as a clearly defined boundary. Only when food fell and rolled beyond that boundary did Plum Blossom, in a flash, pounce and partake without hesitating.

During the winter slaughter, when the bed was covered with horse bones and intestines, the kitten slunk left and right between them, patiently, afraid

The roof of our earthen burrow was Panda Dog's heated flooring.

to touch a single treasure, even when there wasn't another soul in the burrow. In those days, all the unprocessed meat was piled up in the yurt where it was left unguarded. Panda Dog crouched outside the yurt's flap all day, staring in with hungry eyes. She never dared to take even one step closer.

It was not hard to imagine that to have achieved such excellent behavior, they must have experienced countless beatings.

15.

Everyone

CATTLE, SHEEP, CAMELS, HORSES—they all eat nothing but grass. Herding is easy: you take them out in the morning, bring them back in the evening. If that's what you think, then you're a fool! Is there a means of production in this world that doesn't require wisdom and attention to minute details? Unless you were born into a family of herders, mastering their techniques would require massive effort. Even if you could major in herding at college, reading books for four years would get you absolutely nowhere. And if you continued on to a postgraduate degree, it'd still be no use. It's simply too hard....

I asked Cuma, "Why bring the camels home at the end of the day, but not the cattle? Is it because the cattle know the way home, but not the camels?"

Cuma explained, "What do you mean they don't know the way home? They don't want to come home, because the grass is everywhere, and they're not cold."

This explanation left me just as puzzled as before. What did a lot of grass have to do with not coming back? If there were less of it, would they come home? Surely less grass would mean they would have to search for it even longer, right? Moreover, what did "not being cold" have to do with it? Wasn't it just as cold everywhere?

Of all the livestock, cattle and goats feared the cold the most, followed by horses. But the cattle and goats all spent the night in a roofed shelter, while the horses slept in the open.

I asked Cuma, "Why don't the horses have a house?"

His reply: "Because horses have no stomach."

Even more enigmatic. . . .

Eventually, I figured it out. His first reply referred to the fact that camels are greedy eaters so they are reluctant to come home. Even though they wore felt coats that allowed them to stay out overnight, if their blankets were torn or lost, and they didn't return to have it mended, it would have been too cold for them.

His second reply referred to the fact that horses don't have rumens, the large first compartment of the stomach of a ruminant, only intestines that digest grass quickly. They can't be penned in, they have to eat nonstop and excrete nonstop. No wonder there's the saying, "A horse with no grass to eat at night will never grow fat."

PER MY OWN OBSERVATIONS, of all the livestock, the cattle had the best eyesight. During the night, back when we were traveling south, moving from camp to camp, the horses calmly ground their teeth, chewing grass; the sheep opened their eyes in the dark, waiting for the light of day; and the camels lay as still as mountains; only the cattle, one after another, began to stir. First, they edged close to the tent where we were sleeping, rummaging for food, jostling the stove, and making a racket before gradually wandering off into the distance. At three in the morning, when everyone woke up, the men dismantled the tent and loaded the camel, Kama packed the bedding and kitchenware, and I went to herd the cattle. . . . The sheep, horses, and camels were all exactly where they were the night before, only the cattle were already five hundred yards away!

For some reason, calves were always better looking than adult cattle, although it's hard to say why. Upon closer inspection, the biggest difference seems to be in the profiles of their faces—calves have down-turned noses whereas adult cattle have upturned noses. As for why down-turned noses look better than upturned noses, I have no idea.

But what use are good looks? The little calves were the worst! They knew that there was one of me and three of them (two belonged to Cuma's family, one to Shinshybek's). So the moment I started to chase after them, they split up and went in three different directions. Chasing calves used up so much energy that blood no longer reached my stomach, my hunger quickly intensified, and when I got home, I had to eat a huge meal. . . .

Although they were only calves, they were unbearably stubborn. With my hands on their rumps, I pushed with all my might but they barely budged a step—it was exhausting. Cuma offered a wry suggestion: "Climb on. Mount it and it will listen." He sounded totally serious—I almost fell for it.

Ginger gets spicier with age, but cattle only grow more spineless the older they get. When I brandished my stick to chase after the cattle, they would first gauge the thickness of the stick before deciding whether or not to resist. Those hardheaded calves, on the other hand, resisted no matter what. It didn't matter who won or lost, they invariably took it as a victory. It was insufferable.

I eventually learned that when cattle-chasing, you can't just run in a straight line. That only pushed them farther afield. You need to be strategic. First, stroll nonchalantly in the opposite direction until they lower their guards, and when you are far enough away, circle back around until you're directly in front of them—then chase!

What inevitably followed was this: after my Herculean efforts herding them out to the open plains, past the dune ridge to the east, I would turn around and return home. But as soon as I got back home, they would be there too . . . and I had to move them out all over again.

There were many times when, from the top of a sand dune, I'd look around and the calves were nowhere to be seen! Worried, I'd scramble down to search everywhere, looking east, looking north—nothing. Returning home to warm myself up, I anxiously quaffed two bowls of tea before setting out again and kept searching until dark. By the time I returned home utterly exhausted, I'd find them waiting happily in the cattle burrow . . . like a mirage.

The second most annoying thing was the patch-faced young bull that remained under maximum security for the whole winter. This was because, late one night, the beast charged into the yurt and chewed open sacks of corn and flour (we had just arrived and the cattle burrow hadn't been cleared, the temperature wasn't too cold, so the cattle slept outside for the time being). After that quiet night of feasting, the location of that hidden treasure was permanently etched into his memory. Whenever an opportunity arose, back it went to wreak havoc. Our yurt only had a felt curtain, there was no wooden door. No amount of rope or wooden planks could withstand a bull calf. Think of its sheer might! A modest ram was all it took for him to enter. Our only recourse was to always be on guard, beating it back as soon as it got close.

Whenever it wandered within ten steps of the yurt, we beat it and chased it so that, eventually, the notion of "forbidden" was etched into its mind.

Alas, the corn that had spilled everywhere could still be shoveled up and patiently cleansed of sand (which Cuma spent hours separating with water!), but the spilled flour was ruined. What a shame!

THE CAMELS WERE FREE SPIRITS, anarchic and uncontrollable. Otherwise, why was it that nine out of ten visitors we had over for tea were out looking for their camel rather than a cow or a horse? Furthermore, of all the livestock, only the camels had their owners' phone number, name, and village written in big, bright characters on their sides. Clearly, they didn't simply wander off, they wandered *far* off.

Shinshybek had lost three camels in two years. Afraid of losing any more, he monitored his camels even more cautiously than we did our young bull. Every evening he went to the trouble of making sure they spent the night within the burrow settlement. After herding them back, he folded one of their front legs and tied a rope around the thigh and shank so that the camel could only crouch. Even if one managed to stand, it wouldn't get far on three legs.

Herding camels was a source of considerable tension between the two families. Shinshybek's family thought that, like herding sheep, the work of herding camels should be divided equally. Cuma, on the other hand, insisted that since we had far fewer camels than they did, dividing the labor equally would have been outrageously unfair. Besides, Cuma had never lost a camel and often mocked Shinshybek for making a big deal about it.

In the same vein, Shinshybek had never lost a cow to the cold and therefore put little thought into keeping the cattle warm. Unlike our family, who covered the cattle burrow's skylight and hung a padded curtain over the doorway every night, their cattle burrow didn't even have a roof! It was wide open.

In any case, whenever it was Cuma's turn to herd camels, he became grumpy. He complained as soon as he entered the door, "This old brute is spent! Over there—three! Over there—five! There, there, and there—one each!" He pointed every which way and added, "More tiring than sheep!"

Herding sheep, you only had to follow them around slowly, but herding camels required cracking the whip, letting the horse gallop, cursing your ma and cursing your pa, a never-ending contest of wit and brawn.

Camels were an odd bunch, perpetually in a state of discord, forever engaging in separatism; not at all like horses, sheep, or cattle that always traveled in a group.

Besides being members of the free-spirit clan, the camels might also be considered members of the beggar clan. When a flock of camels wobbled their way over, each wearing a patchwork of rags . . . Oy, it was their fault for being too big—where would you ever find a whole piece of cloth big enough to tailor an outfit for them! The only way was to cobble together a patchwork of old cotton jackets, old felt scraps, and old *tekemet*. And the camels never took care of their blankets, always rolling around on the ground (where clothes were most likely to tear off) until they were covered in wet cow dung. Then they'd stand and scratch an itch against a friend's body, soiling the other camel's blanket too.

Further, camels were supposed to be masters at enduring thirst and hunger, but that's not what I saw. On our journey south, the camel bull calves without nose pegs always looked like they were starving. They stopped to eat every little clump of grass bigger than a thumb, constantly falling behind, forcing me, the chief organizer, to work my butt off the whole way! Only the pack-laden lead camel knew how to behave, never stopping to eat or drink all day, keeping onward as always.

On the journey south, I was responsible for the camels. For some reason, the lead camel was always grumbling and grim. It had a special trick, which was to shut its mouth and let out a deep rumble from the back of its throat. Even though it was clearly right next to you, the sound it made seemed to come from miles away.

ANOTHER OF THE CAMELS' mischiefs was to crowd into the middle of the flock of sheep. Especially during the busiest hours of dusk, the wild bunch would try to force their way into the sheep pen! They may have liked the sheep, but the sheep clearly didn't like them. As the sheep filed orderly inside in a line, they were suddenly disrupted by this "death from above" and chaos ensued, wool stood on ends. The camel tried to play dumb; the more you tried to shoo it, the more comfortably it sat, blocking the entrance to the pen. When you tried harder to push it out, it simply rolled onto its side, playing dead, refusing to budge.

Even though the camels were terrible, they still had their cute side. Specifically, these gargantuan camels had the tiniest ears!

WHEN THEY ATE SNOW, the cattle twirled their tongues around, the horses chomped properly with their teeth, but the camels were most impressive of all, lowering their long necks until the bottoms of their chins lay on the ground, then pushing forward like snowplows, instantly plowing up whole mouthfuls of snow! Then they shut their mouths, swallowing it all in one gulp. My guess was that somewhere among their ancestors, there must have been the genes of the *Platybelodon*.

Whether cattle or sheep, if it was male, the time would come when it had to be gelded. Even a giant creature like a camel could not escape such a fate. One golden dusk during the coldest days of January, it was our bull calf camel's turn to suffer the misfortune! Nose peg secured, four hooves bound, it was pushed to the ground with a crash, where its balls were removed. The surgery was simple—after removing the testicles, the wound was stitched up, washed with a potassium permanganate solution, then cauterized with a red-hot pickax. I watched from afar as they stood over the struggling victim. There was blood everywhere; I didn't dare go any closer to look. But afterward, I examined the balls that had been removed and learned that they were olive-shaped!

When the deed was done, Sister-in-law cut a hole in the center of a felt square that she slipped over the poor fella's tail and sewed it onto its blanket to provide the wound with a little protection from the wind. After the final stitch, Shinshybek loosened the ropes and removed the nose peg, and the camel bolted.

UNLIKE THE REST OF the livestock, the horses always ranged free. I never fully understood horse husbandry, only that every evening the mount received a treat—a corn-filled face mask. In addition to the mount, the feeble Young Pioneer and the dairy cow also had face masks tailored to the sizes of their respective faces.

The horse was always highly cooperative while I tied the mask on. If I fastened it askew, the horse would lean its head to one side to inform me: the right side is too loose!

It was such a large horse, but every time, it was only given a tiny amount of corn. Cuma said that it was a good year for grass, so we should save what we could. Suppose there was another bout of disastrous weather; the four bags of corn that we had brought with us might not even be enough!

Cuma also said that, if lost, a herder would loosen the rein to let the horse find its own way home. And why do horses always know where home is? Because they miss the corn! Therefore, whenever a horse returned home, it was fed corn so that it would never experience disappointment. Besides, the horse had worked hard; herding would be impossible without it.

As Cuma explained, horses have no rumen, they digest food quickly and need to eat constantly. The horses' main job was to "eat," which meant they could wander as they pleased. It was amazing how a camel could vanish without a trace after only a day of wandering about, while a horse could spend a whole month unsupervised and still be there.

The mount that the families rode every day ranged free at night as well. Come morning, retrieving the horse was the job of the family whose turn it was to rest. The strange thing was, under the vast sky, with eight directions to choose from, the horse retriever always walked in the same direction. I would have first stood somewhere on high ground to look around before setting out.

Every once in a while, Shinshybek would bring all the horses back. At which point, both families leaped into action, standing on the sloped open terrain by the sheep pen, forming a human net to intercept the horses. Due to my diminutive stature, Cuma told me to wave a polyester sack in the air while shouting at the top of my lungs. When the horses were surrounded, we softened our voices and gently guided them into the sheep pen one by one before shutting the gate. It was unclear why we did this. It didn't seem like it was a body count or health check.

Horses enjoyed the most freedom, running wherever they pleased. Often, horses from other pastures would grace our burrow settlement with their presence. One evening, in the murky twilight, a pretty band of horses emerged on top of the dune ridge to the west, drawing praises from everyone. Though they varied in size, the claret horses all shared the same dark red hue. Their coats were flawless and glistening. Long, white ribbons were tied around their manes and tails as if they were uniformed soldiers at a victory parade—simply dashing.

Just then, our Panda Dog was lying beside a frozen clump of blood not far from the horses, gnawing it with abandon. Nothing would have come of it, except the dog turned and noticed me approaching, so she decided she should fulfill its canine duty. She dropped the frozen clump of blood and charged at the horses, barking furiously. The horses were naturally startled and turned to run. But one foal didn't flinch. It turned toward Panda Dog and took two steps forward, staring menacingly. Panda Dog's ferocity was instantly cut down a notch, but noticing that I was still looking at her, the dog bolstered her courage and barked even more vehemently. At that point, the other horses had also seen through the paper tiger, so they regrouped around the foal. Together, they glared at the dog, very much as if they were forming a united front. The dog turned to me once more, but I shrugged my shoulders in response: *I'd love to help, but*...She instantly extinguished its fire and went back to licking the frozen blood in defeat.

What a brave little horse! The air of a prince, not to mention the long, flaccid penis it dragged on the ground.

FINALLY, ON TO THE SHEEP. But what is there to say about sheep? They may lie at the heart of pastoral life, but they seemed to be relegated to a supporting role, forever patient and silent. About sheep, Cuma had this to say: "Goats are pregnant for five months, sheep for six. Sheep sell for up to a thousand yuan each, goats only five to six hundred." That was all.

Also, sheep are short, so inevitably, they are shortsighted. When they move as a flock, those at the center never know what's going on; they only follow those around them. Only the outermost sheep have a clear view of the situation. Even so, the outermost sheep still insist on squeezing their way into the center. They're all perfectly happy to follow blindly, as if the safest thing in the world is to disappear among the "majority."

The horse stands, waiting for its treat and blocking the doorway.

Only goats had guts, always leading ahead.

As Plum Blossom's horizon, so to speak, expanded beyond the burrow, he turned his attention from Panda Dog and the neighbor's leopard cat onto the sheep flock. Every evening, while we ushered the sheep into their pen, he anxiously charged up and down the flock as if he, too, was lending a hand.

16.

Walking in the Wilderness

B EFORE I LEFT FOR THE winter pastures, my mother wasn't worried about the hardship I might face. The thing she worried about was that I might be bored. Her suggestion: in addition to clothes, pack a few dozen pounds of yarn and knit sweater vests. At fifty yuan a sweater, a winter's knitting should be enough to buy a goat. The knitted vests with colorful wavy patterns flew off the shelves at my family's store. Every time my mother finished one, it sold right away. Supply couldn't keep up with demand.

Cuma was also worried about my getting bored, so he recommended that I open a mini-mart in his home. He'd already thought of the name: "Li Juan's Burrow Retail Store." He even made a list of the products I should carry: ten boxes of cigarettes, one case of liquor (for the man himself, no doubt), twenty pounds of sugar, ten bottles of soy sauce, ten bottles of vinegar, fifty pairs of batteries, twenty pairs of socks, twenty pairs of gloves, ten packs of playing cards, and fifty candles. All I would need to do was send a message and my mother could ask the vet to deliver the goods.

It was a modest proposal. However, only twenty-some-odd families lived in the tens of thousands of acres around us. It was such a tiny market. . . .

So, it seemed that, for the winter, idleness was a foregone conclusion. The sheep were combined into a single flock and the men took turns herding them.

Sister-in-law managed the home and cleaned out the pens. As for me, aside from finding and collecting snow, following the movement of the calves, sewing, and sweeping, there really seemed to be little to do.

But really, there was no need for anyone to worry. Of the many things I feared, boredom wasn't one of them. This thing called "idleness" was something I could never have too much of. I woke at seven thirty in the morning and was back under the covers by ten at night. Of the fourteen hours in between, two were for drinking tea, one was for sweeping the burrow and organizing the kitchen, two were for collecting snow, and one was for helping either Sister-in-law or Kurmash usher the animals into the pen. Aside from the two hours of embroidering and two hours lazing in bed, studying Kazakh, and listening to everyone's chatter, there were only three hours left, during which an aimless stroll was enough to kill the time.

There is no better phrase than "aimless wandering" to describe my slow ambling through the wilderness! Were I in the city, the "aimless" part would have been impossible because of all the traffic lights and the parades of buses, not to mention pickpockets.

Here, wind swept across the open terrain. At noon in January, the temperatures rarely rose above fourteen degrees, like in a freezer. And when your world is a big freezer, your thick layers are your citadel—scarf, hat, gloves are all but indispensable. Invincibly clad in the cold, bright air, I walked safe and free, especially considering how there were no wolves in the daytime.

I wandered the wilderness and there was nothing in my way. When I came across Kurmash on horseback, he asked me if I'd seen the camel calves. I said hadn't. Just then, two young camels cropped up from the dune behind me— but it was only a minute ago that I had passed through there. Impatiently, Kurmash spurred his horse to corral them. Yup, to wander aimlessly means to worry about nothing at all.

Soon, my aimless wandering acquired a new purpose: to collect pebbles. Although the surrounding dunes were made of sand, where the terrain dipped, there were pebbles. The pebbles were tiny, rarely larger than a pea. But they were always smooth, speckled, and vividly colored. Close up, some were semi-translucent, like agate. Their beauty could not be fully appreciated in a single glance. One must study them carefully, quietly, and for a long time. In this monotonous, silent world, the beauty of even a single pebble could send a person into a reverie.

At first, I only collected the white pebbles. The whitest were so white that they would even stand out against the white snow. Then, I found the translucent pink pebbles and yellow pebbles more and more attractive, so I carefully selected a few of those. Finally, I began to collect the colorful, porcelain-like pebbles. When I put them all together, they were as pretty as a handful of jelly beans.

Later, I turned my attention to the variety of landmarks across the terrain.

The largest landmark was the road. Even the shallowest, most inconspicuous road had the power to orient the world—wherever the road pointed was the way forward.

Beneath the broad, empty sky, sand dunes and flat desert scrub were woven together as far as the eye could see. Scanning the land from the peak of a dune, the human body seems no bigger than a leaf. But how can people possibly be considered small in a world like this, where signs of human activity are what leave the deepest marks? Human presence—even when you are still far away from someone's home, you already begin to sense their presence. You notice the tracks of animals becoming cluttered, anxious. The hoofprints become denser and denser until they coalesce into paths. The paths gather from all directions, becoming more and more defined as they close in on their location. Everything leads to them; everything races relentlessly their way. Indeed, the whole world orients itself around them. They are the master of the wilderness.

LAST YEAR'S RARE BLIZZARD resulted in this year's rare lushness. Not only the herders, but the mice too enjoyed the abundance. The open plain was full of their holes, one every few steps. Like our burrow, a passage sloped into each, which on closer inspection, reached deep into a quiet ball of darkness.

Clearly a cautious bunch, in spite of the many holes I saw, I never once saw a mouse. It couldn't have been easy for them, digging holes in the sand at the risk of their whole world collapsing in.

The mouse tracks usually began at the entrances of their holes. After meandering through sand and snow, they eventually led to a distant, mysterious place. To us, the place was nothing but an ordinary tuft of dry grass.

Compared to the delicate precision of a single set of tracks, two sets of intersecting tracks immediately conjured a sense of bustling excitement. Where the tracks crossed, you could almost see how one critter had just greeted another. Often, one set of tracks coming from the entrance of a hole made its way to the entrance of another. A neighborly visit perhaps? Sometimes, a set of tiny tracks circled around the mighty hoofprint of a cow. Just when it appears to have left the hoofprint behind, it returns to circle around it a few more times. The little thing must have discovered something interesting indeed.

A busy traffic route was one that was an inch wide, consisting of dense prints sunken into the snow. Where there was only one set of prints, it was a quiet back road.

The horses, cattle, and camels, on the other hand, left tracks that were rude and brazen.

The tracks of a flock of sheep were a wide, messy stretch that stampeded across the grasslands. Yet from afar, the sheep looked like a fine line, marching in an orderly advance.

And there was another animal, I don't know what it was, with four petals for prints, the front two large, the back two smaller, that seemed to move with a sturdy stride.

Birds appeared ephemerally through spatters of claw marks. Though they belonged to the sky, I rarely spotted them overhead.

As mice leave prints on the ground, the birds leave squawks in the air. In the wilderness, when there is a sudden cacophony of birdcall, a person feels transported to a forest at dawn. But when you look around, there are no birds in sight. The only birds you see from time to time are the massive falcons that quietly land on top of the sand dunes. With their head turned to one side, they stare at you through one eye as you walk closer and closer. Only when you are too close will they spread their giant wings and erupt into the sky.

ASIDE FROM THE CHEE GRASS and the saxaul, I couldn't name any of the other multitude of flora that sprinkled the wilderness. But although I didn't know their names, I was deeply familiar with their shapes and personalities. One thick-bladed, pale green grass with a tip that curled endlessly (like instant noodles) I named "Clingy." A long grass that was elegant, wispy, and soft I named "Fickle." One plant, full of light red and white spindly branches that spiraled upward with evenly spaced inch-and-a-half-long offshoots, I named "Tender." Finally, the pale grass that was densely coated with fine thorns, alert and expectant, I named "Gloomy."

Walking across the sunlit land strewn with Clingies, Fickles, Tenders, and Gloomies, I couldn't help but celebrate: thank goodness I didn't spend this time knitting sweaters!

In the evening, a pack of unfamiliar horses galloped across the wilderness beneath the crescent moon. Though the grasses looked withered, they showed no sign of surrender. Why did people call them dead plants? They were clearly still alive, every leaf and every branch intact.

Underfoot, the sand was a faded yellow. But cupped in your hands and inspected in the light of the setting sun, individual grains gleamed a translucent pink or yellow. Imagine if every grain were a million times its size—what a shimmering reverie the wilderness would be!

It was during that same sunset that I found, on the western face of the northeastern dune, a delicate but tough hedgehog carcass that was perfectly intact. The spines that shot out were as fine and smooth as jade, bearing no hostility. It didn't feel like a carcass, but rather an old shell, lovingly left behind. When I was done admiring it, I placed it back on the sand so that it could continue to sunbathe quietly. Whenever I passed by it again, I couldn't help but say, "Hello!"

At times I wondered what it might be like if I actually opened a store. How at any given time, somewhere in our quiet yet spacious corner of the world, a herder and his wife would be waiting for the right day. On that day, he would wake early to make his long journey here on horseback. As he calculated in his mind all the things he would buy and say, he'd be feeling both hopeful and alone. So, he'd slow the horse to a steadier pace and start to sing. . . . But I never opened a store, never set our meeting in motion. I could only wish that he spent those moments in some other corner, making a happy lone march toward some other hope.

OF COURSE, THESE AIMLESS strolls sometimes led to my getting lost. It was usually on the cloudy days, when no sun shone. The only landmarks were the dummy on top of our burrow settlement and the metal tripod nearby. As I walked, I would turn back to check they were still there. Still, there were times when I looked back to see nothing! Then I found myself walking in circles; I lost all confidence in my sense of direction. The earth undulated under the towering sky. Everything looked the same. There wasn't a horse or cow in sight. . . . I nervously picked a direction and walked until I could climb a nearby dune to scan the horizon—only to find that the lifesaving tripod was in the opposite direction! People have one leg shorter than the other, as they say, so who can blame them for walking circles in the wilderness?

A month passed. The sun's arc shifted slowly northward. Daylight lingered, which meant more and more idle time. Whoever's rest day it was—whether Cuma or Shinshybek—was inundated with idleness, with hours of sleep, and boredom without release. Idle Cuma leaped up without warning, wrapped his arms around busy Sister-in-law, and with the melodramatic tone of a long-awaited reunion cried, "This old woman is the greatest!" His overenthusiastic clap on her back knocked the wind out of Sister-in-law, sending her into a fit of coughing. Anyway, boredom.

What I named "Clingy" grass popped up everywhere.

The bustling world of animal tracks

Only I was as cheery as ever, to everyone's bewilderment. I worked with gusto and ate heartily. After finishing my work and eating my meal as quickly as I could, I disappeared behind a sand dune. There were times when Cuma couldn't help but ask, "Always walking here and there, what are you doing?"

"Playing."

"How is walking here and there playing?"

"I'm playing a game of 'walking here and there.'"

Unable to understand, he simply smirked.

Because I was enthralled by the walks through this boundless land, herding the calves became my favorite chore. The calves plodded slowly, so I plodded slowly behind them. Strolling like this allowed me to look like I wasn't doing nothing.

Before heading home after a stroll, I would climb up a nearby dune to scan the horizon. That way, when I arrived home, I could report to everyone: "The cattle are to the northeast, and the camels and calves too!" It was further proof that I wasn't just doing nothing.

17.

Isolation

IN THE PRESENT ERA, there are no longer any secluded corners. Even the moon's surface has lost its mystery. Even our burrow settlement, tucked in the heart of the desert, maintains a degree of contact with the outside world. This fact was apparent from everyone's day-to-day conversations— always so much to talk about! Chatting in the morning, chatting in the evening, once the chatting started, it never stopped. The speaker alternated from one pitch to another. The listener reacted in varying registers of *hmm*s and *aww*s. There had to be a constant flow of fresh information entering the wilderness for there to be so much to talk about.

Most of the information was passed via conversations between herders on horseback. Then, there was Shinshybek's satellite phone. But how many days would go by before you saw another person? And that junk of a phone hardly ever had signal, a bar or two at most in the middle of the night. Every conversation on the phone sounded like a shouting match: "Can you hear me? I can hear you! What! Come again? I can hear you! Allah! You can't hear me?..." But for the wilderness, it was good enough.

We arrived at our burrow and everything seemed to have settled down; all the important jobs had been finished. It was time for dear Kama to return north to Akehara to care for her ailing grandma. But how was she to make the journey? Where would she find a ride?

When I stitched, my needle moved quickly. Cuma was always praising: like driving down an asphalt road!

The vans that pick up passengers on the pastures were unregulated. Their frightening condition would horrify city folk. The vans crawled slowly through the barely visible sand road at twelve miles per hour. Only when the vans snuck their way onto the asphalt road along the Ulungur River's south bank could they finally enjoy the thrill of being a motor vehicle.

But even the vans were a rarity. If you found one when you needed it, it felt like . . . felt like . . . felt like firecrackers going off! Indeed, only firecrackers, our Han toy, with its maniacal "cracking, popping, snapping" bursts of energy, could accurately express the sense of excitement.

Finally, one day, Cuma came back after helping relatives in the north dig their burrow with news that a car would be passing through a nearby pasture the next day. After dropping people off somewhere to the south, it would return northward by the same route two days later. Kama hurried to prepare.

As I mentioned before, by "prepare," she simply meant washing her hair. I found this difficult to understand. Not merely because we were experiencing drought, so water was precious—but wasn't she about to go home? The banks of the Ulungur had no shortage of water, why didn't she go home to wash? If it was for the benefit of the driver and other passengers, wasn't that a tad vain, not to mention extravagant?

But it was so much more than mere "vanity"! Her life was already so modest that to be careless about a detail like this would have been like shouting, "I'm indigent." Lives of the poor need dignity too, and dignity starts with taking care of the smallest details. Even being clean and presentable for a driver and a couple of passengers for a few hours was nothing to sneeze at!

Just picture it—traveling across a vast, empty expanse, the figure of a girl on the side of the dirt road draws closer and closer. The driver pulls up to look: so neat and elegant! She must have fallen from heaven (not crawled out of the dirt . . .). In this quiet and rugged world, such a sight would be miraculous and comforting, not to mention a reminder of hope and joy.

So Kama not only washed her hair, she also tidied herself from head to toe, unpacking a new pair of socks to wear. Then she sat down for a whole morning putting on makeup, greasing her hair, applying her foundation. She spent half an hour just brushing her hair! And it wasn't some fancy hairstyle either, just a clean, sleek ponytail.

In my view, the information about the van was far too unreliable. It was only hearsay and we had no way of getting in touch with the driver to confirm. There was no way of knowing if there had been a sudden change of plans, and yet nevertheless everyone treated the information as irrefutable.

It was a cold day. That morning, there was only a single set of footprints in the snow revealing the black manure underneath, winding across the burrow settlement before vanishing over a dune. With Kama preparing to leave, Sister-in-law had boiled a pot full of meat the evening before. In the morning, we ate the leftover meat and broth. After that, everyone went about their individual tasks, leaving Kama to pretty herself in peace. When it was time, she put on all her jewelry, a clean coat, and leather flats (so thin!). Suddenly, the girl wrapped her arms around Sister-in-law and kissed her, purring in Mandarin, "Mother, my love!" Sister-in-law smiled and kissed her back.

I said, "It's still early, how about one more haul of snow?"

She turned her hip sassily and ignored me. She was thrilled to be leaving the wilderness.

Kama had already packed her bags the evening before. Sayna brought over a bag of sweets to give to Grandma. Sister-in-law prepared two horse sausages, a bag of cooked meat, two sheepskins, and one *nan* that had been baked in the ashes of sheep manure (*nan* baked this way was the tastiest!). Everything was bundled up in a sheet of white cloth. In addition, Sister-in-law handed Kama a few of the pricier sweets, which made her scream out loud. Then Kama held out her empty wallet to Cuma—she needed money. Without hesitation, Cuma slipped a hundred yuan inside, which made her even happier. She'd only wanted fifty. Finally, Cuma added five hundred yuan for Grandma to use for groceries and medical expenses.

When picking a hat, Kama held out two and asked her father for his honest opinion. Cuma said that the lilac one looked best, so she put it on, low over her forehead. Watching his neatly dressed daughter merrily skipping about, Cuma smiled. He quietly rolled a cigarette while waiting patiently for her to be ready. Next to his well-groomed daughter, Cuma looked woefully drab. He wore his patched-up, oversized boots and the raggedy overcoat that was wrinkled and out of shape. Next to her excitement, he looked down and listless, but explained that it was because he had slept badly: "That meat broth was too invigorating."

Then the two went out the door and mounted their horses. Cuma took her to the road (by "road," we simply mean two car-tire tracks in the desert) to wait. According to the information, the van would be passing through at around noon.

Their horses disappeared behind a dune ridge far to the north. I stood on a dune and watched for a long time.

With the two gone, Sister-in-law and I felt alone. She worked in the sheep pen. After collecting snow, I went over to Sayna's to help with the embroidery, not returning until two in the afternoon. But when I pushed open the door, I found father and daughter sitting around the low table munching on the leftover meat. . . .

They said they had waited four hours at the roadside until they could no longer bear the cold so they came home. The van, it seemed, was either still a long ways off or was long gone.

Kama and I had already shaken hands and said our goodbyes. Now, face-to-face over a plate of meat, we shook hands once more as if it was a long overdue reunion: "Hello! Are you well?" It was hilarious.

Kama changed out of her clean clothes and nice shoes to collect snow. Cuma continued to patch the sheep pen. Sister-in-law unwrapped the white cloth bundle to return the sausages and other treats to the yurt.

I asked Cuma, "Why don't the vans come to pick people up?"

He explained patiently, "If it was your car, would you drive all this way? Fuel is expensive!"

That evening, the money for Grandma and Kama's allowance were returned to Cuma. Though it was agreed that it would be handed over again when it was time to leave, Kama wasn't pleased. I thought it strange as well; why take the money back? Was he afraid that she might spend it? But where in these wildlands would she spend the money?

Days later, a phone call (there had been no signal for over a week . . .) garnered some reliable information: there was a truck heading north delivering ice for the pastures where the drought was especially severe. So, father and daughter made a plan to go to their relatives' home up north to wait for the truck.

But it was far away, about three hours on horseback. Taking into account the time spent waiting for the truck, Cuma most likely wouldn't make it there and back on the same day.

Another round of goodbyes began. The neighbors came over to repeat their well-wishes for Grandma. Sister-in-law started rewrapping the food parcel. Cuma gave the money back to Kama and noted it in his accounts, this time with an additional twenty yuan and a handful of change. Kama counted it twice with a gleeful smile, each time sighing, "So much money, so much money . . ."

With the previous experience in mind, I realized how significant goodbyes were, so I decided to give her something too. After some thought, I decided to give her the small bag I used for storing toiletries. She was surprised and a little overwhelmed, politely declining several times. Until then, she only had a plastic bag with which to carry her small things, which wasn't at all durable. I told her, "The plastic bag could easily break if you hold it in your hand on horseback. Your phone will be gone in no time. Then your mirror too, then your purse . . . and then Kama will be crying!" She hugged me, rocking back and forth to show her gratitude.

Again, early in the morning, she spent a long time brushing her hair, greasing it, applying foundation, clipping in a hairpin. No stage of the process was skimped on.

When father and daughter once again disappeared beyond the distant dune ridge, I thought: Just wait until dusk, I'll open the door and the two of them will be inside giggling. "Hello! Are you well? *Ay*, still no car!"

However, this time, she really left. When Cuma returned around midday the next day, he described the truck that came and said that he watched until it was out of sight before turning to leave. Sister-in-law asked for more details. After that, husband and wife sank into a deep silence.

KAMA WAS GONE! It felt like a hundred people leaving us! How lonely we were.

From then on, the nights grew long and quiet. By the light of the solar-powered lamp, I studied Kazakh, Sister-in-law made yarn, and the kitten practiced catching mice. Cuma pored over a pile of old Kazakh-language newspapers. Every time he finished reading one, he folded it several times and cut it into long strips that he rolled up—for rolling cigarettes. If some item caught his attention, he stopped to read it out loud for Sister-in-law. When he reached the end of the article, Sister-in-law would put down whatever she was doing to quietly read the passage to herself. Husband and wife had learned the Latin alphabet as children, and although both had later tried to learn the Arabic alphabet, they could only sound the letters out.

On evenings like this, Kurmash often came to visit. First, he talked with Cuma awhile, then handed me his phone so that I could help him fix some problem he was having. The phone's operating system was in Chinese, which he couldn't read.

During the day, I helped with the scrubbing, washing, sweeping in the morning before going outside to herd cattle and collect snow. In the afternoon,

I went to Sayna's to help her embroider. Sister-in-law cleaned out the sheep pen and cattle burrow, baked *nan*, and mended felt mats. When it was Cuma's turn to rest, he repaired and patched everything under the sun. Then he slept. Then he sat in a daze smoking for a long time before finally searching for more things to fix. When there was nothing more to do, he turned his attention to the kitten. Once he managed to catch the cat, he pinched its little head between his big hands and "massaged" it because he thought it might have a headache—once, when he had a headache, I gave him a head massage.

When he saw the cat sleeping on its back with both front paws resting on its chest, he waved us over to look. Then, he lay down beside the cat to imitate it . . . anyway, that's loneliness.

Were a guest to show up, it would have been like saving his life!

There's a Kazakh saying that goes, "When there are forty guests, one must be the god of happiness." Which tells us two things: first, Kazakhs love guests; second, there are too few guests.

Yet no matter how plain life is, no matter how little happens, won't there always be something worth sharing, worth pursuing?

ONE DAY WHEN CUMA came home, he was silent for a long time. When he finally opened his mouth, he said, "Li Juan, today, when I was herding, I saw a mouse. It only had three legs so it had to hop." I gasped, desperate to learn more.

When he saw that I was genuinely curious, he began to perform: "Then, I saw another mouse. It only had one eye."

I was skeptical: "Really?"

He said, "And there was another mouse. It had no tail."

I no longer believed him. But he couldn't stop himself. "Then there was this fox with red fur. It was real handsome, but it also had no tail."

I was actively ignoring him now. But he only got more excited. "Last night when I got up to relieve myself, I saw a bear!"

I told Sister-in-law in Kazakh, "He said there are bears!" Sister-in-law warned him to stop.

Over the days that followed, he kept telling the same joke over and over. What lack of imagination. It was like he'd seen every animal on the planet that was missing an arm or leg.

Yet, there was no other news.

Ever since we arrived at the winter pasture, I'd grown an enormous appetite, especially when it came to greasy foods that made my mouth water. At first, I suspected that it had something to do with the lack of a diverse diet. But, on second thought, was it really different from the meals I had back home? They might well have been less varied than what I was eating here. I pondered the question some more and concluded that it must have had something to do with my sense of security. I was subconsciously experiencing an existential crisis—trapped in the wilds with no transport and no way to call for help.

I was lonely, and when there was nothing to do, I took longer and longer walks. Returning home, Cuma would say, "You've been walking for ages, what have you seen?"

I answered impatiently, "A bear, with no eyes!"

One day, Cuma came back from herding and told me, "Seven inlanders coming! They've been walking for days through the desert!"

At first, I thought this was more of his nonsense, but he turned to report the same news to Sister-in-law, in Kazakh. That's when I believed him, though I still couldn't believe it!

Cuma said that they were out here for trade, mainly to sell clothes. Since entering the desert, they had stayed with one herding family. Every day, each of them set out with two or three poly-weave bags toward nearby pastures to peddle their wares. By "nearby," he meant more than six miles on foot! They couldn't leave until they'd sold everything. When Cuma met them, he invited them to show their wares here. But when they heard what direction we lived in, they shook their heads. That's too far, they said, it'd take five hours to walk and they wouldn't make it back that evening.

I couldn't believe it!

They must have faced great difficulties in the outside world to want to give the wilderness a try. To them, this must have seemed like a thoroughly isolated world (not far from the truth), a market that they could monopolize. In any case, their willingness to put themselves through so much trouble must mean that there's some hope for them yet.

LATE ONE NIGHT, Shinshybek flew in the door with news: "Quick! Kama's calling! Quickly!" Any delay might mean losing the signal.

Husband and wife sprang up from the bed and ran out of the burrow before they had a chance to put on coats.

Kama told them on the phone that Grandma was alone at Ciakutu township hospital, where she was recovering steadily. She was taking care of the cows and goats at home on her own, milking them daily, managing the housework. She added that she'd sold the sheepskins she brought home for a hundred and forty yuan each.

Cuma and Sister-in-law discussed the phone call for days, savoring every word their daughter had said.

Soon thereafter, the vet arrived with a package from Kama, packed to the point of impenetrability. It took the couple ages to open it. Inside, along with several *baursaks* and two pieces of raw sheep hide cut by Grandma, were two items that Cuma had long been dreaming about: a channel changer for the TV and the missing parts of the satellite dish.

In that moment, the great silence was ripped asunder. We could watch TV!

18.

The Only Television

EVERY MORNING, THE SUN ROSE in the southeast, and by four thirty in the afternoon, it set in the southwest. After a stingy, shallow arc across the southern sky, it considered the day's work complete. One couldn't help but be reminded of the phrase "Full of sound and fury, signifying nothing."

Short days and long nights—a proportion that I'm perfectly happy to entertain. Plenty of time to sleep eagerly! Every time I woke up, I found myself still enmeshed in darkness.

But not everyone felt this way, especially Cuma; for him, idleness meant destruction!

As a result, dinners always seemed never-ending. When the meal was finally over and the bowls and chopsticks were put away, Cuma would declare, "Tea time." So out came the recently folded tablecloth and *nan* was cut, bowls were placed. It felt a little like the reluctant musician in the poem who had to come out for one encore too many. But how many more bowls of tea could we really drink at that hour? When Cuma finished his tea, he didn't hand the empty bowl back to Sister-in-law but spun the bowl on the table like a top instead—as if to remind us how bored he was. Sister-in-law didn't bother taking his bowl. When he grabbed the yogurt bowl nearby and started spinning that too, Sister-in-law simply ignored him. Then there was the butter bowl. And if she hadn't put away the wooden spoon and pieces of *nan* . . . what a child.

Then he returned to his newspapers. He had many newspapers. After he read them, as I mentioned, he used them to roll cigarettes. He not only had Kazakh newspapers but a few Chinese ones too. Although he generally didn't use the Chinese newspapers to roll cigarettes because Chinese characters have too many strokes, resulting in lots of ink on the page. Smoking a paper like that would make you cough.

Of course, Cuma couldn't read the Chinese newspapers, but he could always pretend. Pointing to the sports page featuring photos of three gold-medal athletes, he explained to Sister-in-law, "This one, he's just died. He did a good thing, everyone should learn from him. This one, also died after he did something good. And this one . . ." He scrutinized the photograph of a swimmer before finally declaring, "Inland is flooding, he drowned."

I couldn't help but laugh: "*Koychy!*"

Then he turned his attention to the doctor providing free medical checkups in the community: "This famous doctor inland works for free. Everybody went to see the doctor, and he told them all they're sick. It's free to get a checkup, but the medicine's not free . . ." and on he rambled. But in a way, what he said had some truth to it. There really have been medical scams like that. Cuma must have been tricked once when he went into the city.

Anyway, that was what life was like before television. But, if you ask me, I thought it was rather enjoyable. Those who wanted to concoct news stories could concoct news stories. Those who wanted to read books could read books. Those who wanted to write could write. Those who wanted to do laundry could do laundry. Once Cuma finished deciphering the newspaper, he pondered for a while as to what to do next, finally settling on turning on the stereo. He skipped one song after another until he found his favorite, then let it play while he lay in bed to rest. When the song finished, he got up and started skipping through the songs again. A lonely evening. I worked on my Kazakh exercise book for a while, drifted off for a while, flipped through the Chinese newspaper for a while, and lay down for a nap. I was the only one who didn't mind doing that.

Fortunately, we had neighbors. Cuma always waited until he couldn't bear it anymore before letting out a final groan, throwing on some clothes, and running off next door to play cards. There were two other men there after all. And sometimes Sister-in-law would slip out with her spindle to go chat with Sayna. When both husband and wife were gone, Kama and I would put on a dance tune like "Black Horse Trot" and boogie to our heart's content. At this point, Kama would gossip about the lives of the young people. In the end, she would suggest that I may as well marry a Kazakh man. All the sheep and cattle and horses I could want. What could be better!

But in mid-December, when Kama left, I started to feel like the slow, dark nights really were getting "slow." Think about it: every day, the world was dark for twelve hours!

And before long, Kurmash left the wilderness as well, leaving Shinshybek as Cuma's sole companion. How interesting can a two-person card game really be?

THAT WAS THE SITUATION until our second month in the wilderness, when, having returned to the banks of the Ulungur, Kama asked the vet to deliver the channel changer and missing parts for the satellite dish. It was the day Cuma had been waiting for. He quickly set up the mesh satellite dish (which had previously hung haphazardly on top of the burrow) and connected it to the black-and-white television inside (until then I thought it was just for decoration). He then cut open the wires of the TV and of the receiver and twisted them to the two terminals of the battery (we had no sockets). Then, while one of us was on the roof adjusting the dish, the other kept an eye on the signal strength on the screen inside. We fiddled and fiddled until eventually, we had access to two Chinese-language channels! The signal was weak, a mere 20 percent, and the image kept freezing, but we were already very happy.

Ay, I'd really lucked out! I never thought that I would be living in the only burrow in the whole winter pasture with a working television set! It was probably because most of the herders were simple people. The clever and ambitious ones like Cuma had long run off somewhere to do business and make their fortunes. He was the only one left on the pasture cleverly tending to his flock. He had nowhere else to make use of his cleverness, so he ended up contriving a television. To watch TV in a burrow—how extravagant! Watching TV in the desolate wilds was nothing short of surreal . . . how lucky that I would never get a good night's sleep again.

We huddled together in front of the box and watched until the battery ran low and the image flickered, turning white, but we kept on watching. We watched until the image became blurry and shrank, but we kept watching. When all that was left was a postcard-sized rectangle displaying a scrambled mess, we kept watching. Even when the postcard was gone and the screen turned black, leaving only the sound, we kept watching—no, listening, listening as if it was a radio drama. We listened until the solar battery began beeping its warning before we finally felt that it had been enough and turned the thing off. But that wasn't the end! After that came a round of tea and a rehash of the plot until eventually, we cleared the *dastarkhān*, brushed the bed, and laid out covers for bedtime. How infuriating.

IN THE EVENINGS, the Shinshybek family would come over, carrying Karlygash, to watch TV. When the kids were home for winter break, the bed platform was so crowded that there was no room to lie down for a nap. Besides, I had an important job to do, so dozing off was out of the question. I was responsible for explaining the programs to Cuma. In turn, Cuma explained them to everyone else.

Mostly though, they weren't interested in the plot but rather the visual details. For example, a pretty girl is weeping because of a broken heart, a Japanese imperialist is slapped across the face, a group of villains step on a landmine . . . these were the scenes that everyone savored, evoking sighs and laughter.

Everyone felt sympathy for the girl from Beijing sent to the northeast to herd sheep (an "educated youth") because of her beauty and her misfortune. However, one thing that confused the audience was that if she'd been sent to herd, why were there no sheep from beginning to end? At last, during the next evening's episode, there came a shot—the girl holding a lamb, gazing into the distance. With a collective "ooh," the audience felt their skepticism alleviated. They waited for the frame to zoom out or pan so that they could see even more sheep. But the director let them down. Clearly, due to their tight budget, the production had only rented the one little lamb.

Watching these trashy TV shows in the city is a fine way to kill time while you digest dinner. But in the wilderness, they failed to pass scrutiny before their attentive audience. The scenes showing snowstorms were so fake that even Karlygash could see through them—only handfuls of snow sprinkled in front of the camera lens, while the actors who struggled against the storm didn't have a flake on them!

In another scene, the lead character's horse broke a leg, stranding both horse and man in the middle of a blizzard. Everyone felt terribly sympathetic. But soon after, another man rode the same horse to save the stranded man. They all cried out, "The leg's fixed!" Silly director, he didn't think to cast a different horse.

To poor city folks, all horses look the same. But for a herder, the difference between one horse and another is as obvious as the difference between two people.

IN SHORT, THE TV had brought the outside world into the wilderness, tearing asunder its tranquility. And while TV allowed the herders to marvel at that outside world, it also made that world seem laughable. There were the commercials for snacks that despite their attractive packaging, still seemed like nothing special compared to our freshly fried *baursak*. When I tried to translate a commercial, it was met with a series of "*Koychy*s." TV brought the outside world into the wilderness, but as a result it made the wilderness even more isolated.

How unrealistic! The capricious love and hate, friendship and animosity, the lies as clear as day, the crocodile tears and gratuitous intrigue, the budget-busting deus ex machina . . . even the herders in their tiny little world had to grumble, "Change the channel!" As for me, sheer boredom and despair: TV is like a tractor rumbling along, tearing up the land, leaving a mess in its wake. There's always the same trash on every program, as if that's reality.

It couldn't have been further from our reality. We put one foot in front of the other, never missing a beat, slowly but surely traversing the seasons. We heeded the laws of nature and rules of tradition; like newborn calves, we understood nothing, worried about nothing, nothing other than growing up, for which strongheadedness was everything. And yet, who is to say which reality is more fragile?

When Cuma returned after a day on the pasture, Sister-in-law, who was preparing dinner, asked, "Should we have some tea first?" His response: "Tea's unimportant. Let's see how Qiao Haiyang is first!" Qiao Haiyang is the male protagonist of a series we were watching. An enjoyable series to be fair, even if the plot was all over the place. But the most incredible thing about it was that from age eighteen to over forty, the main character lived in a perennially snow-covered world, supposedly the country's northeastern territory. Cuma asked me, "Why is it winter every day?" I said, "TV shows are filmed quickly! They finished shooting in one winter so they never got around to summertime."

After watching one series set during the War of Resistance, everyone managed to learn a Japanese song, "*Sakura, Sakura* . . ." They sang it in the morning and sang it at night, breaking into a dance whenever the song was sung. Kama (she had returned with her brother Zhada for winter break) pulled me around the room, jumping up and down, while Sister-in-law danced with Karlygash, her hands holding the infant's little arms, and Cuma with Plum Blossom, gripping on to the cat's paws. Those were happy times.

There was another program called *Two-Gun Li Xiangyang*. When Cuma was fixing his saw, he suddenly grabbed two triangular pieces of wood, one in each hand, and strafed left to right, up and down, and front to back, "*pew pew pew . . . !!*" terrifying the little girl Nurgün. From next door, both of Shinshybek's older children had arrived for winter break as well.

After having watched three Communist-revolution-themed series, everyone seemed to have grasped the tropes. Around the breakfast tablecloth, Cuma assigned each of us a role. I was from the Eighth Route Army, Kama was a guerrilla soldier, Zhada was a little Japanese invader, Cuma was a Kuomintang officer, and Sister-in-law was the officer's wife. Only Sister-in-law couldn't figure out the scene, refusing to play along, but the rest of us threw ourselves into role-playing and were carried away by our performance.

MERCIFULLY, WE WEREN'T stuck with only trash to watch. There was, eventually, a genuinely interesting show, *My Brother Shun Liu*.

What's more, we began to receive signal from the Kazakh-language channel, and there were Chinese subtitles, so everyone was happy. Everyone was mesmerized by the series and we all loved the character Shun Liu. I'd seen one or two episodes before and knew certain elements of the plot. When I told everyone that Erlai dies in the end, they scolded me for talking nonsense.

Sadly, the solar-powered battery was limited. With the incessant ads, we could only watch half an episode at a time.

The situation was as follows: after fully charging the battery, we could watch for three hours on the first day; after charging it all day the second day, we could only watch for two hours; the third day, the charge would only last one hour; on the fourth day, we had to take a break; that way on the fifth day, we could to watch for two hours again. If we rested for two consecutive days, then on the sixth day, we could watch for three hours. At any rate, it was bad. And that's upon the premise of having no cloudy days. That, and that Sister-in-law didn't make a mistake wiring the battery—which she often did, because in the absence of plugs and sockets, all the appliances had to connect to the two terminals, above which hung coils upon coils of wires. Each set of coils presented the possibility of having its negative and positive ends mixed up . . . it was a real head-scratcher. There were times when even I couldn't work it out.

In order to save electricity, the moment the commercials started, we removed the wires from the battery. We waited in the dark (lights would waste electricity too), then reconnected the wires after five minutes. If we did that, at eight thirty we could watch an episode and half of *Shun Liu*!

Turning on the light before eight thirty was not allowed even if there was an emergency. We all sat in the dark, chatting about this and that. The children huddled beside the stove's faint light to make shadow puppets. When Kurmash played music on his phone, the children danced and sang, taking turns to perform.

In those final moments of power, shrouded in darkness, the room silently listened to the radio drama. If anyone dared to speak a word, they were immediately reprimanded.

Everyone felt deep a sympathy for Erlai's fate, talking about him nonstop during the day. But in the end, we never saw the finale. It had been snowing for days, always overcast, giving the battery only enough electricity to power the TV for thirty minutes. We were so disappointed.

The neighbor's boy couldn't let go. He fashioned a wooden gun with a strap and a twisted-wire scope that he carried with him all day. Every so often, he dropped to the ground and positioned the gun for an ambush. If I ran into him, he would hide his weapon behind his back and gradually retreat, an embarrassed smile on his face. He was determined not to let me see his treasure.

Before long, the gun ended up in Cuma's hands, and he brought it home for us to see. We all took turns holding it and aiming it for a good laugh. The next morning, suited up and ready to head to pasture, Cuma went to his horse, grabbed his whip, and then, on second thought, decided to sling the gun solemnly over his shoulder before mounting. We laughed uproariously.

Even Kama sank into a quixotic mood. When the two of us went to haul snow, she suddenly charged down the snowy slope to secure advantageous terrain. Behind cover, in a prone position, she fired pistols from both hands like a consummate soldier, while adding sound effects, *"Puchka! Puchka!"*

Sadly, when *Shun Liu* ended, there were no more shows like it. They were all abysmal, but we had no choice. We watched whatever was on. Annoyingly, this often happened: we would spend an hour watching something terrible, then a Jet Li action flick would come on for thirty minutes. Of course, just when it got good, the battery would die, sending Cuma into a rage. Had he known, he would've skipped the first hour.

19.

Rahmethan and Nursilash

ONE FINE EVENING in early January, the setting sun was exceptionally bright. Even halfway hidden beneath the horizon, you couldn't look straight at it. It was unlike the sun of previous days, soggy, placid, like—to use that tired cliché, duck egg yolk.

We were about to head out to round up the cows for milking when Cuma, back from fetching the camels, opened the door before us. The moment he was inside the burrow, the man started his griping, complaining that the ten camels had run off in five different directions, forcing him to chase them everywhere until he became an icicle! Sister-in-law wasn't one for honeyed words, so she simply held the poor man's head for a kiss, "mwah," on his forehead, before returning to the task at hand. Like that, Cuma's weariness evaporated. Happily, he took off his hat, his coat, and lay down on the bed to rest.

Just then, the sound of a car engine came from the northern sand dune. How unusual! We hurried out to look. Before we reached the sheep pen, a child emerged from the golden halo behind the sand dune! With a bag over his shoulder and a big polyester sack as big as he was in his hand, the boy tottered through the sand toward us. Sayna dropped the cattle reins and rushed up to greet him. That's when I realized that the most momentous event of the winter was underway—the children were coming! That was when the wilderness said goodbye to its cold silence.

Moments later, Sayna's little girl appeared above the dune wearing a flashy new outfit and bright red boots, pulling so many pieces of luggage behind her that she could barely move! I quickly ran to take the luggage from her. What a beautiful girl, no more than eight years old.

Next to appear on the dune was Kurmash, who had vanished for more than half a month. He was also sporting a set of new clothes, looking dapper and lively.

The exhausting journey only just behind him, the young boy exchanged his fancy new coat for his mom's large vest and joined the others in rounding up the livestock with practiced hands. When the camels drifted too close to the flock, he let out an experienced whistle to warn them back.

After I asked his name and age, he shyly asked for my name. Getting his answer, he gently turned the sound over twice in his mouth like a lollipop—hearing him do this was just as sweet. Then, a moment later, he asked me about my profession—in Mandarin nonetheless! But I soon realized his Mandarin wasn't all that great—for the rest of the winter, he kept asking me this same question. But no matter how many times I answered, he couldn't make sense of it.

It was Shinshybek's turn to herd the sheep that day. When I went to meet the flock on their way back, I thought I could be the first to give him the good news. But his reaction was calm, as if he already knew. Before long, the boy caught up to help me herd the sheep. After half a year apart, father and son exchanged a polite greeting, as formal as one between two male acquaintances.

The girl ran out the burrow, still sporting her lovely new outfit, and watched us from afar.

It was the liveliest moment in the wilderness so far that winter, even considering that the children hardly spoke.

The boy, who was eleven years old, was called Rahmethan. The girl was nine. Her name was Nursilash, but we all called her "Nurgün." Both children looked younger than their age. After we rounded up the sheep, I couldn't resist taking a photo of the brother and sister against the golden twilight. When I showed them the pictures, they let out exclamations of wonder and whispered at length to each other.

The following day, the little girl came to our burrow three times in the morning. The first time was to bring a plate of candy and *tary* (a traditional

Kazakh specialty that reminded me of a coarse grain like millet), then to borrow a roll of clear tape, and another time to return the roll. Each time she sat for a while at my side, staring at me, making no attempt to hide her curiosity. I pulled out my camera and snapped a picture of her. She really was a very pretty girl! Her eyes and brows were adorable. Her smile dazzled like a flower in bloom. Her manner was that of a young lady, courteous, reserved. Sister-in-law treated her with the same respect as she did any adult. When they chatted, they spoke matter-of-factly and as equals. Sister-in-law poured her a bowl of wheat porridge. As soon as she finished it, she put the bowl away and said goodbye. Although reluctant to leave me and my camera, she didn't linger a minute longer because that would have been considered impolite.

From then on, I had a sidekick. Wherever I went, she followed, sticking close behind even when I went to the toilet. She was my little assistant—after every end stitch, she offered me a pair of scissors; when I washed my hands, she hugged the kettle to pour warm water; when I carried snow, she helped support the sack; when I wanted to go outside, she zipped in front to open the door. In short, she took every opportunity to do something for me, as if that was the only way to show her friendship.

She always sat beside me quietly when she sipped her tea. When I got up from the bed-stove, she leaped to straighten out my shoes on the floor—it was a bit too flattering. In the past, setting out shoes for others had been my job.

Because I was helping Sayna with her quilting, I spent two hours in her home every day. Under my influence, the girl soon grew fascinated with sewing too. Besides, she was a big girl now, about the age when a girl should start learning needlework. Sayna selected a piece from the freshly boiled red felt, sketched a simple ram's horn using soap, and began teaching the girl stitch by stitch. Her big brother sat beside her as her adviser, eagerly pointing out her every mistake while laughing mercilessly.

Sayna had a short temper. If it took too long for her daughter to learn a lesson, she would begin to scold. With mom yelling and brother sniggering, Nurgün felt depressed. Yet, in spite of the challenges, the girl persevered through to the end of her vacation. Even if the final product was a mess, at least she had grasped the needle's logic. In my view, children should be encouraged, so I pointed out her best stitches and said, "These are good!" But she only looked more defeated . . . turns out those weren't her stitches after all. Still, the blacksmith's granddaughter continued undeterred, fortified, no doubt, by her iron will.

But my needlework was superb, which made the girl exclaim repeatedly, "Wow! So pretty! Wow! So pretty . . ." Her brother was impressed as well. At some point, he fished out an old coat and bashfully asked me to mend it.

I could see straightaway that the coat had been patched up dozens of times before, and each stitch was near an inch long! *Ay*, Mama Sayna wasn't much of a blacksmith's daughter after all. But I soon learned that the little lad had mended the coat himself! As the children spent most of the year at a boarding school without mom and dad around, they learned from a young age to take matters into their own hands. Big Brother mended not only his own clothing but his sister's as well. I couldn't help but feel a profound respect for him, so I made sure to mend the coat meticulously. Unfortunately, the yarn Sayna provided me with was too thick (if it had been ten times thinner, it would have still been too thick), so there was no way for me to display my talent. But Sayna insisted, the thicker the yarn the stronger the repair!

WHO IS THE HAPPIEST woman in the world if not a mother with her three children at her side? As Sayna sewed, she unwittingly hummed a tune. Soon, the two children started to hum along. Then, Shinshybek, waking up from his nap, joined in. The family chorus made the whole burrow vibrate. The kids sang and danced. Little Karlygash, excited by the sounds, wanted to stand up and dance too, but because she couldn't, she cried. When she cried, everyone else laughed uproariously. Their laughter bewildered the baby, so she stopped crying and began to laugh along. In comparison, how dreary the household had been—as dreary as the bottom of a deep well.

Yet, this home—now full of song and laughter—also felt like the bottom of a deep well. Outside, yellow sands rolled in waves, extending winter's icy grip. The family huddled together around a warm stove, laughing and cheerful. It was a lonesome sort of joy. The children growing up were everything; nothing else mattered.

Inside the dark burrow, a single shaft of light beamed through the only window. The sight of Rahmethan planting little kisses on the baby's bottom; the sight of brother and sister discussing the changing of the baby's diaper; son holding on to father as he cuts strips of cowhide, the two slipping in and out of song together; the little girl Nurgün squatting with dripping-wet hair beside the stove, washing clothes . . . these scenes moved me immensely. But I didn't dare to photograph them for fear of disturbing them.

Besides, the burrow was too dark anyway. People in the photos would have turned out looking like ghosts. As for using a flash, one had to consider the baby; besides, using the flash ruins the colors. . . . I began to muse: when I'm rich, I'll buy a new camera with a lens the size of a plate!

With the presence of two students and a cultured person like me, the household quickly acquired an atmosphere of learning. Mother, father, and uncle began to develop an interest in the children's Chinese textbooks and took turns poring over them. As soon as I stepped through their door, I was barraged with questions about the word for this or that utensil in Mandarin. Of all the members of the family, Sayna was the fastest to pick up new words, followed by Rahmethan, with Kurmash and Nurgün tied for third, and Shinshybek in last place. Shinshybek spent most of his time herding sheep or chasing camels, so his slow progress was understandable. Anyhow, each person set his or her own learning objectives, then proceeded to memorize words and quiz each other. Their conversations became a mixture of Mandarin and Kazakh, putting what they learned to use.

Most interestingly, Rahmethan was always reciting the textbook loudly, focusing especially on the phrase "Children are young, they don't understand, so let's just forget about it!" which he repeated all day, saying it and writing it, as if he was preparing for the day when he would need to beg for mercy on behalf of his two little sisters.

Rahmethan was a handsome child, though a little pale and ordinary compared to his younger sister. But he was exceedingly bright. When Sayna sat down to teach Nurgün how to weave a patterned belt, he learned it after watching for a bit, while Nurgün still wasn't clear what went where. When Sayna lost her patience and gave up, he stepped in to save the day, showing his sister how it was done, weave by weave. But Nurgün still couldn't figure it out.

He had a strong sense of responsibility, always proving himself an indispensable member of the family. He never hesitated to haul snow and manure, and at every dawn and dusk, no matter how foul the weather, he helped out with cleaning the sheep pen and padding its floor. Wielding a shovel taller than himself, he worked like a pro. Hard work certainly makes a person stand tall and proud!

Of the two siblings, brother worked outside while sister worked inside. Nurgün was responsible for sweeping, dusting, washing dishes, and cleaning diapers. She hardly had a moment's rest all day long, always singing as she worked. Whereas Rahmethan was shy and introverted, Nurgün was cheerful and easygoing. While she didn't possess the sharpest brain or very good grades, and while she couldn't learn to sew or weave a belt, she was a wonderful singer and dancer, a highlight of her school's entertainment programs, I'm sure! Especially when it came to singing, she could even deliver that nasal, sobbing timbre found in pop songs.

As the eldest, the male, the heavy lifter, and the smartest, Rahmethan didn't miss any chance to boss his little sister around: "Shut the door!" "Bring the scissors!" "Put your schoolbag down!" And she always complied without complaint, even if it was in the middle of an argument or if she was in the middle of another chore.

Likewise, as the stronger of the two, he made sure to look after his sister. In the middle of dinner, when he heard that the calves had returned, he left fried meat fresh out of the wok behind, grabbed his hat, and ran out. (After Rahmethan arrived, I was relieved of my calf-herding duty. He was much more responsible than I was!) Sayna saved an extra-big bowlful of the meat off to one side, which his little sister couldn't take her eyes off. When the young lad returned and noticed his sister's mouth watering, he ate less than half of it and gave the rest to her, much to her delight. Seeing her so happy, he acted like it was nothing.

Of course, there were occasions when the siblings argued. Sometimes they even insulted each other in Mandarin. Sister would shout, "*Ben dan!*" (idiot) and brother would shout back, "*Wang ba dan!*" (bastard)—which amused them to no end. . . .

Then, they both turned to ask me, what do "*ben dan*" and "*wang ba dan*" mean? For the sake of complete honesty, I offered them a boring literal explanation: a *ben dan* is a chicken egg that's gone bad. And a *wang ba dan* . . . luckily, I had just seen "The Tortoise and the Hare" in Nurgün's Kazakh textbook, so I pointed to the tortoise: "This is *wang ba*." They let out an "oh." Then I added, "*Wang ba dan* is its child." A disappointed "oh"; they were unable to understand what was so special about a bad egg and a tortoise's child that these terms could be used as insults? Thoroughly underwhelmed, that was the last time they insulted each other using these words.

BOTH SIBLINGS LOVED THEIR baby sister, Karlygash. They came up with all sorts of ways to make her laugh because her happiness gave them joy. Compared to Nurgün, Rahmethan was the more affectionate. He played with her patiently and gently. When Nurgün thoughtlessly placed the scissors she was using while embroidering a little too close to the baby, he would scream and move the scissors far away while giving Nurgün an earful. Nurgün responded with an apologetic smile.

Before heading out for work, the little lad always sternly bid his sister to take good care of the baby. And when he returned, he first shed his icy clothing and warmed his hands near the stove before picking up the baby. He kissed her greedily and sucked on her ear, nibbling it. And that soft little ball of flesh, that enchanting smile, that tiny living thing always gazed trustingly back into his eyes. . . .

Karlygash was the family's center of gravity. Her favorite activities were playing with a ball of yarn and ripping pages from books. When she was kept from those games, she cried woefully. They had no choice but to let her have her way, handing her balls of yarn to unravel, which Sayna would have to then rewind. Pages of the homework book were handed to her to rip apart, only for Rahmethan to have to tape back together. All the unraveling and rewinding, ripping and taping led to endless hours of amusement.

There was a chess set in the house. The men used it to gamble. Karlygash used the pieces for chewing. The brother and sister threw them at each other. It was another source of endless amusement.

And the siblings' faces were never without injuries. When I asked, they would calmly say, "Karlygash!" followed by a resigned, generous smile. And poor Nurgün, whose pretty little cheeks were marred with three deep red streaks. I jokingly called her "class captain." Instead of outright denying it, she proudly informed me that her big brother was the actual "second captain" of his class!

When they first arrived in the wilderness, the two children were handsomely dressed. A few days later, they had changed out of their outfits. The brother wore his dad's big shoes and the sister wore her mom's big shoes. Above those, they both put on their mother's old coats (Sayna is very petite). As for their own nice clothes and shoes, those had to be saved for when school started.

At first, Nurgün only did housework, no heavy lifting. But after two weeks, she began to haul snow and manure alongside her brother. I felt touched every time I saw the brother and sister tottering through the wilderness with sacks of snow on their back, one in front of the other. As they neared, I could see the little girl's back hunched like an old lady's, her face barely a foot from the ground! As she struggled past me, she offered a shy smile to make light of her awkward stance. Her cheeks were frozen red and frost covered her eyelashes.

Even when the load was too heavy to lift, she never gave up or asked for help. She would drag the sack if she had to because there is nothing more shameful than giving up! As a result, after spending five minutes dragging a sack of manure a dozen meters, she was panting for breath. After I finished herding the cattle out to pasture, I hurried to help her pull—the heft! Even I couldn't carry or drag it very far!

WITH THE ADDITION OF two little helpers, life became easier for not only Sayna, but me as well. I no longer needed to deal with the calves or clean the sheep pen. Besides carrying snow and tidying the burrow, most of my day was spent embroidering. And soon, my first work of the winter was complete—a soft black woolen shawl with eight symmetrical flowers and a floral edge. I wrapped it around the little girl and took photos of her in the snowy twilight. How glamorous! Rahmethan rode by on a white horse bareback. After a moment of watching his sister posing like a model, he snickered and kicked the horse, trotting away. I immediately took the opportunity to snap a few photos of his parting silhouette.

20.

Kurmash

TWENTY-TWO-YEAR-OLD KURMASH WAS like a shadow, flickering in and out of view. His speech quivered, his eyes fluttered; even his purpose was as mercurial as the clouds. It was like he was never fully present. That is, unless he had put on a new set of clothes.

The one thing that signaled Kurmash's presence was music. The moment you heard music playing from a cell phone, you knew that Kurmash was about to appear. Kurmash was passionate about music. Then again, it wasn't just him—all Kazakhs are passionate about music. The memory card on Kurmash's phone was a veritable library of every Kazakh pop song currently in fashion. There were two things that he did every day: one, play with his cell phone; two, charge the battery.

Because of his cell phone, he and I learned quite a bit about one another throughout the winter. He couldn't understand the phone's Chinese notifications. Whenever he found himself with an error, he immediately came to ask for my help.

The young man didn't know a sentence of Mandarin so when he tried to explain what was wrong with his phone, the only thing he could do was to press various buttons while muttering, "This, this, this..." But, somehow, I was able to send him away satisfied every time. Heaven knows how we understood each other.

Once, I considered teaching him the Chinese characters in the phone's notifications, but soon abandoned the idea. Just the thought of the vocabulary— "personalize," "background theme," "time settings"—how much Kazakh would I need to know to translate that!

Late one evening, Cuma and Sister-in-law were next door drinking tea, leaving me alone in our burrow. Kurmash came over again. This time, he hadn't come for his phone, nor was he playing music. He sat next to the bed and said some words to me. After several attempts, I still couldn't understand what he was saying and there was no way to pretend like I'd understood, so I told him outright, "I don't understand." After that, I ignored him and went back to reading and writing.

He sat quietly for a while, then suddenly pointed at the stove, asking me the word for it in Mandarin. After I answered him, he asked for a sheet of paper and pen that he used to write down the word's phonetic spelling. Then he asked the same thing about the shovel.

After that, this young man pointed at all sorts of everyday objects and wrote down their names using the Arabic alphabet, numbering and noting their meaning at the side, eighteen words in all. I was baffled—what had possessed him to study Mandarin all of a sudden? Was this some pretext to come chat through the long nights? He seemed so serious about it.

The next day, when I watched the young man, fully clad, ride into the wilderness behind the flock, I finally understood—herding sheep was excruciatingly boring so he wanted to study something to occupy the time. The previous day had been his first time herding sheep. He felt lonely.

It's easy to sympathize with loneliness, but not taking herding seriously can only rouse anger. Every time the young man herded, by four in the afternoon, he was already lingering at the edge of the burrow settlement, looking for a chance to come home. Even the cattle weren't back yet! Furious, Cuma complained. After that, the neighbors never asked the young man to herd sheep again. They told him to take care of the bigger livestock, chase camels, clean the pens, help Sayna haul snow, and other simple chores.

But he didn't take any task seriously. Building a three-square-meter pen for the calves, he was as slow as a lackey, spending a week on the job only to produce a leaky structure! Even I could have done it in two days.

On top of that, he was always running off to visit relatives. Apparently two cousins of his lived in the pasture to the west of us. Every time he left, he would disappear for two or three days at a time.

Cuma said that he was off playing cards and gambling, adding with disdain, "Young men like him don't feel the need to work anymore. Give them a phone and they think that's life!"

But what could we really say to him? He was still young, with no girlfriend or property to speak of.

And then there was the solitude. Despite being with his brother and sister-in-law, he was still living under other people's roof. While the family sang merrily, Kurmash was off in his corner, lost in his cell phone as if he wasn't there. Sometimes, they really did forget that he was there.

During the quiet hours of morning tea, Kurmash would suddenly charge into our burrow and collapse onto the bed. He did nothing, said nothing, and after drinking the bowl of tea Sister-in-law served him, he lay down for a while longer before saying goodbye. I asked what he was up to. He replied, "Looking for camels." During dinnertime, he would return. Again, he said nothing, ate very little, and after sitting around for a bit, left. I asked him again what he was up to. He replied, "I have to tie up the camels." How lonesome.

After our TV was set up, Kurmash's evenings became substantially enriched. Every day, after he tied up the camels, he arrived early, eager to reserve a good spot close to the screen. He watched and watched until the screen became blurry—still, he refused to leave, even when the show was so terrible that no one else was watching—still, he wouldn't leave, even when the whole family was asleep, sprawled across the bed—still, he wouldn't leave, and after Cuma pointed the flashlight at the clock, showing how late it was—still, he refused to leave. Eventually, Cuma couldn't take it anymore and complained. Right away, Rahmethan and Nurgün stood up and went home. The young man, however, simply made himself even more comfortable and continued watching. Half an hour later, when the picture on the screen had shrunk to the size of a palm, Cuma finally exploded. He stomped over to click on the light, turn off the TV, and shoo the young man out.

CUMA TOLD ME THAT KURMASH wasn't helping his brother on the pastures for free. For the winter, he would earn a horse or a cow. In the future, his parents, brother, and sister-in-law would pay for his marriage. He didn't have to spend his own money.

Because he was still a bachelor, even though he was twenty-two years old, his status at home was still that of a child. Before the siblings arrived, whenever they ate hand-pulled meat, it was his role to pour water for everyone to wash their hands. A kettle in one hand and a basin in the other, he served us, one at a time. Having a young man of his age to wait on everyone was a little awkward for everyone involved. Further, when Sayna invited Sister-in-law for tea, she was still asking Kurmash to deliver the message.

Bolat, who lived in the western pasture, was the same age as Kurmash. As a married man and a father, his visits were greeted with respect and courtesy. He stepped around Kurmash with dignity to take the seat of honor while Kurmash could only sit in a corner and play with his phone.

Whether it was because he felt out of place or because of a genuine preference for being alone, like a child, he never joined the conversations.

It wasn't until Shinshybek's two children arrived in the burrow that Kurmash was able to find something new to do with his days. Every day, he studied the siblings' Chinese textbooks, a crash course of sorts (of course, the eighteen words that I already taught him were long forgotten), and humbly asked the children for guidance. But his questions were so basic that the children couldn't stop laughing and they didn't bother to answer him.

Nonetheless, the young man's desire to learn was admirable. When he had a free moment, he laid a small plank over a corner of the bed, took out a pencil stub, and set to scribbling line after line on a crumpled elementary school student's workbook. His approach remained the same: first, spell a word out phonetically in Arabic, note the meaning at the side and add a number, then review and test himself. Quietly, I thought to myself, if only he'd been this industrious as a kid at school, he might have a different life now. . . .

The black sheep of the family, Kurmash saved his warmth for Karlygash, whose name he'd gently call when he passed her. And only Karlygash was willing to smile and giggle when she heard his voice. Only Karlygash treated him as an equal, being unaware that he was somehow different.

Aside from Karlygash, the only other person he enjoyed interacting with was Kama. It was probably because they were about the same age, so they had shared concerns and topics of conversation. Even though Kama didn't think much of him behind his back, face-to-face, she was very polite. One important element of their relationship was the exchanging of memory cards so that they could listen to each other's music.

Less than two years ago, when young people visited each other, they still swapped cassette tapes. In a mere two years, it had become memory cards. The times really are changing.

Another person with whom Kurmash shared a close bond was Rahmethan. The two often laid out the chessboard to see who was better. As it turns out, the two were quite evenly matched. It was clear that Kurmash liked to listen to the things Rahmethan said, quietly admiring him. Rahmethan was a clever student full of knowledge that might impress a herder. He demonstrated a trick: lighting a candle under a paper box filled with water, yet the paper never burned, much to everyone's amazement.

Besides Karlygash, Kama, and Rahmethan, Kurmash had two other true friends, which were the cousins that he often (often meaning three times) visited in the pastures to the west of us. Like Kurmash, these two young men often came to visit over the winter (often meaning twice). The two young men were humble and timid, always smiling, never speaking. They looked different too, dark-skinned, curly hair, like Indians or Tajiks, which is why Cuma dubbed them the "foreign Kazakhs." When they were here, the trio did everything together, herding sheep, chasing camels, and so on. That or they did nothing together, quietly standing in a row on top of the northern sand dune.

Anyway, that's all I have to say about Kurmash. I knew so little about him, which could be why he seemed like a shadow to me. But don't all living things need to manifest themselves somehow? No matter what, for better or worse, this young man didn't seem like he could ever leave the pastures or leave this life behind. What else could he do? He couldn't speak Mandarin, and he wasn't a child anymore. I can only hope that he will have his own family and his own cattle and sheep someday, that he will find a life that suits him, that he will no longer be so lonely, so dejected, so lost.

ONE DAY, WALKING IN THE WILDS, after skirting a sand dune, I bumped into him. He was holding several large sacks under his arms, heading west to collect snow by himself. After waving hello, he asked me if I wanted to join him. I asked if it would be far. He said it would be far. Then he set out by himself, slowly shrinking into the distance. Deep into the wilderness, he continued walking slowly, determined to reach his destination. That scene left a deep impression on me, like a blade slicing softly across my skin. In that moment, Kurmash was no vague shadow.

When I asked if I could take a picture of him, he said, "Wait a second." Casually, he took out a comb and a mirror from his jacket, took a look at himself, combed his hair a bit, looked again, then turned to me with a smile. In that moment too, he wasn't a shadow.

21.

Zhada

NEAR THE END OF JANUARY, Kama returned to the wilderness, having spent over a month at the summer encampment. Dressed in green, she emerged over the peak of the sand dune to the north, hands full, slowly descending. I was off in the distance hauling snow. The moment I saw her, I dropped the sack of snow and scooping plate and dashed toward her, shouting her name. I shook her hands, hugged her, then took her luggage from her. Together, we walked back to the burrow. Kama asked, "Li Juan, no me, good or bad?" I cried, "Bad!"

Kama arrived with her fifteen-year-old brother, Zhada, Cuma's only son. Our burrow had gained a new member.

Even though I had never met Zhada, I already knew everything about him. There were clues all over the burrow—a heart-shaped wooden ladle he had carved, with a little heart engraved into the handle and painted red. The redbrick oven to the right of the door was his handiwork. Even though it was never used, no one wanted to tear it down.

The burrow's floor was made of a mix of sand and soil. When we first arrived, Cuma coated it with a precious layer of mud, but after days of people walking in and out, not much was left. As a result, some amount of sand had to be swept up every day. Would the floor sink lower and lower over time? At this point, the doorway was already a foot and a half above the floor. You had to hop down every time you came home. A trench was beginning to appear along the base of the walls. Every few days, Cuma would fill in the trench with sheep manure, then coat it with mud. But how long would that last? I suggested taking apart the brick oven and using the bricks to pave the floor. But that proposal was quickly dismissed, the reason being, "Zhada built it when he was thirteen; just look at how perfectly the bricks are laid!" I could only agree: "You're right, it's perfect, what a talented kid." Cuma said proudly, "Like father, like son."

Starting about half a month in advance, Sister-in-law had begun to wear the boy on her lips, counting the days on her fingers until winter vacation. To prepare for her children's arrival, she carried all the rugs and wall hangings and blankets outside to be beaten clean; she swept the whole house and even fried fresh *baursak*.

No one was as jubilant as Sister-in-law. Her eyes sparkled with joy. As soon as he came in through the door, the boy embraced and kissed his mother, though not without a hint of self-consciousness. With his father, he kept a respectful distance. Zhada sat quietly near the tablecloth and listened while the adults spoke. Once the driver who had brought the siblings back had finished his tea and left, the room quieted down and the son at last shuffled his way over to the tablecloth. Suddenly, Zhada wrapped his arms around his father and kissed him. Cuma couldn't help but pull him in close.

At this point, Kama began unwrapping the packages, pulling out all sorts of treasures as if they were tributes. Mostly, there were bags upon bags of candy sent over by the throngs of aunties. Neatly wrapped and tied in handkerchiefs, they were salutations from afar. Then, there was the *bolangu*, a two-headed toy drum with beads attached by threads to the handle, clearly a present for Karlygash. We all gave it a whirl, "*gu dun gu dun*," before tying it back into its original packaging. This entire time, Cuma didn't manifest any of his usual tomfoolery. Solemn and patriarchal, he sat at the host's seat and received his children's reports.

With the addition of two able bodies, the evening's milking and herding chores were finished quickly and easily. When we all returned to the burrow, the light was turned on right away—previously, only what little electricity was left after the TV was turned off was used for the light!

While preparing dinner, Sister-in-law snatched a brief moment to embrace her son, rocking him back and forth while kissing him. Kama took the opportunity to dive into her father's arms while chirping, "In that case, you can kiss me!" But Cuma pushed her away, feigning anger: "Go away, you're no daughter of mine! Not a single box of cigarettes for your daddy, or even a lighter! Even Li Juan helped me herd the calves and sheep and mended clothes. . . ." Kama protested childishly and everybody laughed. The kids were back. It was like a family again.

ZHADA WAS A TALL, handsome, and rather serious lad. Padding the floor of the sheep pen at dusk, he threw himself into the chore with a boyish pride, eager to prove himself through his hard work. Before long, he and Kurmash became buddies. After the pen was padded, the two climbed up the sand dune to the east and made their way up the metal tripod, where they perched beneath the moonlight. There, they exchanged words about this and that as they stared off in the direction from where the sheep would return.

When he first got home, Zhada was as fashionable as a city kid. It wasn't until work time that he traded his cool new coat for a green plush jacket his mother made, which instantly transformed him into an ordinary shepherd boy. Cuma picked up the new coat that had been discarded on the felt mat on the bed and studied it from every angle before asking the boy how much it cost. It was moments like these that revealed that his boy was slowly becoming a stranger.

That evening, Sister-in-law boiled a huge pot of meat, the biggest pot of meat so far! Of course, Shinshybek's family joined us for the feast. The burrow was bustling. With the ten of us and a baby, we could barely fit! During the banquet, the youngsters seemed especially courteous and serious. At home, Nurgün was always a hungry girl. But as a guest, she insisted on sitting behind the grownups, refusing to sit at the tablecloth even when invited. Before the mouthwatering hill of meat, which the grownups urged her to eat up, she slowly nibbled only a few pieces—reluctantly. Clearly, she had a strong intuition for feminine grace! Zhada was just as courteous too. When he saw his sister wipe her hands, he promptly followed—a signal that he was full and would retire from the meal early.

Later events proved that in the absence of guests, the boy's appetite was second only to Cuma's.

When there were too many people at the tablecloth to eat mutton on the bone, the women and children would crouch in a corner and eat from a smaller bowl. On such occasions, Zhada would want to sit with me, Sister-in-law, and Kama, but Sister-in-law would insist that he sit at the main *dastarkhān*, like a real man.

When it came to eating noodles with sauce, Sister-in-law would add a hefty portion of meat and vegetables to Zhada's noodles and only a small amount to Kama's noodles. Though there is a saying, "Girls shouldn't eat too much," this was clearly favoritism! Kama lived in the pastures all year round; how many opportunities did she have to eat anything good? But she didn't think much of it. Even if she did complain once in a while, Sister-in-law firmly rebuked her.

That said, as a boarding student, Zhada led a spartan existence too. The free canteen meals were likely no more substantial than the food served at home. And he was a growing boy after all.

One evening, while everyone else was busy working outside, I was in the burrow preparing dinner. I had decided to make dumplings for everyone. Soon enough, Zhada, who had finished his work, came in to help, full of enthusiasm. I rolled the dumpling skins, he wrapped them. In the dimly lit space, he sang as he wrapped, then joyfully announced that dumplings were his favorite; then he asked me what my favorite was. I listed off one dish after another, unable to help myself. Of these, hot pot and fried rice noodles were things he had never heard of before, so he asked for more details. When I mentioned noodle salad, he shouted excitedly in Mandarin, "Yeah! Noodle salad! Mine like it too!" And so his gaiety continued. . . .

When I went to collect snow and saw Zhada, distant and tiny, patiently trudging toward me from the dune to the north with a saxaul branch in hand and Panda Dog tailing him, framed against a background of boundless white—I found it deeply moving. Those hushed hearts in the most distant crevices on earth.

AFTER THE TWO CHILDREN had returned home, every day the boy hauled manure, herded sheep, and cleaned the pen; the girl tidied the burrow and cooked. I gathered snow and embroidered. Cuma exclaimed, "Tomorrow, me and Sister-in-law might as well head back to Akehara! What are we still doing here? There's nothing for us to do!" Yet, on his face was a look of sheer bliss.

When Zhada was away, Kama was Mom and Dad's only spoiled child. Now that Zhada had returned, Kama readily stepped aside. She held her tea bowl gracefully, looking on as her little brother nuzzled into his parents' bosom like a piglet, and occasionally offered a mocking "*Koychy.*"

Sister-in-law thought the world of her only son. She regularly dropped whatever she was doing to hold him. Kneeling behind him, she would hold his head and smother it with a hundred sweet kisses.

And don't be fooled by the siblings' endless bickering. When they weren't arguing, they also found comfort in each other's embrace. Those long hugs said all there was to say about their silent, loving bond.

But most of all, the boy wanted to be close to his father. The moment Cuma lay down to rest, Zhada would instantly creep beside him, hugging him tightly while playing on his phone.

But Cuma preferred teasing his son. Zhada wanted to turn the handle of a broken trowel into a door handle. Cuma said, "Let me see." Zhada quickly handed it to him. Who would have thought that Cuma would snap it in two and admonish, "You should be studying, not tinkering with nonsense." Zhada instantly burst into tears. He threw his bowl of tea on the floor and sat down in the far corner to grumble. But after only a few minutes, he had forgotten all about it. After leaning in to kiss his dad, he picked up the empty bowl and handed it to his mom for a refill.

After our TV program ended one night, Zhada was already fast asleep. Cuma crept up to his son and suddenly let out a piercing whistle in his ear. The prank left the child bawling with indignation. While scoffing at his son, Cuma told him to go relieve himself in preparation for bedtime. As he spoke, he slipped a jacket over the boy's shoulders so he wouldn't catch a cold when he went outside.

I rarely let people browse my camera's photos, in order to conserve the battery. On one of those rare occasions, I had only flipped through a few photos before Cuma said, "That's enough, turn it off." I was taken aback because he was always the one who enjoyed looking at photos the most. By way of explanation, he added, "Zhada's outside. Wait until he's back and we'll look together."

Zhada was the family's center of gravity. They were a bit overprotective of him, but not to the point of being indulgent. He loved being the center of attention, yet he did not become a brat as a result. In short, he was a good kid (aside from always sleeping in) who never shirked on his chores. He was brilliant too, able to disassemble a cell phone down to its keypad, then put it back together again (it was Kama's cell phone he disassembled, resulting in some harsh words from her). He could also take a battery from a broken MP3 player, the bulb from a broken flashlight, and a switch from some other piece of electronics, and voilà, a functioning flashlight. And a bright one at that! In short, he was the pride of the family. But this clever boy, for some reason, ended up with bad grades.

Of course, Zhada had his defiant moments too. When everyone was busy with no hands to spare, Sister-in-law told him to quit whittling the piece of wood and go out to collect some snow. He complained for ages, and after some more procrastination, he reluctantly went out with a sack. An hour later, there was still no sign of him. Sister-in-law asked me to put down my needlework and go look for him. As soon as I stepped outside, I spotted the kid in the clearing just beyond the burrow settlement drawing on the ground with a shovel! The sack, bulging with snow, lay by his side.

The clearing where he stood was covered in a fresh layer of snow. The snow was white and the manure beneath it was black. The image he "drew" with his shovel had the effect of crisp, clear black lines against a white page. It was the face of a giant monster with bulging eyes and a thick beard. I praised him, "It looks just like your dad!" He said, "*Koychy!*" before smudging it out with his shovel.

IT'S HARD TO SAY if this thing called "childhood" is interesting or boring. There are many pointless activities that, when they were done by Zhada, became fascinating. For example, one day he decided to fill a bottle of his eldest sister Sharifa's expired liquid foundation with hot water, then walk around squirting the milky-white liquid everywhere. When he ran out of hot water, he used tea from the thermos. Like that, he whiled away a whole hour; what kind of pleasure could he possibly have gotten from it?

Other equally pointless activities included:

- Cutting up a piece of white cloth that Kama intended to embroider onto a cushion and turning it into a Japanese flag. Then cutting a sleeve off one of Sister-in-law's old red tops and turning it into a red flag. Then Zhada and Rahmethan held one flag each high above their heads and charged up a sand dune for an all-out war.
- Draping a large bundle of ready-to-spin wool over his head as a wig and strutting about like a model. When Sister-in-law saw him, she laughed out loud. Once she collected herself, she scolded the rascal for tangling up the wool that Li Juan had spent all afternoon straightening.
- After seeing a news anchor from southern Xinjiang wear a black lamb's leather fez on TV, a light went off in Zhada's head and he rummaged through chests and boxes until he found an old coat with a black leather collar. He tore off the collar, sewed both ends together, and slipped the tube-shaped hat over his head. From then on, he wore this topless southern Xinjiang fez every day as he worked.
- Zhada was busy every morning sawing a small length of wood or knocking off a red brick. One would think that he was working on some

small project to contribute to home improvement, but as it turns out, he was making a little wooden car with four bottle tops for wheels; that or he chiseled a lovely round hole in a brick.

- Once he brought home the stiff, frozen hide of a dead horse's head and softened it in the oven. Then he retrieved an intact horse skull that was hanging on the tripod on the dune and wrapped it with the softened horse hide. After carefully sewing the seams together, he had produced a horse-head taxidermy. His craftsmanship was flawless. Even the gaps in the hide were carefully patched and sewn.
- Another time, after connecting countless insulated wires together into one cord over thirty feet long and attaching a small light bulb to one end, he then hooked it up to the battery to light up the bulb.
- And having tied a flexible blade of grass around a white pebble, he created a ring.

But it was only a few days before the carefully sewn horse taxidermy was taken apart by no one knows who. The hide was returned to the yurt where it came from, becoming, once again, stiff and frozen. The skull was found hanging from the tripod once again. The wooden car was tossed to a corner of the burrow with three of its wheels missing. The power cord that once stretched over thirty feet long shrank by the day until eventually the broken bulb was tossed into the oven.... Only the fez from southern Xinjiang survived—he wore it every day. The boy certainly was clever, applying himself to everything he did, only most of the things that he made were of no use to anyone at all.

Although the nose pegs he whittled for the camels were useful. Upon Cuma's request, he ran out to retrieve a bundle of saxaul branches. Sitting by the bed, he whittled and whittled, producing twenty-six units in one sitting! But they only had three camels....

When Kama painted her fingernails, he begged to paint his too. But what would a boy do with painted fingernails? So he painted his toenails....

ON A WARM DAY in the middle of February, Kama and I made a visit to the family that lived in the pastures northwest of us. When we returned, I couldn't stop talking to Cuma about how many children the family had. Cuma griped, "They don't follow the two-child policy! They have a relative in the family-planning department!" Because of the policy, Zhada exceeded their family quota, leading to a fine of over ten thousand yuan, a fact that Cuma was still upset about.

This only son of theirs wasn't particularly healthy. He was often plagued by fits of coughing. It was especially bad at night. Even when he ran out of breath, he still couldn't stop coughing. Lying in darkness, we listened quietly, having long gotten used to the troubling sound. I urged Cuma to make Zhada visit a doctor in case it turned into something more serious. Cuma said, "I gave him the money, he bought a cell phone." I was speechless. But how can you blame him for wanting to be cool? He was young and lived in a world of shiny objects far from home.

On another warm day in the middle of February, Zhada donned his father's getup and went herding. I could hardly believe it, so I asked, "Will he come back by noon?" Cuma replied, "No way! No earlier than eight!"

Out with the flock, it was critical that Zhada had his cell phone. That way, he could listen to music while the sheep grazed. On top of that, he had to have Kama's phone too. This way, when one ran out of battery, he could continue to listen to music on the other.

I suggested taking his school bag instead—study while you herd. He giggled and acted as if he hadn't heard me.

The neighbor's boy, Rahmethan, envied this little lone shepherd so much that he climbed on a white horse bareback and followed Zhada out to the pastures with the flock. From the top of a sand dune, I watched the two kids ride side by side into the distance. Even though I couldn't hear their conversation or see the expressions on their faces, I could nevertheless sense their excitement and joy.

Just as I expected! By twelve thirty, the boy came home for tea, having left the sheep behind. Like a decorated hero, when he ate fried noodles, he insisted that his mother should add extra sugar.

I was sure that Zhada wouldn't be able to keep it up for more than a few days. Who would have guessed that from that day on, whenever it was our family's turn to herd, the boy rushed to volunteer. His enthusiasm was quite remarkable.

It wasn't until school was starting up again and the boy was sorting through his inventory that he would be taking north to school with him that I finally understood—Cuma had promised to give him five yuan every time he herded. . . .

Cuma exclaimed, "He arrived at the burrow with only fifty cents on him. Now he's leaving with more than sixty bucks!"

Zhada had a head for business. He even pocketed the cash gift left in exchange for Panda Dog's puppies. Outrageous! He never even fed the dogs, yet he took the money when they were sold!

What's more, he sweet-talked Kama into trading her new phone for his secondhand one. Kama quickly came to regret the decision. When she wanted to trade back, the rascal said, "Sure, but you have to give me twenty yuan on top!" He even explained his logic, which left Kama thoroughly confused. As Cuma savored the siblings' dispute, he said to me, "The first time they traded, I told them to write a contract. They didn't listen. Now they are having ding-dong [trifling] problems!"

AS ZHADA'S DEPARTURE approached, Kama became deeply anxious, often mumbling to herself, "The twentieth, Zhada will be gone! . . ." When the parents heard her, they had nothing to say. But the boy thought nothing of it and seemed even more chipper than usual. Of course, he was leaving this desolate place soon. More importantly, his wallet was bulging. . . .

During those last few days, when I was teaching Kama Chinese, for some reason the boy suddenly felt inspired. He took his Chinese textbook out of his backpack and started to read. Normally, at that hour, he would have had his wallet out to count his money. Cuma exclaimed, "A month, after a whole month! This is the first time I've seen him open his backpack!" Zhada paid no mind, transfixed by his textbook.

On the day before his departure (apparently a car would come pick him up), Zhada sang compulsively all morning. Everyone sat around the tablecloth eating last night's leftover meat on knife-cut noodles. While eating a piece of backbone, Cuma said, "Why wait for a car? You can fly there in an airplane!" With a pair of wing bones in his hands, he made a humming noise indicating that the "airplane" was taking off. Everyone laughed. But the sadness of separation still hung in the air. Only the person of interest was distinctly cheerful, carefully chewing the bones, worried that he might get grease on his new clothes.

Those last few mornings were shrouded in fog. By the time the fog dissipated, the blue sky was once again obscured by the rising mist. The day remained overcast. The solar-powered battery barely charged, so we couldn't watch TV in the evenings. Add to that the fact that the car was several days behind schedule, and Zhada grew anxious—he would herd the flock to earn some extra cash, but he was afraid that he might miss the car; or maybe he wouldn't, in which case it was another day wasted waiting. . . . From a high vantage point, he watched the two flocks (by that point, our new neighbors, Kulynbek and his family, had moved into one of our burrows) as they walked far away, slowly converging to the same distant point. He watched for a long time. Zhada was the son of a shepherd, so of course he loved the land, but what truly inspired him was the glittering life beyond the pastures.

PART

THREE

Serenity

22.

Twilight

I T'S HARD TO PUT into words just how long twilight lasts. From when the sun weighs down on the western horizon like a hefty pile of golden ingots to the luminous glow after sunset, and then, when the constellations begin to light up and the world fades into serenity—in this stretch of time, we are able to do so many things! Drink tea, herd cattle, milk cows, add "bedding" to the sheep pen, prepare dinner. Then we climb up the northern dune again and again to gaze toward the direction from which the flock will return . . . then meet them along the way . . . then slowly accompany them home. . . .

Whenever I walk alone into the wilderness, enveloped by dusk, I watch as the celestial halo hardens into a sharp, silvery disk. The silver moon grows heavier and heavier, deeper, bigger, and rounder, its cold light radiating . . . and just like that, another day has passed. As the long night thrusts forth slowly and forcefully, the earth turns away. Darkness, like a kettle of water, fills the world . . . no, I can't describe the power of dusk.

To a herder, wouldn't the experience of dusk feel even richer and more profound? Alone, he leads the flock slowly back to camp. Cold and hungry, he hasn't said a word all day. Beneath the stars, white kitchen smoke rises from the direction of his home. The sheep are even more eager than he is, their heads low, trotting quicker and quicker. If in this moment, the herder sees his family approach him from the distance to greet him, what comfort and delight would that bring! He cannot help but sing.

AT DUSK, AFTER THOSE who remained home finished their day's work, they retreat to the burrow to rest and wait for news of the flock's return. I stood at the top of the northern dune by myself, scouring eastward. Far in the distance, it seemed that the sheep were approaching. I watched for a long while before I could clearly see the outline of the flock moving. They were a little over half a mile out, so I ran home to bring the news. Once I had returned to the dune, I picked up the long whip I'd stuck in the sand and fixed my eyes on the flock as I set out to greet them.

After trekking over two small dunes, I noticed that the flock had scattered in place. They had decided to continue grazing in the dark night air. Shinshybek sat still on his horse, apparently unable to bring himself to disturb the feeding sheep. So I stopped too and watched from afar, afraid to startle the flock and interrupt their feeding, sending them hurrying homeward.

When Shinshybek saw me, he dismounted and walked over, leading the horse along behind him. He spoke his first words since leaving the burrow that morning: "How are you, young lady?" I quickly returned his greeting, but then found that I had nothing else to say. The two of us stared at the flock in the twilight.

A while later, he spoke his second sentence of the day: "Sheep, eat!" in Mandarin, by which he meant the sheep were still eating, let's wait a little longer. The sheep were startled nevertheless by his words. They raised their heads and crowded together nervously, gradually nudging one another toward home. The two of us stood side by side in the gloom, still with nothing to say. Suddenly, he kicked the sand with his felt overboot and asked, "How to say this in Mandarin?" I said, "*Shazi*." He repeated the word to himself. Then he asked me how to say "snow" and "grass," then waved the whip in his hand and asked me what that was called. I answered him one by one, but I knew that it would be hard for him to remember all the words. Maybe it wasn't so much about learning as simply wanting to say something. After all, he had just returned from a long, lonely day.

We walked on either side of the flock, slowly accompanying them westward. It was getting darker and darker. The sheep began to quicken their pace.

All of a sudden, from the other side of the flock, Shinshybek started bellowing a song: "Every day, ah, every day! Every day, ah! Every day . . ."

In the distance, the dummy we erected on the top of a dune looked as if it was approaching us—shoulders slumped, listening, trying hard to identify us.

If Cuma had been the person I had gone to greet, he would have talked endlessly, teaching me everything he knew about herding. It was because he assumed that the only reason I had come to the winter pasture was to learn to herd.

When he returned home in the evenings, he would say to me, "One should always walk slowly, never rush." This was because the sheep had been eating grass all day, and their stomachs were stuffed. If they ran, their stomachs will catch cold at night.

With that, he would kick his horse and gallop home, leaving me to walk the sheep back by myself, slowly.

After only a few steps, he turned to remind me, "You must not run!" And off he went again while bellowing a song.

IT WAS STILL EARLY. Alone, herding the flock beneath a solitary moon, I climbed over the last dune. In front of me was a lonesome sunset. They say the shape of the moon comes from the earth's shadow as it blocks the sun. But it looked like the sun and the moon were right next to each other, while the earth was all the way down here where I was. The three objects clearly sat on a plane, forming an acute triangle. . . .

And yet, even after the sun set, the crescent moon remained at the same angle in the sky. Why didn't the moon also turn? It was a mystery to me. . . . Then I thought, astronomers couldn't possibly be wrong about these sorts of things. Maybe it has something to do with the way the earth's atmosphere refracts light?

After the sun had fully set beyond the mountains, the sky, like a pristine lid, covered the earth. Where sky and earth met was a gradient shifting from cyan to red. Then it turned gradually white, then blue, until there was no more daylight. Above, the only things visible were the bright moon and the lonely *Chulpan* (Venus).

As I walked, I couldn't help but sing too.

SOMETIMES, KURMASH WOULD JOIN me in welcoming back the flock. Along the way, the young man would ask me about everything, not caring whether or not I understood his questions. There was nothing I could do about it. Whatever he would say, I would reply with a smile, which seemed to satisfy him. After that, we made our way in silence.

One time, he suddenly asked, "How much was your coat?"

I said it cost one hundred and fifty yuan.

He waited in anticipation.

So I asked, "And how much was your coat?"

He said, "Mine was a hundred."

Then he pinched my arm. "Not bad, thick material."

I didn't know how to reply, so I felt his sleeve as well. "Not bad either, pretty thick too."

Then, silence. The flock was still nowhere to be seen.

He started to sing.

Walking through a hollow, he suddenly stopped and pointed at a trail of Ping-Pong ball-sized footprints stretching across the snow. He said to me that, not long ago, a black-tailed gazelle had passed through.

He had never seemed as lonely as he did in that moment.

EVER SINCE THE NEIGHBOR'S son, Rahmethan, had joined us in the wilderness, it was usually the two of us walking together. Oddly, he also kept asking me the same questions: "How much were your clothes? How much were your shoes? How much do you make a month?"

Moreover, he really wanted to know what I did for a living, but I couldn't explain it very well. So every day, he would ask again.

One day, out of nowhere, he asked me where Huanghe, the "Yellow River," was. I pointed toward the southeast. Then he asked me where Beijing was and I pointed in the same direction. His steps slowed as he stared in that direction, as if he could really see the Yellow River and Beijing. It wasn't a yearning exactly, more like astonishment—*so far away!*

It reminded me of a joke. An old shepherd went to Beijing as a model of an ideal worker. When he returned, everyone asked him, "Is Beijing as good as they say?" With a sigh, he said, "It is good, but, sadly, it's just too remote."

That's right. Beijing, so what? Yellow River, so what? In that moment, the burrow settlement upon which the dummy fixed its gaze was the center of the world.

GOING WITH NURGÜN to greet the sheep was a much livelier affair. The little girl sang and skipped and talked and played. She was constantly asking me if I knew so-and-so. I would say no. So then she would ask, how about so-and-so? But I still wouldn't know this person. After that, she rattled off a long list of names, all which, of course, I had never heard of. She was disappointed that I wasn't a part of her social circle.

Walking in the dusk with Kama was a rare occurrence because she had chores to do at home—like cooking and looking for the camels.

On those rare occasions, she was always singing. What little confidence she had to perform could only be expressed in the wilderness. Yet, even there, she still felt awkward about it and pretended like she simply wanted to hear some singing—so she asked me to sing. I said, "Why don't you take the lead?" She sang one song after another, each with more passion than the one before.

I adore the way Kama sings. Her voice, though plain, is full of feeling. The melodies she weaves are always so graceful. Out on the open plain, the sound was especially powerful.

We walked along on opposite sides of the silent flock. From the other side, her voice flowed steadily and soulfully, an outpouring of feelings that could not be put into words. Once, as she sang, she suddenly stopped to say to me, "Out here, when Kazakh girls reach twenty-two, they are considered old maids." And she was about to turn twenty. . . .

Kama was suspended in that delicious limbo of youth, after which she would either become a wife or an old maid. But sadly, she still didn't have a boyfriend, or even anyone to pine for. She said her family didn't receive many suitors because they were poor and she wasn't exactly a catch herself. . . .

Immediately, she changed the subject and began listing off all the places where the flock would go next: in March, once the snow had melted, they'd head north. After a few days camped beside the Ulungur River, they would cross into the wide-open desert scrubland and slowly make their way toward the "ninety-two-kilometer point" of Interstate Highway 216, where they'd wait for the lambs and calves to be born. A month later, they'd wade through the Irtysh River and stop on its south bank in Danawuzi. After that come the rugged hills of Kiwutu. Then, they would follow the Xalasu southeast of the township to enter the Dongquer Valley. Then into the mountains until they reach the end of the mountain range at Gieles. In short, all sorts of open steppes and rugged mountains. Throughout the entire year, the amount of time the flock spent in populated areas (nearby two or three villages) totaled to about ten days across spring and autumn. In short, they were in for a lot of loneliness, a lot of waiting . . . but then she started singing again.

That's right, like Kama said, an old maid at twenty-two, which made Big Sister, me, feel rather self-conscious. . . . I was thirty-two years old. Did that make me ten years older than an old maid?

THEN THERE WERE THE LONG, anxious nights waiting for the flock to return. Stationed on the eastern sand dune, Shinshybek held up his binoculars, scouring the wilds. He would see me approach, and casting about for something to say, would start pointing every which way, telling me where the camels were and where the horses were.

After the sun had fully disappeared, darkness rose from the earth, skyward. The moon was almost full, but it was still too dark to see much. There was only enough light to see the sky and my hands. I turned my head to listen carefully and heard nothing. But Shinshybek kept pointing east: they're here. Sure enough, I began to hear Cuma's shouts. Then, gradually, I could make out the undulating flock. But the camels were still crouching in the sheep's path, with no intention of moving. When the flock reached the camels, they hesitated for a moment before splitting up to move around the obstacle like water down a stream. Under the moonlight, the camels poked out of the flock like dinosaurs raising their long necks, bulging their big eyes, acting like nothing was happening.

WHAT KIND OF STAGE was that high dune to the east? Was the world around it the curtain? I always stood center stage, turning my body to see in every direction. The scene to the west was the most spectacular. Pink clouds flowed like rivers toward the sunset. It was a vortex sucking up the world, and the sun had already been sucked in some time ago.

In the twilight, I saw a figure on horseback come to a halt on a distant dune ridge. After a short pause, he climbed down from the horse and stood next to it for a long time, shoulder to shoulder. My face felt so cold that it hurt, but the man and the horse just stood there, without moving.

In the distance, I saw Zhada walk toward the flock, singing as he went. Soon, he was nothing but a speck, but I could still hear him singing.

I saw Shinshybek gallop toward the dune ridge to the southwest, where the camels stood in twos and threes.

I saw Kama squatting by the burrow, looking at the ground. Making use of the last remnants of daylight, she was practicing her Chinese characters in the sand with a twig of dry bramble. Now and then, she took a piece of paper out of her pocket to check her work. Then the character was rubbed out in the sand and she'd try it again.

I saw Sister-in-law swaying her hips as she walked, leading the cattle herd out of the white snow into the black burrow settlement.

I watched as darkness continued to blanket the sky. Less than half a moon hung on the southwestern sky. The snow on the ground was glittering. Up above, the deep blue space. Down on the ground, glittering white stars.

All that time went by, with me standing there, watching, and I still couldn't see the flock. Suddenly, I noticed a faint flickering light in the wilderness. At first, I thought something was wrong with my eyes. But a moment later, there was another flicker. As I focused my gaze, I noticed the flickering more and more frequently and regularly. Eventually, the light grew brighter and brighter until I was sure that it was a vehicle! By now I could even hear the hum of the engine. Was it a motorcycle or a car? I waited patiently as it carved a wide arc through the wilderness, closer and closer. It was a car! How exciting . . . who could be coming to visit our burrow settlement? And by car no less, how fancy! But, right before my eyes, the car turned eastward and soon disappeared, even as the engine's thrum continued to reverberate.

I was so fixated on the car that I forgot about the cold. Shinshybek said we should go, the sheep had arrived. I quickly asked, where? He pointed into the twilight. I took a look and there they were! When had they managed to get so close to us? So quiet.

*Waiting for the flock to return, time and again we would
climb the sand dune to scan the horizon.*

23.

The Cattle's Winter

WHEN WE FIRST ARRIVED in the pastures, after having helped with the calves for three days, Cuma announced at dinner, "From now on, the calves belong to Li Juan!" What a big responsibility. So every day, whenever I had a free moment, I would climb the sand dune to the east and keep my eyes on the whereabouts of the troublesome trio. At the slightest sign of trouble, I charged in to intervene. By trouble, I mean calves and cows reuniting before it was time to go home.

There were two close calls, when over a low dune ridge to the north, the calves and cows caught sight of each other! Frantic, I chased after them desperately. My lungs stretched like a bellows and my tonsils were ready to explode. From a distance, Sister-in-law watched as I chased after this or that calf, running in circles like a headless chicken . . . she couldn't help but shout, "Good enough! That's enough! Oh Allah . . ."

Only later did I learn that these situations require a strategy. How can you possibly force cows away from their calves? The trick, instead, is to let them reunite. Once calves and cows are walking shoulder to shoulder, the rest is simple—just walk them home. While in motion, calves can't make any mischief.

But what mischief could a calf really make? Indeed, it was nothing more than drinking their mothers' milk . . . but if we let them drink up all the milk, then we'd have to drink our tea black. Sorry, little calves, even though you're still young and growing, we need the comfort of milk too. We're living a rough life too, so we have no choice but to embezzle some of your rations. . . .

Yet, for some reason, when the calves returned home at night, they still carried a pungent, milky aroma. I always secretly suspected that they had stolen milk from their mothers. But I had kept such a close eye on them—when would they have had the opportunity?

FOR BOTH CATTLE AND CALF, returning home at night was a happy process they were eager to begin. Back home, there was a warm cattle burrow and delicious nutritional supplements. For the calves, it was also where they found their beloved cow mamas; for the cow mamas, that's where they found their precious baby calves.

Every evening, the first to begin heading home were always the nursing cows. Once they began moving, the other cattle had no choice but to say goodbye to the dry grass and follow suit. The closer they got to home, the more excited the cow mamas became. For the last few hundred yards, they began to sprint, mooing as they ran. The calves returned the call with just as much fervor, each charging toward its respective mother. . . .

Reunion! But then what? The moment they found each other, they would be tied up by the herders, and Sister-in-law would proceed to milk the cows. Before milking them, she would lead a calf over for a few sips, then tie up the calf and milk its mother as it watched. After the cow was milked, the calf would be free to feast on the very last drops left in the udder. Poor, wretched thing. . . .

Milking was the busiest time of the day. All the kids joined the fray, yelling and screaming, herding and lassoing. They had to get the whole herd settled in before it was dark. Cuma looked especially content during that hour, unable to peel his eyes away from Sister-in-law, who was kneeling on one leg below a cow, making a "*psshh, psshh*" sound with every squirt. That one frame seemed to contain all the treasures that he had come to find in this life. He walked over to a calf and slapped it on the belly, before sarcastically mocking, "Seems like you've been eating well!" He then slapped another calf on the belly, but this time, he kept quiet.

He pointed at a patch-faced cow that was in the process of being milked and said, "Last year, it was so cold, three of its nipples froze. Even now you still can't milk 'em. . . ." One could only imagine the pain!

He then pointed to a piebald cow that was pressing tightly against a young calf and said, "Last winter, its baby died from the cold." Then he pointed at the calf and said, "Its mother died from the cold." So then everyone had tried to lead the pitiful calf over to suck on the equally pitiful cow's udder. For some reason, the cow had accepted the calf immediately. From then on, they became a real pair of mother and child. All day long, the piebald cow missed its calf just as much as the other mama cows. On their way home, it ran ahead of the whole herd. When it saw its baby calf in the distance, it was so happy—so happy that there wasn't anything else in the world that could make it happier! Why can't cattle stand upright? Why don't they have arms? If they did, mama cow would show the world what a real hug looks like!

Just imagine: being driven out to the pasture first thing in the morning, unable to see your mother or offspring. Only during milking were they allowed to interact for ten minutes. Of the twenty-four hours in a day, ten minutes was all they had. . . .

YET AS THE WEATHER grew colder, there were days when the calves returned early and—without even waiting for their mothers—filed straight into the calves' pen, where they refused to budge. They were so cold, they couldn't even bring themselves to drink their mothers' milk!

The calves were perhaps the least cold-hardy of all the livestock. Whereas even on the coldest days, the cattle, on returning, would circle around the sheep pen and their own burrow a few times, looking for dried cow pies and horse dung to eat. When there wasn't enough grass to eat, they had to make do with manure.

But on the very coldest days, even the cattle couldn't handle it anymore. The neighbor's cattle looked for all sorts of ways to get into our cattle burrow because their burrow still didn't have a roof . . . it wasn't just me, even Cuma was upset about it. He said, "It's just a plastic tarp, a few bucks at most, so what if it breaks, it's not a big deal!"

Even though the calves were the naughtiest, most annoying, unreasonable things, they were also the most pitiful. Unable to see their mothers all day, they were only allowed a few sips of milk. On top of that, they had to suffer the cold and ended up growing dirty-looking blisters all over—I don't know what kind of blisters they are, rough and hard like dried, crusty mud that oozed blood whenever they popped. It must have been awful. . . . The only remedy Sister-in-law could come up with was to melt a small block of butter and rub it on the wound.

And then, there were the unforeseen accidents. Once, the rein around a calf's neck came loose and the knotted end dropped to drag on the ground, where it somehow got caught in the cleft of the calf's hoof. The rope was so short that the calf limped hunched over with its head pulled toward its rear, which left it straggling at the back of the herd. When it needed to climb a sand dune, it was practically walking on its knees . . . and the rope still wedged in its tender cleft hoof, how it must have hurt! How long it remained in that state I cannot say. . . . After that, every morning, when I herded the calves out of their pen, I took care to check the reins to make sure that they were all nice and tight.

THROUGH THE VERY coldest period, the piebald cow became conflicted about the adopted calf, and was no longer willing to feed the youngster, head-butting it away whenever it got too close. Then, one evening, another calf inadvertently ate some of its mother's extra snack and became immediately hooked, outright refusing to drink milk no matter Sister-in-law's efforts to push its head toward the udders. Sister-in-law was furious.

However, the two calves had recently turned a year old, so it was time for them to be weaned off milk regardless.

Milking, from then on, was a much easier chore—now that there was no need to tether the calves anymore, and the long-fought battles at dusk had come to an end. But the calves and cows still had to be kept far apart through the day. In fact, the calves hardly ever saw their mothers again, something they seemingly had an easy time getting used to, whereas the mothers struggled without their babies. . . . Come dusk, the mothers were still first to rush back toward camp; they still started their anxious, incessant mooing the moment the burrow settlement came into view. Even long after the split, when they too had forgotten about their calves, the deep-seated memory of what coming home once meant still played out.

One evening a month later, when the calves returned particularly late, they passed by the piebald dairy cow that was waiting to be milked. Somehow, the mother suddenly recognized its calf, as if in a flash everything had come back to it. Instinctively, the mother dashed toward the calf to smell it, lick it. The calf, however, couldn't have cared less. Clearly, it no longer remembered its mother.

Although an inevitability in the course of life, it was nonetheless painful to see.

PUTTING THE CATTLE to bed at night, Sister-in-law arranged them according to their ability to withstand the cold, with the back of the burrow being the warmest and the entrance being the coldest. Farthest back were the

nursing cows, then the cows, then the young bulls. But there were always indi-
viduals who were unhappy with their placement and insisted on shoving the
others. And once said individual reached the back of the burrow, it defended its
territory with all its might, ramming anyone who came close. For Sister-in-
law, putting the cattle to bed was always a battle. Fists were swung, feet were
kicked, curses were shouted.

One thing that puzzled me was why Sister-in-law always led the big black
cow in first, giving it the best spot. It looked plenty big and strong. . . . It
wasn't until one day when it gave birth that I understood—it was a pregnant
mother!

The black cow's calf was born early one morning in the middle of January.
When Sister-in-law went to let the cattle out of the burrow first thing in the
morning, she came right back to bring us the news. Thrilled, I put down my
tea bowl and ran to look. So—a newborn calf is no bigger than a dog. It was all
skin and bones with huge, bright eyes. Dragging from its belly was a long,
slimy umbilical cord. All of a sudden, the black cow's belly deflated, drooping
loosely over its pelvis. It had been a skinny cow all along!

The black cow licked its calf with love and affection, not the least bit put
off by the slimy, ugly little thing. The calf's four hooves were so thin that it
couldn't stand straight. Even though it could hardly keep its body off the
ground, it still tried its best to avoid me.

Cuma happily remarked, "Don't be fooled by the fact that it can't walk
yet. Tomorrow, it'll be walking slowly. The day after tomorrow, it will be
walking quickly. Then, the day after that, Li Juan, even you won't be able to
catch it!"

The cattle burrow was too cold, so Sister-in-law brought the calf back to
our burrow. The big black cow was furious. It refused to eat and stood outside
our door, screaming for days. (There was one thing that perhaps Cuma and the
family did wrong. They threw away the placenta instead of giving it to the
mother to eat. According to them, if the cow ate it, it wouldn't produce milk,
but as far as I know, it's mammalian instinct to eat the placenta after giving
birth as the first boost of postpartum nutrients. . . .)

The calf was probably unaware of the fact that it was the subject of all the
protestations outside. It was unaffected by its mother's call, crouching listlessly
on the manure floor under the window. With its jaw on the ground, nose
scrunched up, it spent all day doing nothing.

For two days, the black cow decided to block the entrance to our burrow and give everyone coming and going a mean look. It even chewed up the thermometer I had hung outside, broke the plastic sheet over our window, and knocked over our satellite dish. On the third day, it was so hungry that it had no choice but to follow the others to graze. But after only two hours, it returned by itself to continue to protest. After another long demonstration, it felt hungry and joined the herd once more. As soon as it had filled its belly, it rushed home to take care of its unfinished business . . . what a persistent gal!

That very same day, the black cow started producing milk. I carried the calf out of our burrow to suckle. It was a hefty little thing, about thirty pounds! Carrying around such a heavy load must have been tiring for mama cow, not to mention having to walk a long way to find grass. . . .

Since the black cow was producing milk, Sister-in-law decided she might as well squeeze a small potful! And that was the first time I tasted cow colostrum. It's hard to believe, it was yellow and thick—impossible to boil, you had to steam it. Once steamed, it looked like egg custard but much heartier and more potent. And it tasted like egg custard, not at all like dairy! The treat sat at the center of the table. Everyone shared it using the same spoon. The calf crouched grumpily by the bed, probably because it knew that we were eating its lunch.

But whose fault was it that it didn't finish its meal? It was so much more interested in this strange new world than in its mother's milk. Each time, it would get distracted after only a few sips. It was always running off, forcing its mother to chase after it, calling and running.

Cuma was right! By the fourth day, not even I could catch the little guy. It ran all over the place! On the fifth day, it learned another new skill: jumping. It bucked its hind legs as it jumped, which was quite the performance. All the other cattle and calves turned to watch in amazement. And yet, it couldn't recognize its own mother! As it passed by the other cattle, whether it was a bull or a cow, it would kneel down to look for teats. But often all it found was a headbutt. Good thing it was born a fighter. The moment is saw the other three calves, it charged forth to challenge them (it seemed to have known not to mess with the cattle . . .). Unfortunately, its head was bald, without any horns to speak of. Clearly, it was no match for the other calves!

In short, the calf quickly fell in love with the world. Whereas at first, it needed to be picked up and taken outside, now, as soon as the door opened, it would leap outside. As soon as it was out the door, it began to run in circles. Its anxious mother chased after it, circle after circle, mooing all the while. Alas, there were only a short few hours to run wild; of course it was too busy to drink milk! It was a cause for concern. Even little Karlygash knew to drink milk several times a day. Yet this newborn, barely a week old, only drank milk once or twice a day. It sure could handle hunger.

Cuma said that in ten days, the calf would begin to eat grass. So Zhada gathered a big bouquet of "Fickle" grass and hung it from the window. The soft "Fickle" grass was the best fodder winter had to offer; all the cattle loved it. On the other hand, it was just dried grass, coarse and hard—whereas the calf's tongue was so tender. Alas! Lucky are the calves born in the summer pasture, where the earth is covered in tender green grasses.

Sure enough, after the grass had been hanging there for a week or so, the calf poked its head up to eat it! The first time I noticed, I quickly ran to tell everyone. With everyone watching, the calf stretched its neck to take a second bite. Everyone was thrilled.

By day twelve, the calf's frame had filled out considerably and its coat had grown thicker, giving it a glow of confidence—a black, shiny snout, eyelashes thick and long, and a pair of perky ears like a dog's. But it was still ever so petulant. When it was out frolicking, it was always puffed up with pride, unwilling to answer to anyone.

As the sky comes to light, the cattle set out to pasture.

Thanks to that little calf, our standard of living had greatly improved! Every day, we were able to drink creamy milk-tea . . . a cow who has just given birth is highly productive!

Sadly, the good times didn't last. On a warm day in the middle of February, Cuma's relatives from Akehara arrived in a rented jeep to pick up the black cow and the calf. They had a newborn child back home who needed the milk more than we did. In the winter, milk is a precious commodity.

At that point, it wouldn't be long before we picked up camp and migrated north. Such a young calf may not have been able to handle such a long journey. It was better off in the care of the relatives. As for the milk, I suppose that would have to be considered the caretaker's compensation.

The men tied the black cow to the hatchback of the Beijing jeep and covered it with a felt mat to symbolically protect it from the frigid journey. The calf was tied into a ball, wrapped in felt, and stuffed into a polyester sack, which was then stuffed under the back seat . . . its own fault for being so compact! It couldn't have been a comfortable ride. Had it been a person curled up like that for the whole journey, their limbs would have gone numb and fallen off.

Knowing that the black cow was leaving us, Sister-in-law figured she may as well squeeze another small pot full of milk! It was enough to keep our tea creamy for three days.

24.

Food

WHEN I FIRST ARRIVED in the pastures, the moon looked pale and elegant. But before long, when I looked up, all I saw was a crispy golden pancake, fried just right . . . not to mention everything else that I could put in my mouth or, better yet, my stomach! Confronted with the vision of such delectable treats, I froze as if caught in a gun's sights.

During teatime, I usually politely declined refills after three bowls by saying, "Satisfied!" But once, after only my second bowl, Cuma spoke on my behalf: "*Ja, boldy!*" (Enough, satisfied!). Feeling panicked, I quickly corrected him: "*Haide boldy?*" (What do you mean, satisfied?). Everyone laughed. So it was that Cuma gave me a nickname: "*Haide boldy.*"

From then on, if I was full from a meal but the cook was offering more, I would politely say, "*Toydym!*" (I'm full!). Cuma went out of his way to mishear my words as "*Toyjadymu*" (I'm only half-full). Which was how he gave me a second nickname: "*Toyjadymu.*"

I had to live with these two nicknames all winter.

IN THIS DAY AND AGE, perhaps it is only out here in the wilderness, living a life simple enough to split with an ax, that food is still just food—and not some sort of pretty composition or novel distraction. It's there, on the tablecloth, on the plate. Between you and your food is the shortest path between two points. It only has one purpose: eat me! Food appears in the oral cavity the way love appears in the spring! There's nothing more natural, nothing more perfect.

Question: What kind of food is the most delicious?

Answer: The food of a quiet and peaceful life is the most delicious!

In a quiet and peaceful life, even a handful of cracked wheat can smell like paradise. Soak the cracked wheat in some tea with milk, then mix in some butter—your heart and soul will surrender to it! More specifically, it's the kind of deliciousness that after every gentle chew sends another wave of ocean tide passing over you, a tide that sweeps away all the scattered footprints cluttering the sand.

Or what if you added a handful of crumbled *irimzhik* (cottage cheese made from sour cream) to your tea with milk? Then you would have even more to chew on. You are struck by an aroma like a welcome home from your two-hundred-and-sixty-pound wife, as she stands there with open arms, full of warmth and comfort. And if the tea happened to have been boiled with some cloves and black pepper, then she would be smiling a deep, meaningful smile.

There is only one reason to eat noodles in sauce: to make your belly as round as you can!

Wheat porridge, on the other hand, acts like a clothes iron that smooths out all the crinkles from your stomach. And if that wheat porridge has been cooked in lamb broth topped with yogurt, then all the digestive enzymes in your stomach will raise their banners like a welcome parade!

When you eat *baozi*, *baozis* are the most delicious things in the world. When you eat mutton on the bone, the most delicious food in the world becomes mutton on the bone. There's not even the slightest contradiction between these two truths.

Let us consider the *baozi*'s filling: diced potato, minced meat, pork rind. Now let us reconsider it: soft and flaky potato mash, a meatball bursting with juices, golden brown rind . . . Then let us consider mutton on the bone: think about how after Cuma quickly completes the *bata* (so simple you might say he never even started it), he picks up the knife and starts shaving slices of meat; think of how bright and shiny the slice of bread becomes after it has fully soaked all the meat's juices, how pleased with itself the bread feels, being held in the same regard as the slice of meat. In the end, what the *baozi* and the hand-pulled meat have in common is that even when you are gorged up to your uvula, you feel like you still want to eat more.

Can the leftover filling from the *baozi* be used to stuff more *baozi* later? No!

Sister-in-law was much more resourceful than that. The next day, she shaved a few more fatty slices of meat into the filling before kneading two steering-wheel-sized flatbreads. She stuffed the middle with the filling, sealed the edges, then threw the whole thing into the piping-hot oven the same way she baked *nan*. That's one serious baked *baozi*—the size of a steering wheel! When it was time for the *baozi* to come out of the oven, everyone was waiting eagerly at the sitting area. The neighbors' kids weren't going home no matter what. They could wait forever if they needed to. When the steering-wheel-sized *baozi* landed on the tablecloth, its glory lit up the whole burrow! When Sister-in-law sliced it up like a birthday cake, grease poured everywhere! Rahmethan's hand was as quick as his eyes, instantly reaching out to grab the largest slice. He ate it slowly and properly, then declined a second slice with just as much decorum.

After having munched all the meat from a horse femur, Cuma would pull out his butcher knife and hack off the two dumbbell-shaped ends of the bone. He had Kama and me chew on the pieces and suck out the marrow from hollow bone. When someone is cruel, we say they "suck a person's marrow dry"; in other words, they are very violent. But to be honest, sucking horse marrow is . . . oh that flavor! It's impossible to pass up—even if chewing on the pieces of bone only yields a teeny, tiny amount of marrow.

The cheese soup Sayna brought over from next door was one of life's pleasant surprises. Better yet, she generously added lots of sugar!

And there was the thin *nan* baked in sheep-manure charcoal—Sister-in-law would fire up a pile of manure until the flames died down. Then she would pry apart the smoldering charcoals and lay them out flat. After that, she would knead a prepared dough into a large flatbread and throw it in the center of the smoldering charcoal. Finally, she would move the charcoals back to cover the pristine white dough. Once the charcoal had cooled, she would use her tongs to pull out a perfectly golden brown, porcelain-hard flatbread—yum, the smell . . . what more can I say?

Likewise, what can I say about beef *plov* or meat and potato *kuurdak* stew? And strangely enough, even dry *nan* soaked in breakfast tea, maybe with half a spoonful of butter—even that's so delicious it leaves me speechless.

And if there was a handful of *tary* in the tea, then speechless would be an understatement. You pretty much had to weep, it was that delicious. . . .

We only had two heads of cabbage in total. Every day, we peeled off a few leaves to boil with our dinner. This way, the two cabbages lasted us two months! Why were they able to last us so long? It was because in addition to cabbages, we had over twenty potatoes.

The scene of someone frying *baursak* was as festive as New Year's Eve: an iron wok bubbling with oil, a kneading board filled with snow-white dough patties, a whole pot and a bowl full to the brim with golden brown squares!

There was nothing more than a pinch of salt added to the *baursak*, yet it was rich with flavor. The fried dough leaves rolled in raw brown sugar were enticing, like the nouveau riche; the dough nuggets rolled in sunflower-seed oil were classy, like old money. First taste the nouveau riche, then wait for the old money—it was just like New Year's.

But, for some reason, whenever they made deep-fried food, everyone ate it as soon as it was ready; they never bothered to wait for me. . . .

And yet, the hand-pulled meat and *baozi* and *tary*, both the new money and the old . . . in our everyday life, they were seldom seen. More often than not, there was only *nan* on the tablecloth, paired with small dishes of butter and mutton fat. This simple combination must have gone unchanged for hundreds of years. And as for me, I don't pine for hand-pulled meat, nor do I especially care for *tary*; the only thing on my mind is that day-old, half-golden, half-tan piece of *nan* sitting alone on the kitchen counter. That is my one and only! That is my rock-solid truth, the thing that keeps me pondering, even in my sleep—what hasn't it been eaten yet? Give it another day, it'll get even harder!

If, when you reach for a piece of *nan*, you happen to pick one that is only two days old (the rest are all three days old!), it's even more exciting than winning five bucks at the lottery.

Sometimes, Shinshybek would stop by after dinner. As a sign of respect, Sister-in-law would take out a piece of freshly baked *nan* . . . at which point, even if I had just finished dinner, I wouldn't be able to stop myself from returning to the tablecloth for another round of tea and *nan*. Screw it, so what if I have to double my trips to the toilet in the freezing cold!

Regarding that really old *nan* that even the hottest tea can't soften, Sister-in-law had a special trick. She would break it up into small pieces and toss them into the wok when she was stir-frying meat (with the lid on). Out of the wok, the broth-soaked *nan* was tender yet chewy . . . even tastier than the meat itself! Noticing how much I enjoyed it, everyone gave me their *nan* bits. As thanks, I gave everyone my meat in return.

I ASSUME EVERYONE HAD noticed how obsessed with food I was. If I woke up a half hour early one day, Cuma would say, "Stomach must be grumbling early today!"

He's one to talk! He's the gluttonous one. Whenever food was prepared, as soon as the meat was done stewing, Sister-in-law would serve a small bowl of unseasoned meat just for him. Then she would take whatever was left of his meat and stir-fry it with vegetables or add it to noodle soups—even if there were kids or guests watching. Even if everyone was staring at him, the man they call Cuma could still swallow every last bite, unfazed. As a parent, he was about as responsible as a politician!

On these occasions, Kama, who was usually the greedy and petulant daughter, acted like she hadn't seen anything! But young Zhada wasn't quite as disciplined. One time, he slowly edged up to his father, quickly snatched two pieces of meat, and fled as he chewed.

Kama showed her true nature when she asked Sister-in-law for a couple of pieces of candy, every day. When Sister-in-law refused, she would steal her mother's health tonic, "Mind-at-Ease." She drank it like a soda because it was sweet. But Kama's favorite magic trick was to pull a potato out from the manure charcoal in the stove. My, the decadence! We split it in half and shared it. The moment the potato split open, the grainy flesh emitted a gust of steam that could take a bite right out of the coldness of winter. . . .

Kama reached the peak of excitement when she discovered a small bag of sugar that Sister-in-law had carefully squirreled away. She screamed! Then she scooped a mean spoonful into a mutton jar. She stirred and stirred until the sugar and fat coagulated. Then, she spread this strange sugary mutton grease on a *nan* like strawberry jam, and chomped down.

Zhada went to school in the outside world, so he had the opportunity to taste many things that the rest of his family had never tried before—such as mushrooms, tofu skin, and fishball soup. Relegated to the monotonous menu of the winter pasture, he often tried, as if his life depended on it, to describe the shapes and flavors of the myriad strange foods. But in the end, all he did was torture himself, ending up with a mouthful of drool and nothing he could do about it.

As for me, for the sake of food, I too was willing to give up a little status. When the little girl Nurgün suddenly called me over from afar, I suddenly had a good feeling! I ran over to ask, "What is it?" She whispered to me, "Come." I hid my excitement and took a step closer—aha! She grabbed my hand and surreptitiously stuffed a piece of cream candy in my palm! Beyond my wildest dreams—I couldn't help but pinch her cheeks and kiss her, then scoop her up and spin her in a circle three times.

Over the course of the winter, sweet little Nurgün gave me two candies and a cracker!

IN THE DARKNESS after dusk, I often gaze up at the steaming-hot, delicious moon and think about the other moon waiting at home—that fresh new piece of *nan* baked during the day . . . oh, what does that make me? An empty sack with two legs that is endlessly stuffing itself with more and more food!

The power of food is that it does so much more than merely please the taste buds. The reason for our overly voracious appetites must be more than simply that life has gotten dull. I think all the creatures that live out in the wilderness feel the same way about food. Out in the wilderness, there are no outside powers coming to your rescue. The instinct to survive is so strong that we all live in a constant state of near insanity, an eternal emergency.

Think about life in a city. Among the crowds, should life start to look hopeless, you can always reach out and beg, you can look for garbage in dumpsters. There, people always have a minimum level of guarantees, there is always the possibility of survival—out there, "living" is never the end goal, the end goal is to "live a better life." By contrast, here in the wilderness, humans can only rely on the plants and animals. Out here in the wilderness, there is no lucky break, not a single extra thing just sitting around.

In short, I felt insecure. Aside from eating like my life depended on it, everything else was out of my control. It was as if I only felt the confidence to face challenges when my belly was full to the point of bursting.

Anyway, "eating" became the number-one item on my agenda. My stomach was a bottomless pit that never once reached its limit. It was there, once and for all, that I got over my bad habit of being a picky eater. . . .

ONE DAY AT NOON, Kama went to the yurt to grab a length of fatty sheep tail. After chopping it up, she threw the pieces into the wok to render out the fat and make chitterlings. She said to me with an air of mystery, "Today, we will eat this thing that isn't *plov*! Isn't stir-fry! Isn't noodle soup! Isn't a stew! . . ." on and on, listing all the things we ate day to day. I asked, "So what exactly is it?" She pondered for a moment and explained, "Well, this thing isn't a *plov* or a stir-fry or noodle soup. . . ." It must have been lost in translation.

After a bowl's worth of fat had been rendered out, Sister-in-law took over, scooping out the chitterlings then adding a scoop of flour directly into the bubbling oil! She stirred it, mixed it, adding more flour as she went along until the flour and oil reached just the right consistency. Then, she put the wok on a small flame and fried it some more, before finally adding two spoons of sugar. During teatime, she poured a shallow half bowl of the fried flour into everyone's tea bowl, packed it down to the very bottom of bowl, then poured the milk-tea over it. She then instructed me to drink the tea first before eating the flour underneath. I took a sip—the fragrance! In addition to the aroma of the milk and the tea, there was a powerful hint of wheat. By the time the tea was finished, the surface of the fried flour layer had turned into a gelatin, whereas the bottom was dry and sandy. A taste—my, it tasted like cotton candy! If the aroma of the milk-tea could be compared to a charming hiking trail, then the aroma of the fried flour would have to be compared to a boulevard downtown! It really was a thing that "wasn't this thing or that thing"; I had never tasted anything like it before in my life. . . .

The dumplings were also like nothing I had ever eaten before. This was because Kazakh dumplings are different from Han dumplings. The meat filling is much chunkier. Sometimes there was only one chunk of meat inside a dumpling. The skin was different too. First, they rolled a big, flat sheet; then they cut out small square skins. The shape of their dumplings was also different from Han dumplings—they resembled little fish. When it came time to wrap, Kama, Sister-in-law, and I were responsible for making the dumplings. Cuma was responsible for lining up the raw dumpling-fish on the table into formations, making sure they were all lined up straight and pointing in the same direction. Two battalions of dumpling-fish stood face-to-face, ready for battle. And it was Zhada's responsiblity to watch and roll his eyes, offering a *"Koychy"* from time to time, because his father's childishness was just too embarrassing. But when all the dumplings were wrapped, we couldn't help but play with them for a while before tossing them into the boiling pot.

THERE WERE THINGS they hadn't eaten before either. One evening, as we were winding down for sleep, someone brought up *liangpi*, cold wheat-starch noodles. Kama and Zhada, who had eaten them before, were so full of praise that Sister-in-law and Cuma became curious about how it was made. I began offering a lecture on the topic, but as they listened, they became skeptical. Kama insisted that I should demonstrate for everyone the next day. Zhada applauded, cheering me on. But Sister-in-law said, *"Koychy!"* and Cuma said, "A waste of flour!" What they meant was: it sounds impractical.

The next day, Kama urged me to demonstrate in earnest. While enduring Sister-in-law's skeptical *hum*s and *haw*s, I began the demonstration, mixing the dough, rinsing the starch from the gluten, letting the starch water settle, boiling the gluten sponge, steaming the settled starch . . . even making a sauce out of the starch water left from the rinsing. Throughout the whole process,

Zhada showed incredible interest. There was nowhere else he wanted to be, so he stuck around and helped out. There were only two iron plates for steaming the noodle skin, so there was plenty of work for him to do. Once a layer of noodle skin was done steaming, he would take the plate out to cool in the snow. In the next moment, he brought the cooled plate back in exchange for another hot one. During the whole process, the boy listened and did as he was told. He ran in and out of the house being as helpful as can be.

Even though I only rinsed one bowl of flour, it yielded enough *liangpi* for everyone to try a small bowl, as well as a bowl for the neighbors. Everyone ate in silence, offering neither praise nor criticism; it was excruciating. But then, on second thought, no matter what we ate, people rarely offered passionate comments. That calmed me down a bit. But soon enough, the nerve-racking feedback process began. After Kama finished her portion, she announced with confidence, "Tomorrow she will make it, she'll get the hang of it!" But Sister-in-law immediately disagreed. She said it tasted good, but that it was too much work!

Indeed, the menu in the winter pasture was humble. There was only one proper meal a day, and the rest of the time it was *nan* and tea. As for the proper meal, we ate meat once every three to four days. The rest of the time, it was either sliced noodles, pulled noodles, or steamed rice. Whatever we ate, there would always be a bit of vegetable garnish. Cuma was always complaining about how produce was getting more and more expensive, and even went so far as to blame my family's shop for it. How infuriating.

In this family, everyone had all sorts of problems. Cuma's feet stank. Sister-in-law and Kama had gnarly nails that were seriously misshapen. Even my nails were starting to grow horns. Once, when I was embroidering a felt mat, I punctured one of the fingers on my left hand. It was only a tiny little wound, but it never seemed to heal. Slowly, the cut spread along the ridges of my fingerprint, deeper and deeper. When I was out working, even a small amount of pressure could cause it to bleed. In addition, my canker sores were getting worse. When one healed, another would pop up on the other side. My mouth was never without a sore. I had to drink tea out of the corner of my mouth. I assume these are all effects of vitamin deficiency?

In any case, I braved the winter, took it in stride, and avoided any other form of ailments. Even on the coldest days, when I was as cold as a monkey, I still managed to ward off the cold. But somehow, during the last week at the burrows, perhaps because I was anticipating the departure, my body suddenly let down its guard. It was as if other hopes and demands had overcome my immediate needs, smashing my body's equilibrium with a flood of com-plicated concerns. At any rate, during those last couple of days, my digestive system, which had been running full steam all winter, suddenly cooled. At the same time, I came down with a bad cold.

WHEN I FIRST STARTED living with my new family, Cuma noticed by solid appetite and said with confidence, "When you go home, your mother will be shocked. She's gonna think you were drinking chemical fertilizers at my house." But in reality, I didn't fatten up at all over the winter—my weight even dropped down to below eighty-eight pounds.

Because I slept in a sack, Cuma often called me "gunnysack girl." Then as I became thinner, he changed it to "half-a-gunny girl." That was my third nickname in the wilderness.

25.

Visitors (1)

O NE DAY, CUMA STERNLY tugged on my jacket and said, "This is for old woman, not young lady!"

I looked down. The shiny silver down jacket was exactly what young people were wearing. It didn't seem particularly old-fashioned. . . .

Then he added, "So dirty!"

True . . . it was filthy.

Because it was the only light and easy-to-wear jacket I owned, I refused to wash it. Washing it would have been a big commitment. It would have meant the pain and misery of living for a week without a jacket. Besides, the amount of water Sister-in-law gave me for laundry would have only been enough to wash one sleeve.

I bucked up and retorted, "And who am I trying to impress?"

Cuma said, "See, I told you, an old woman."

Hearing something like that said about you, how can you not feel embarrassed?

It didn't matter that I dressed like this when I was herding sheep, collecting snow, or shoveling shit. But the moment I saw someone headed my way on horseback, my first reaction was to take a detour. Should that same person shout a greeting to me, I would keep my back toward them and only turn my head for a quick response.

Had a visitor showed up at the door, it would have been a more frenetic situation. It would have involved me quickly taking off the jacket, rolling it into a ball, and stuffing it under a blanket. That would have been the quickest way to distance myself from the thing.

Bringing a light-colored jacket into the wilds, yet another bad idea!

Fortunately, we were in the winter pastures, with a population density of one person per every square mile and a half. How many visitors were we expecting to see in a winter? And in the middle of the winter, even when there were visitors, nine out of ten times it was people looking for their lost camels. The passersby stopped for a drink of tea, which could hardly be called a visit. So we didn't need to treat it with such seriousness.

Although in my view, camel seekers could be considered an important form of networking as well. When the herders looking for their camels entered the burrow, they sat and drank tea for at least two hours straight—but what about the camels?

When we first settled in, our neighbor Shinshybek lost two camels. He spent a week looking for them, during which he came home only twice. Every time he came back, he still hadn't found the camels, but he smiled as usual. Before we even had a chance to ask, he would grin: "Nope, still didn't find 'em!"

WHILE NINE OUT OF TEN visitors were on the lookout for camels, the remaining one was either passing through on their way to hitch a ride or had missed that ride and were on their way back home. That's life: once you're in the wilderness, leaving isn't so easy.

The latter kind of visitor tended to be young people with beautifully polished shoes. Some were even wearing shoes that were obviously new because their soles were spotless.

After saying hello to the hosts, they would proceed to lie down for a nap on the bed. Sister-in-law, who would be in the middle of boiling or cutting patches of felt, would carry on with her work as usual. While waiting for the tea to be ready, the guests found things to do like play with the cat or flip through an old, wrinkly newspaper that had been tossed beside the bed.

Had I been a competent official, observing life in the wilderness, I would have asked in a politely patronizing tone, "What is your name? How old are you? Is your home far from here? What is your business in the area?" But I was too lazy to bother with all that.

Generally speaking, the younger visitors were always very curious about me. They stared at me with eyes like convex lenses that focused laser beams on my body. Wherever they looked, I felt a burning sensation. Needless to say, it made me feel very uncomfortable.

To solve this problem, I stared back at them just as intensely. Soon, it was their turn to feel uncomfortable. They returned my fixed gaze with a look of embarrassment.

In spite of her lack of interest when guests first arrived, Sister-in-law never neglected her duties as host. Once she had finished with the task at hand, she laid the tablecloth, cut some new *nan*, and even asked me to fetch some *baursak* from the yurt. Normally, our tablecloth did not hold such nice things.

But until then, as Sister-in-law quietly finished her work, the guests plonked side by side on the bed, waiting. It was rather awkward. However, once tea was served, the atmosphere warmed up immediately. Sister-in-law asked the guests all sorts of questions with keen interest. The guests chatted without pause, thanking their host for every bowl of tea. They could have all used some company, after all.

AS FOR THE GUESTS who were not at all surprised by my presence, it was either because they had visited before or because they had heard all about me before they arrived. When this one man entered, he greeted the hostess and sat down on the bed without so much as a glance at me. He took off his magnificent fox-skin hat and laid it next to him on the bed, revealing the small white skullcap underneath. His beard was gorgeous, and there was a sort of magnetism about him. I took the initiative to talk to him, asking if he would allow me to take a picture of him. Unbelievably, I was rejected! Cuma quickly explained to me that the man wanted to be on horseback before taking the photo. That way, he would look even cooler.

After tea, he offered the most gracious thank-you and bid farewell. He put on his hat and strode out the door. We accompanied him outside. There was a coat lying in the snow that was too raggedy to wear inside. He picked it up and put it on. Cuma grabbed the horse's halter to steady it while giving the man a hand as he climbed on. The man turned the horse toward me and waved. I snapped photos, as many as I could. But after only a few shots, he kicked the horse and rode off. Cool indeed!

AND THEN THERE WERE the familiar guests, like Bolat—the elder brother of the girl Kaziyman, whom I'd met on the Dongquer summer pastures. His home was far, a day by horseback. I never did figure out why he showed up there. It wasn't to look for camels or to catch a ride.

Though we already knew each other, the boy never once greeted me in front of the family! What was there to be shy about?

One afternoon, an elderly visitor suddenly appeared. He was of medium stature with a long face and a big nose. He was shabbily dressed, aside from the pair of binoculars around his neck. Binoculars were considered precious items. Many shepherds bought sleek and stylishly embroidered leather cases for them. But this old man's binocular case was a leather satchel, and a patchwork one at that. Rustic and flamboyant, it was clearly the handiwork of his missus. I stared at the swanky satchel for a long time; ah, an old man with a satchel like that, honestly ... but the more I thought about it, the more I realized, huh! What's there to be ashamed of? At least he had a case. Our Cuma didn't even have one. He just wore the binoculars around his neck.

Even though the old man was shabbily dressed, his shoes were unusually new, and stylish to boot! But were they really necessary? He was out looking for camels, why the new shoes? I imagined that perhaps in the morning, he had an argument with his wife over that very decision. Chances were, they were his one nice possession, like Cuma's new jacket that he insisted on wearing when he went to herd. People with nice shoes never took them off when they climbed onto the bed platform. Not only didn't they take off their shoes—they would stomp their feet as they climbed on.

Though I found the old man charming, little Karlygash thought he was frightening. Head tilted, she stared and stared at him. The old man stared back in the same way. After five minutes, the baby suddenly broke down in tears! It was the first time something like that happened. Everyone laughed. Having failed to win over the baby, the poor old man clearly looked embarrassed. He never turned his gaze to the child again.

FOR SOME REASON, I always felt a deep gratitude toward those who made an effort to greet me when they came in through the door. It felt as good as having been offered friendship or assistance. I remember one quiet guest with pale eyes, who was always on the verge of saying something. I thought that perhaps he had something to say to me or perhaps even sought my friendship. He leaned in intently, ready to listen. I could feel his anticipation, but I was tongue-tied, unable to express myself. Before he left, he turned his attention toward me once again, but I was still at a loss for words. It wasn't until I walked him out to his horse that I could bring myself to holler, "Farewell!"

There was another young man who, without a word, picked up Plum Blossom with one hand, a Chinese newspaper with the other, and pretended to look very busy. Surprisingly, he could actually understand it! He slowly read the news out loud to me. Out of every ten characters, he knew at least three—impressive. I offered him my most sincere compliments. He then told me, in what words he could muster, that he had gone to high school and it was a small city high school no less.

So we began chatting. I complained that there were too many letters in the Arabic alphabet. He told me that I didn't need to learn all of them—four of the letters weren't used in Kazakh—and proceeded to point out which four. Wonderful news! Those four letters were the worst. I was immediately filled with confidence.

He offered me some advice: "The winter is long. Learn one letter a day and you'll have learned everything in a month."

I said, "I'm old. I need two days to learn one."

What more could he say?

After he left, I hoped that he would one day return. Some days later, he really did return. I rushed over to talk to him, but for some reason, the young man completely ignored me! I couldn't help but feel a little hurt.

THE GUESTS WHO ARRIVED dressed in thick layers came by horse. Those dressed in extra-thick layers came by motorcycle. And if they wore thin layers, they must have come by car—if they had to resort to using a car, how many camels must they have lost?

And then, there were those three who came by car—acting like they were about to starve! They ranged over the tablecloth, picking and choosing. I had to watch as they picked out the last three pieces of manure-baked *nan* (mixed in with the regular *nan*) and gobble them down. . . .

One evening a guest came. He was far more amazed by my presence than your average herder and stared at me unrelentingly. When I couldn't bear the awkwardness any longer, I tried my old trick and stared right back at him. But for whatever reason, I couldn't outdo the intensity of his stare. I was outmatched. . . . During dinner, he kept his eyes on me while he asked Sister-in-law all sorts of questions about me. I supposed he must have come from very far away. Most herders in the nearby pastures had either met me already or, at the very least, heard of me. He must not have known about me at all, which was why he acted so surprised.

As soon as the guest finished his tea, he returned his bowl, stood, and took

down the white cloth that was hanging over one *tus-kiiz*. . . . I didn't understand what was happening when Kama reminded me to move aside. Only then
did I realize that this man wanted to perform the *namaz* (the formal prayer).
Devout Muslims observe the *namaz* five times a day.

So that's what the white cloth was there for. I thought it was only
decoration.

He laid out the cloth, and while facing west, he began, "*Wula wula*," reciting
the scriptures. Every now and then, he would prostrate himself and pray.

Zhada, being a child after all, couldn't help but snicker at the sight of someone so seriously antiquated. He tried to contain his laughter, but it continued to
escape him.

Yet, at the end of the *bata*, when the man raised his palms to start the closing
words, Zhada instantly raised his palms too, while nudging Kama, who was in
the middle of embroidering. At this time, Sister-in-law stopped what she was
doing too, and the three of them all raised their palms to utter the final word
together, "Allah." The *bata* was completed solemnly.

The man stood up, said his goodbyes, and immediately rode off by himself.
Later, as I stood on top of a sand dune looking for the cattle, I saw him gradually
disappearing to the west. Like all shepherds, he had a long, thin leather strip
dragging behind his saddle. He would bring news of me far and wide.

ONE AFTERNOON, SISTER-IN-LAW and I were cutting a black velvet
cloth that we planned to use to trim our new *syrmak*. Suddenly, the door
swung open, and *plop*, in fell a little boy. After regaining his balance, he
stared at us in a daze. Sister-in-law laughed, called him over, and found a
piece of candy for him. The boy was no more than five years old, quiet, gentle,
and shy, with dark cheeks. Cuma said that he was a relative Kurmash had
brought over from the pasture to our west. He would be staying with us for
some time.

That day, the flock returned late and everyone was rushed off their feet.
After tethering the calves, I bumped into Rahmethan, who was returning
with the sheep. It had only been a day since I had last seen him, and all of a
sudden, he was exceptionally polite. He graciously extended a hand toward me
and said, "Hello." I obligingly stepped forward and shook his hand. Suddenly,
the little boy I had met earlier in the day appeared from behind him and said
softly, "Hello." So I had to shake his hand too. Such grown-up gestures made
the little guy giddy. Energized, he worked extra hard ushering the flock into
their pen. He stood behind us and screamed vehemently, slapping the obdurate

sheep with all his might, refusing to return home until all the work was finished. It must have been freezing.

It wasn't until the next day that I learned he was seven! The poor little chap looked much younger. . . .

Those were Cuma's rest days, which he spent sawing and hammering, and he managed to fashion a series of makeshift items, including a saw handle, a dagger handle, and a cleaver handle (for some reason handles were always breaking). The little boy gawked all day, mesmerized. Cuma told him in a serious tone, "In my family, we have a twenty-year-old baby and a fifteen-year-old baby, all we're missing is a seven-year-old. Why don't we go have a word with your ma and pa, see if they'll give you to us?" The child thought hard about the proposition but in the end decided, "No." Cuma added, "I know your ma and pa, I'll speak to them, they'll be thrilled. In the future, when my family has some new babies, your ma and pa can pick one in exchange!" The boy suddenly fell silent and left. Apparently, after returning to Shinshybek's, he cried all night. The next day, he demanded to go home. Kurmash had no choice but to take him back.

Cuma could be really loathsome sometimes. In addition to bullying children, he also made up nicknames for the older guests. Kurmash's two chubby friends, who looked a bit like Indians, were dubbed "foreign Kazakhs." The two had thick, black, curly hair and round faces, which were darker up top and lighter on the bottom, the result, I assume, of wearing face masks.

Cuma named a skinny old shepherd "old man flower" because the man's sweater comprised a patchwork of various yarns and threads.

In spite of being rather shallow, he was still quite a welcoming host. In these wildlands, who could afford not to be? Perhaps all the people who live in such remote, sparsely populated corners of this world are the same way? The herder's welcome comes not only from his loneliness, but also from the need to forge a network of people who could help each other. Everyone is at once a host, providing food and warmth to others, as well as, inevitably, a guest in the care of others. The sense of equality between guest and host is what keeps the social life of the wilderness predictable, sincere, and simple. Whenever a guest walks through the door, the tablecloth is promptly laid, and tea served. If it happened at dinnertime, the guest sits to eat as well. Even if the host is eating meat, the guest would not act polite and refuse. Likewise, if the guest arrives in the middle of work that requires muscle, there is be no escaping it either. Off the horse and straight to work.

ONCE, WHEN I WAS OUT gathering snow, I tripped and tore my pants. My other pair had recently been washed and were not yet dry (despite having been hung up for a week . . .). So, as soon as I got home, I began mending my pants. We'd had a long series of quiet and peaceful days, but just my luck, guests started to show up. They came one after another like a school of fish. One was looking for lost camels, another was waiting for a car back to Ulungur. Yet another was seeing off the one waiting for the car, and another two were acquaintances of the one waiting for the car who ran into him on their horses, so they all came in to catch up.

While shouting, "Wait, wait!" I wriggled back into my pants in such a hurry that the needle was still hanging from my butt. But the guests had no intention of looking away. Instead, they all squeezed onto the bed as usual and made a joke of me. The whole thing became a classic joke about Li Juan, one that Cuma repeated to every visitor. He's told it at least five times.

On the other hand, I have been puzzled ever since. What happens when these people who just barge into people's homes encounter an even more awkward scene? I suppose it would be considered the host's lack of foresight. That's why out there in the wilderness, no matter how hidden and remote a burrow, it remains perpetually neat and proper, ready to welcome a guest at a moment's notice. Even if only a single guest appears all winter, the burrow will maintain its immaculate state for that one occasion. It isn't a matter of vanity but rather respect for one's self and others.

FOR SOME REASON, after the guests had greeted the host and everyone found their place around the tablecloth, the first ten minutes of the gathering were always silent. As the guests gulped their tea, the host would quietly keep them company, as if they were all laden with weariness. Suddenly, someone would begin the conversation and everyone around the table would instantly come to life, chatting more and more enthusiastically until they could no longer stop themselves.

It was the same way even when the guest was there for a particular purpose. First there was silence. Then, after twenty minutes of drinking tea, when I threw the guest an unconscious glance, he quickly explained, "Your mother asked me to bring a crate to you, it's sitting outside. . . ." What if I'd never looked at him, would he have continued to wait for an opportunity to tell me? It was as if the long stretches of time that separated the contact between people, as long as the desert was wide, made it hard for them to reconnect when they finally met.

BUT MORE OFTEN THAN NOT, people passed by our burrow at a distance. Whenever we saw figures slowly traversing the land nearby, we'd climb to high ground to observe their movement. It wasn't until the figures disappeared completely in the distance, with no intention of ever turning around, that we would finally return home, disappointed.

Our most common visitors were the livestock from the neighboring pastures. There were always occasions when, upon leaving our burrow, I was met with a startling surprise! Outside the door was a gathering of more than twenty camels draped in festive colors. Who knows how long they had been there? What a festive sight!

When cattle from the neighboring pastures got lost, they would grace our burrow too. Perhaps it was because they could smell their own kind there, and perhaps they were attracted to the thick bed of sheep manure, which offered a precious bit of warmth. They camped out outside the sheep pen, and by dawn, they were all covered in a thick blanket of snow. . . . Most of them were pregnant, with bulging bellies. It must have been a difficult night for them in this cold and strange place. On the other hand, it must have been a relief compared to being stranded in the middle of the vast desert.

But our most frequent visitors were the two brothers, Shinshybek and Kurmash. Kurmash came over most every evening around dinnertime to trade news and enjoy a bowl of noodle soup while he was at it. And Shinshybek came over every morning during tea to discuss the day's grazing plans with Cuma and enjoy a bowl of last night's noodle soup while he was at it.

26.

Visitors (2)

I N EARLY JANUARY, we were graced with a guest of honor. This visitor was very distinguished—he was neither looking for camels nor passing through: he was the veterinarian!

The veterinarian was the guest who had traveled the farthest and who was also the most important, so far. From the banks of the Ulungur, he drove down in a pickup to complete four important tasks: one, vaccinate the sheep; two, geld livestock; three, act as deliveryman for incoming and outgoing parcels; four, give everybody a haircut.

Whenever guests turned up at our door, Cuma would ask them if they knew how to give haircuts. He was always asking me as well. How could I? Cutting hair is a highly technical endeavor. It's not like stir-frying or cooking rice, something that anyone can master.

Time and again, I told him, "You're out herding every day, who are you cutting your hair for?"

I even advised that he stop shaving. A long beard could keep the wind out and his neck warm.

But when it came to these rubbish theories of mine, Cuma felt nothing but scorn.

Anyhow, the vet arrived. Cuma and Shinshybek wrapped their wives' headscarves around their necks and had the vet clean up their facades.

Watching the vet cut hair left a deep impression on me—who said hairdressing required a three-year apprenticeship? Nonsense! I watched him do it once and I learned it.

Then the vet helped us castrate our camels. It's called surgery, but from beginning to end, all he did was make one cut, sew two stitches, then cauterize the wound. And to facilitate this work, the whole family had to help. He didn't have to do any of the chasing and hobbling and tethering of the camels, yet he still charged fifty yuan. So expensive!

Then again, camels are rather large animals. Perhaps the price was based on size.

After inquiring, I learned that castrating horses and cattle cost fifty yuan as well, which left me puzzled once more.

THE VACCINES NEEDED to be administered at sunrise before the sheep left to graze, so the vet spent the night in our burrow.

The next morning, we woke up half an hour earlier than usual. The sun was still below the horizon. The sky was gloomy. Steam billowed out from the sheep pen. Shinshybek and Cuma caught the sheep; the vet gave them a shot; Sister-in-law painted a red line on every vaccinated sheep using the red dye that she boiled wool with. The whole process took an hour in the freezing cold. A layer of ice formed on Sister-in-law's basin of dye. Our hats and collars were coated with frost.

It cost one yuan to vaccinate each sheep, which felt quite reasonable. The haircuts were free, as were the deliveries. In addition, the two families boiled a pot of horsemeat and a pot of cattle head respectively in honor of the guest. Before he left, they each gave him a bag of *kurt*. The perks of being a vet. . . .

ONLY A FEW DAYS LATER, we welcomed the winter's second-most-important and honored guests—the horse traders.

In fact, they were only passing by in their big truck, but when Cuma, who was out herding, saw them in the distance, he intercepted the truck and invited them home.

When I climbed up a dune and saw a big truck tottering through the wilderness toward our burrow, I was thrilled! I immediately rushed home to report the news. Everyone followed me back up the dune. As our eyes followed the truck closer and closer, we made guesses as to what its business was. Cuma was galloping behind the vehicle. The flock had been left far behind in the distance.

When the truck finally stopped in a dip to the east of the dune, I saw that there were already two camels and some cattle and sheep tied up in the truck bed.

While Kurmash and I went to herd the flock that Cuma had left behind, we discussed the topic of the horse traders. Cuma had long wanted to sell a horse so that he could buy a car. I first found it hard to believe: How is that possible—the price of a horse is enough to buy a car? But later, when I actually saw the selection of beat-up old vehicles, I changed my mind.

There were four people in the truck: a boss, a hired hand, a driver, and a person hitching a ride to his spring and summer encampment (for a fifty-yuan fee). In the evening, Sister-in-law boiled a large pot of mutton and wheat porridge to treat the guests. Shinshybek's family came over as well, making it a full house. Because at the time, no one from the younger generation was around, it fell to me to carry the kettle and basin for everyone to wash their hands with, as well as a towel draped over my shoulder for drying. I thought nothing of it, but the guests were clearly uneasy, quickly washing their hands and thanking me when they were done.

Because we couldn't all fit around the *dastarkhān*, Sister-in-law and I sat down in the right-hand corner of the room with a small basin of meat. Though everyone else sat all the way across the room, their faces were all turned our way, watching me slice meat with fascination, smacking their lips in approval. I did as the locals would, holding down the meat with my thumb while slicing the blade toward me. The meat fell slice by slice and quite ceremoniously at that.

In the company of so many well-spoken and worldly guests, lonely Cuma was ecstatic. While he conversed normally at the beginning, his conversation quickly turned into a monologue. The distant visitors, weary from their long journey, were exhausted, but they forced themselves to listen late into the night. After a round of tea came a plate of meat, then another round of tea. There was no end in sight to his monologue even as the guests were so tired they could hardly keep awake. When one guest went to the toilet and Sister-in-law took the opportunity to start making the beds, Cuma continued to sit next to the quilts, rambling, unwilling to move aside. And after the lights went out, when everyone was curled up beneath their quilts, he continued to prattle in the dark, laughing at his own jokes. For a while, he even acted out two different characters, impersonating their dialects to great effect, as if he was performing for an auditorium rather than an audience that was deep asleep. To be polite, at the end of every story, one of the guests would say "*ye*" in the dark (*ye* means something like "*uh-huh*"). But gradually, even that came to an end. Sometime later, someone shouted in panic, "Allah!" before mumbling a final "*ye.*" He'd woken up startled.

The next morning, while those in bed were still lost in their dreams, Cuma began telling his story again . . . for half an hour in bed, then another hour while we drank tea. His appetite for talk was finally satiated. . . .

Because it was too cold, the truck's diesel engine wouldn't start. Someone came in to ask Sister-in-law to boil some water. Even though water was hard to come by at the time, Sister-in-law still boiled up a whole kettle without second thought. Although the whole kettle was poured onto the engine, it didn't work. Cuma then brought over a big bag of sheep manure. The driver jacked up the front of the vehicle. They lit a fire underneath the truck and moved it around to several spots until eventually the engine started.

Elsewhere, people were frantically trying to lasso the horses. First thing in the morning, Kurmash went out to look for the horses. An hour later, he returned with five of them. Then both families jumped into action, luring the horse with a corn-filled mask, then encircling it until it could be roped in. The horse had no idea what was coming for it. It chomped on the corn blissfully. If another horse approached to sniff the mask, it would snarl and try to bite the intruder through the mask.

Yet, in spite of having mingled for a night and a morning, no deal was struck! The horse trader felt the horse's stomachs and his face immediately soured. He would only offer fifty-five hundred, but Cuma wanted at least fifty-six hundred. They reached an impasse. The short-tempered trader took his money, climbed into the truck (its engine had been rumbling for a while now), and drove off. Cuma was stubborn too. Without a word, he proudly, albeit disappointedly, watched the truck drive away . . . it really left! Both parties were probably waiting until the very last moment for the other side to give in, but neither did. They both had their pride.

Back home, husband and wife said nothing, a sudden and complete silence.

Hours later, Cuma said to me with a strained smile, "No matter, if we can't sell them this year, there's always next year! All the same . . ." and gulped down two bowls of last night's leftover meat porridge before quietly going out to herd.

In my opinion, next time you are selling horses, first agree on a price, then boil the meat! To treat them so graciously, then have it all come to nothing. . . . Yet even if a deal had been struck, after expensing the cost of the meat, we still wouldn't have made much of a profit. Besides, I felt like the horse trader was a wily fellow, asking for help to start his engine before discussing prices . . . perhaps he was worried that if a number couldn't be agreed upon, he wouldn't have been able to ask for help?

On second thought: that would be too petty! In the wilderness, courtesy is far more important than profit. Sitting together, every kind of guest is still a guest. The joy of coming together is more important than anything else. Moreover, on such a cold day, to leave someone stranded because of a disagreement would have been immoral. You'd feel nothing but shame if word got around!

The only thing I couldn't get over were the livestock that were already tied up in the back of that big truck. It was so cold and they had already been tied up for a night and a morning, which was to be followed by another day of hunger—if only the truck had been filled up already so that they could all go back. . . .

AT THE END OF JANUARY, on a warm and cloudy day, Cuma returned with another group of visitors, the most we'd had at any one time—seven adults and a child! Add to that their thick coats and our burrow was ready to burst.

Cuma had been gone for five days—he went to Akehara for some business. That afternoon, after finishing all the work, I took a walk north. Before I knew it, I had walked several miles to an old burial site that Kama had told me about. Right there by the burial site, a white car suddenly appeared. It was like I had seen a ghost! Like the car had fallen from the sky and appeared silently right there next to me . . . but really, it was just Cuma's ride home.

Even though with Cuma gone, there was no one to talk nonsense or grumble all day, and at night we could sleep peacefully until the morning, I was still happy to see him back. Wanting to accompany him home immediately, I had to impose myself upon the Beijing jeep already fit to burst with seven adults and a child, and cruelly shove my way inside . . . the child cried and cried. The driver took us all the way to the door of our burrow.

Cuma was more spirited than usual, having just gotten a haircut back in the village. Shoes polished, clothes ironed, he looked a new man, beaming with confidence. And now, having returned to his own turf, he was even more magnanimous, ardently welcoming everyone into his home for tea. So the entourage poured out of the car and into the burrow.

Once inside, the guests all offered their greetings before flooding onto the

bed, leaving a mess of shoes on the floor. Sister-in-law hurried next door to borrow bowls, Zhada zipped off to hide, and Kama swiftly tidied the burrow. Soon,
food covered the tablecloth and a multitude of conversations broke out, sharing
all sorts of news from up north, by the banks of the Ulungur, all the things
that had happened over these past two months. It was so exciting. Then, someone even went to the car and brought back a *dombra*, a long-necked lute.

Tall and fat, not to mention old, Cuma couldn't possibly squeeze in the back
seat of the car with the others, so for the whole trip he had sat alone in the front
passenger seat. Likewise, the *dombra* couldn't be squeezed either, so the whole
way, Cuma had to hold it carefully. Even though it had no carrying case, the
lute still managed to arrive in the wilderness in one piece.

Those who could play took turns showing off their skills while those who
could sing let their voices loose, singing one song after another. Sister-in-law
was both audience and waitress, endlessly offering more food to everyone. Not
a single person questioned the moment—even though it would be pitch-black
out if they didn't soon hit the road!

The driver even tried to get me to leave with him. He said that the four
groups of people he was scheduled to drive next were all heading to different
corners of the land, no less than a whole day's drive. That night, he and his passengers would seek shelter at the next destination (the poor family, six adults
and a child). When they would arrive, there would be a whole night of music
and song, very exciting (the poor family!).

He spoke to me as if offering advice: "Someone like you, who wants to
write about our winter pastures, can't just stay in one place. You should
go here, there, then another place, and somewhere else after that; you've got
to take a look everywhere." He even made a promise: after dropping off this
carload and picking up another carload, he would bring me back home. And
added, "It's on the way!"

At the time, I was tempted. But because I didn't have anything decent to
wear, nor did I have any gifts prepared for my new hosts, I thought twice about
it and eventually declined the offer.

Good thing I didn't go—by the time the car came back to our part of the
pastures, a week had gone by. As soon as he had dropped off one carload, he
picked up a new carload. Meanwhile, it was probably music and songs every
evening, then crashing the night wherever he ended up.

IT WASN'T UNTIL the middle of February, when the days grew longer and
temperatures warmer, that we finally welcomed our first visitors, in the true

sense of the word—who came neither for money nor entertainment. Gifts in hand, they came specifically to see us—us! Specifically!

They were Kama's old classmate Azila and Azila's mother. Azila had been studying at a medical school in Altai for the past two years. It was winter vacation, so she returned to the winter pasture to see her father and mother. At this point, she had been in the winter pasture for two weeks. Being used to life in the city, she was perhaps having trouble coping with the isolation of the wilderness. As soon as the days warmed, she began to pester her mother to go visit neighbors together. Truth be told, the two girls were acquaintances rather than close friends, and their mothers hardly knew each other. It was only because their homes were close, a mere hour's ride on horseback.

The arrival of the two guests came suddenly, catching Kama and Sister-in-law completely by surprise. When they pushed open the door and entered, the mother approached Sister-in-law right away to shake her hands, as if it was a much-anticipated occasion. And the first thing Azila did upon entering was to ask where the mirror was. She tidied up her bangs and, once satisfied, asked Kama a second question: Where is the toilet?

Azila's hair was jet-black (from the looks of its luster, recently shampooed with "Instant Black"), thick, with a stylish slanted bang. Her eyebrows were thick, her skin fair, and her teeth white and straight. But, how shall I put it—though the individual features on her face looked nice, when they came together, there was something mean about it. . . .

Though not particularly attractive, Azila wore heavy makeup, dressed in a set of blindingly white coat and sweater, as well as a vest that served no purpose other than decoration, and covered herself in strong perfume. Her meticulous efforts accentuated her "femininity." In comparison, Kama looked like a noodles-in-water plain Jane.

Azila's mother clearly had nothing to talk about with Sister-in-law, but she sat happily at the tablecloth anyway. There, she admired her diva of a daughter's every gesture. The humbly dressed woman had a tan, weathered face and a personality as open as the plains. With a satisfied smile, she said to me, "She, my daughter; me, old lady!"

While the parents stayed home drinking tea, the girls went outside, hand in hand. They sat down on a log next to the sheep pen below a sand dune to sun themselves and eagerly shared some girl talk. Blue sky stretched over the vast land. Though there was clearly no one else around, the girls nevertheless spoke in their softest voices. One could only imagine the exciting secrets! Then, young Kurmash butted in. After saying hello, he sat down next to the girls and silently listened in on their conversation. From beginning to end, he didn't say one word or show any indication that he had found what he heard to be interesting. Anyway, he just sat there quietly to a side as if that was all he needed to do to feel part of the group. After that, Rahmethan and Nurgün also joined the group, and so, having nothing better to do, I went to check it out as well. With everyone sitting in a big circle, the girls stopped whispering among themselves. It was a "stop" that felt natural and welcomed. All the young people were gathered in one spot under the sun, whimsically kicking the sand. The days really were getting warmer. The coldest of days were gone, never to return!

Sister-in-law heated up a pot of meat and cabbage over rice for the guests, also inviting the neighbor, Sayna, to eat with us. With the exception of Zhada, there were only women around the tablecloth. The conversations became varied and effortless. Our little banquet lasted for a long while before drawing to a close. When it was over, mother and daughter stood and said their goodbyes— the sun had passed its zenith. By the time they reached home, it would be dusk.

After the guests left, we laid out the tablecloth once again and started a new round of tea. Sister-in-law and Kama had a long discussion about the visitors. Kama turned to me and asked, "Did you think she was a good girl?" Before I had a chance to reply, she expressed her criticism: "No good! She has so many boyfriends! Even though she kept going to school, she can't even speak Mandarin!" This second point was a fact. Whenever I asked the girl a question, Kama had to interpret for her. She had spent two years living in the city, yet her Mandarin wasn't even as good as Kama the herder's! Perhaps she really did spend all her time dating?

ONLY A FEW DAYS LATER, two more special guests arrived. They were two cousins from the pasture to the east. That day, they were only passing through our part of the pasture on their way north. Why do I call them "special"? In reality, the younger one looked like any other herder guy with a beard and ruddy cheeks, shy and quiet. But the older one was exceptionally dapper. Even though his down jacket and leather shoes weren't new, they were neat and clean. His hands were also clean, not like the hands of someone who did manual labor. His hair was clean-cut and his manners refined . . . in short, he didn't look like a herder! When I took out my camera to take a picture of him, he took out a camera to snap me back—and his camera was better than mine! My camera was only worth a thousand yuan, his was worth two thousand.

I suspected that he was a cadre from the office of rotational grazing. But to my surprise, he was a teacher! He worked at an elementary school to the northwest of the city, in the village called Danawuzi by the Irtysh River, though he usually lived in the city. He was a guest visiting the pastures to our east and had already been there for twenty days.

I asked him why he was visiting the winter pastures. He said, as a matter of course, "For fun! I've never been here before! I wanted to see what it was like." Certainly an unusual idea for recreation, so I didn't believe him. Only later did he admit that he was out there to lend a hand. Only one family comprising two unmarried brothers occupied that enormous pasture. Normally, the older brother herded while the younger brother took care of household chores and camels. Then, when the older brother went into the city for three weeks to take care of some business, the younger brother couldn't handle all the work by himself, so they invited this cousin to their winter burrow to help out (probably of all their relatives, the only one with free time was this cousin, who was on winter vacation). Each day, the younger brother herded the flock and the teacher took care of the housework. By this point, the older brother had returned, and with the days getting warmer, the younger brother took the cousin around to explore the area and see family before he left the pastures. For those couple of days, the older brother must have been scrambling at home, all by himself!

I was impressed. "Twenty days, not bad at all! As a city boy, how did you adjust?"

He asked me back, "And you, as a Han, how did you adjust?"

That's when Kama introduced the bearded herder to me as Cuma's younger brother. But a younger brother from which branch of the family? I decided to get to the bottom of it, but the teacher saved me the trouble of asking: "They're from the same clan." *Clan!* What an apt word.

The more we talked, the more I was surprised—this elementary schoolteacher wasn't just knowledgeable about ordinary things. Never mind chatting with me, he could have delivered work reports to the county party secretary! I couldn't help but ask, "What do you teach?"

He smiled. "I'm the school's party branch secretary."

My first reaction was sheer respect, the second an urge to laugh. I imagined this party secretary spending all day kneading dough, baking *nan*, pulling noodles, milking cows, and chasing down camels.

As time went by it become clear that he wasn't our visitor but rather my visitor! I kept him yapping away without pause. Soon, I had three questions cleared up: first, our pasture was roughly thirty thousand *mu*, not two thousand *mu* as Cuma insisted, two thousand! I had always had my suspicion. Even simply eyeballing it, the pasture seemed like it was at least ten thousand *mu*. Second, there was indeed a new policy that this would be the last year during which the nomadic herders would be allowed to graze the winter pastures (good thing I made it just in time!). The government subsidy was seven yuan per *mu*, not six as Cuma had told me, and the subsidies would last for seven years! These two bits of information were related: if the policy is implemented, Cuma's family would receive several hundred thousand yuan in subsidies (bearing in mind that his family only owned a third of the pasture).

The final point that was clarified had to do with the children's schooling. Cuma said that each child's schooling cost, on average, three hundred yuan a month, which was hard for me to believe. Could rural education really be so expensive? Now I knew for certain that this was more of his nonsense. According to this teacher, the policy of free tuition and board had been enacted years ago. Each student paid only forty-five yuan a year for their uniform. If they grew slowly and could hold on to their uniform for two years, they paid forty-five yuan every other year. All other items like tuition, books, meals, and board were all free, totally free. Old Cuma sure knew how to cry poor. . . .

Of course, under the current circumstances, his family wasn't exactly wealthy. But there was no need to keep so much from me. Didn't we already tell him that his debt would be canceled?

The cousins sat for no more than an hour before leaving, continuing on their way to the north. They still had an hour's journey ahead of them. That night, they would stay with the relatives they were visiting before heading home the next day.

It was almost too sad to see them go. . . . I walked them all the way to their horses.

Just as they had buttoned their coats and put on their gloves, ready to mount their horses, Sayna's two children came back carrying sacks of snow. As soon as they noticed who I was with, they disappeared inside the nearest cattle burrow. The school party branch secretary smiled awkwardly. "Both of them are my students. . . ."

What a riot—he must have been quite the authority to have instilled such fear in the children!

SEVERAL DAYS LATER, the school secretary's cousin returned, on his own this time. He wanted one of the puppies. Without his older cousin, the official, at his side, he was much chattier—turns out that his Mandarin wasn't bad either!

The young man was around the same age as Kurmash, yet he seemed much more refined and courteous. When it came to selecting his pup, he was very particular, from the size of its claws and head, to the evenness of its coat and markings, to the length of the tail. We crouched by the dog burrow conferring for quite some time. The dog he settled on at first happened to be the same one that I fancied, but he barely hesitated before deferring to me. Then he asked me for advice on how to raise a dog, what I fed it, what it could survive on, where it should sleep at night. It was very comforting to know that the little dog he eventually left with was going to a good home.

He told me that aside from several older brothers who lived far away, his family consisted only of his mother, one older brother, and one younger sister. Because of the winter pasture's harsh conditions, his sickly mother and younger sister didn't come along. Then, full of optimism, he said, "It'll all be better in the summer! In the summer Mother can join us in the mountain and make *kurt* and all sorts of dishes. . . ." The two brothers must have been very lonely, with only each other for company morning and night, watching over their pasture of over ten thousand *mu*. During the day, after the older brother went out with the herd, the younger brother was the only one home. After finishing the housework (did he decorate their burrow lovingly like the girls?), and there was time to spare, what did he do? But the days ahead will be a little better because now he had a little dog, a little buddy to keep him company.

IN LATE FEBRUARY, as the temperature continued its slow ascent, and the day of the many flocks' northern migration drew ever closer, more and more people started to arrive on our doorstep, mainly herders looking for pups. And the two other groups of guests who came to visit Sayna's home were all female. It seemed like women were more eager to make social calls. But on second thought, that wasn't right—all winter, the men had plenty of opportunity to look for camels, and stop by a burrow or two for a visit. But the women couldn't go anywhere, so it was about time for them to get out for some air!

It was around then that Kulynbek, who had herded the flock south with us, along with his family, moved into our burrow. All of a sudden, there was another couple, a young man, and two kids in our lives, not to mention all the relatives from the neighboring pastures coming to visit them . . . the door to our burrow was constantly thrust open with a bang. The children were always running in and out. The young people were always playing cards and gambling. Sister-in-law was always offering everyone tea, and I was always washing dishes, and Kama was always cleaning up . . . it was so hectic! But the most frustrating thing of all was when the female guests saw the half-embroidered felt that I left on the bed, they would first fawn over it (my needlework was incomparable, even better than Kama's!), then immediately try to continue the pattern that I started. This inevitably ruined the pattern, leaving the felt looking like it was embroidered by a dog! After they left, I spent hours pulling everything out.

During that whole period, Zhada didn't dare to sleep in. He had no choice; there were always guests in the morning.

The truck that came to the winter pasture to buy livestock. The animals in the truck bed had already been freezing there for a full day and night.

27.

Peace

CUMA SAT NEXT TO ME watching quietly as I was sewing a pair of leather pants for him. Suddenly, he said, "In the past, people used bark from the larch tree to smoke the leather, giving it a smooth auburn color, which is more beautiful."

In the past, life in the wilderness must have been even more difficult and isolated. But even in a life like that, beauty was a necessity. When people finished their work and found a moment to spare, they stripped the damp tree bark and carefully smoked their simple leather clothes. When a figure on horseback would slowly emerge out of a forest—his red, not the red of his clothes, but the red of his mind . . . the red satisfied the world's tiniest desire for beauty. Even as I sat in this distant burrow across distant time, I could still sense that the man was content and at peace.

In late January, Kama finished embroidering a *gül* (a "rose") on a white scarf. As this type of fine white cloth scarf always comes in pairs, she had one more to embroider. After cutting the cloth, she asked Cuma to heat the edges with his lighter so they wouldn't fray, then she started to repeat the first scarf's pattern. Completing these two scarves took up every second of her free time. When they were finished, they would be hung up on each side of the *tus-kiiz* to further decorate their home.

When he wasn't herding or working, Cuma spent long stretches of time watching his daughter embroider, occasionally offering to help sew a few stitches. His daughter said, "*Koychy*, go stitch mom's *syrmak* or something."

Having been rejected, Cuma turned to me with hurt pride, "I know how to do everything! There's nothing I can't do!"

Then, as if suddenly reminded of something, he dug through boxes until he found a plastic trowel. (It was truly baffling; he wasn't a bricklayer and there wasn't any mud in the desert anyway, so why did he bring the thing all the way there?) He sawed off the trowel's handle, then sawed the remaining plastic plate in two. Next, he sandwiched an old dagger with a missing handle between the two plastic pieces and tightly wound a copper wire around the pieces to form a stylish new handle.

The dagger now had a handle, but the trowel was destroyed. It was like tearing down one wall to patch another. But ultimately, one of life's cracks had been filled in. And besides, the trowel had been lying around for ages, which made it a burden.

Fortunately, life never ran out of cracks to fill. Or else, once the dagger was fixed, Cuma would have been right back to complaining, "Dagger's fixed, now what?"

He shined everyone's boots until they sparkled; trimmed the *syrmak*'s frayed edge and wrapped it with a strip of red cloth that was then sewn up securely and elegantly; when he noticed loose threads on Sister-in-law's clothes, he quickly pulled them off. Filling the cracks. Must fill cracks.

PLUM BLOSSOM FILLED in many of life's cracks too. After a long period of being quiet and bored, Cuma suddenly grabbed the cat by his hind feet, raised him high in the air, and let go, forcing Plum Blossom to quickly spin his body like an acrobat . . . more exciting than the ten-foot dive.

Then he threw the cat toward the post, letting everyone admire the cat's agile turn and ease with which he grabbed onto the wood—as opposed to hitting his head and seeing stars. Good thing he was a cat. Had he been a dog, it would have been a tragedy.

Also, Cuma was always forcing Plum Blossom to sleep on his back, legs sprawled. And often, the cat even cooperated.

When Cuma slept during the day, the kitten slept next to him. Their postures were always the same—lying on their sides, heads resting on their arms.

MOST OF THE CRACKS were filled with silence. One morning, when the mount went missing, Cuma woke up early to look for the horse. He walked slowly along the sand ridge to the east, a lone grim figure shrinking into the distance. We were all waiting for him to come back to have tea together. Sister-in-law spun thread. I read. Kama embroidered. By the time the pitiful man returned, his hat and neck were covered in frost . . . and the cold and pain that he had just endured subtly but bitingly seeped into the morning tea. No one spoke. It wasn't until Cuma suddenly put his bowl down and declared that last night, he'd taken seven trips to the toilet, that the rest of us let out a "*Koychy!*" and burst out laughing.

At the end of January, life's cracks grew bigger and bigger. The days grew long and warm. And with the kids around taking care of most of the little jobs, Cuma had even less to do. So, when some insignificant little thing came up, he decided to make a trip back to Akehara!

After finding out that a car might come in the next two days, he began to make preparations to depart at a moment's notice. He cut up an old, broken poly-weave bag to patch another, less broken poly-weave bag. One patch over another, the bag was as strong as can be. Everything that he intended to take back to the permanent encampment was stuffed inside: a part for the satellite dish (in need of repair), a broken spade (to be welded), a goat hair comb, a large roll of camel fur (which was clearly brought there from the encampment, so what was the point in taking it back?), and some old clothes.

Additionally, Sister-in-law wrapped a few candies in gauze for him to take back, to be given out when visiting relatives and neighbors. She also baked two *nans* in sheep-manure ash to give to Apa.

At three in the morning, Cuma was woken up by Sister-in-law, who had him wash his hair and body in the dark (normally, there wasn't the opportunity . . .). Then, Cuma put on that new jacket of his, carefully stacked his cell phone, address book (why not enter the numbers into the phone?), and sunglasses into his pockets, and was ready to head out—a proper man.

I said, "When you get back to Akehara and they look at you, they will say, he couldn't possibly have come from a winter burrow, he must have come from Kazakhstan!"

Soon, in the morning glow, a green Beijing jeep took Cuma away. Sister-in-law, leaning on one side with her hand on her hip, watched for a while from on top of a sand dune.

After that, Kama began herding the flock for her father. As she set out in the morning, Sister-in-law would stop her, "Wait a moment," and run back inside to fetch a few candies, rush outside, and hand them to her daughter on top of the horse. Gleefully, in Mandarin, her daughter said, "I love my mother. Bye!" before kicking the horse and galloping over the sand dune. Sister-in-law clambered slowly up the dune where she stood in that same pose and watched.

WEIRDLY, WITHOUT THAT busybody, everyone kept on doing what they were doing and no one seemed the busier for it. Only now, it was just much quieter. Only now, the Indian singer's bewitching voice coming out the speakers sounded all the more bold. Only now, we didn't boil tea as often and the tea was much milkier. The three of us who remained quietly drank tea, with nothing to say.

It was only in the evenings after the cows had been milked that the children came to life and started to play a game of hide-and-seek—truly a game that will never go out of fashion anywhere in the world! But where was there to hide? In this world, there was nothing but sheep pens and cattle burrows. Nevertheless, everyone relished the fun times, a cacophony of squeals.

The nights were especially quiet. The dinner of rolled noodles required considerably less dough than before. I thought about the *baozi* that we had eaten the day before. At around the same hour, everyone sat together wrapping them in an assembly line. Kama cut the dough, Sister-in-law rolled the skin, Cuma added the filling (this specialization seemed unnecessary . . .), I folded and pinched the edges, Zhada nitpicked. Whenever one of Sister-in-law's skins wasn't quite round enough, he'd "*Koychy*" at it.

Bedtime was so quiet that it was eerie. There was no one repeatedly going to the bathroom, no one snoring or violently coughing, no one waking up in the middle of the night to roll a cigarette, drink water, or take painkillers.

As usual, at six o'clock in the morning, when the world was still wrapped in darkness, Sister-in-law quietly climbed out of bed. Since the ashes in the stove were cool enough to be moved without billowing, she cleared out the stove before filling the chamber with more sheep manure. Then, she went back to sleep. At seven, as the world outside brightened, she rose once more to add manure into the stove's waning flame. On top of the stove, she placed a kettle to brew a strong tea. A new day had begun. By the time everyone woke up, the burrow had warmed to a comfortable temperature and the tea was waiting for us.

Morning tea became a pleasant time once more. We played the game that we never tired of—when Sister-in-law said, "Karlygash, dance!" I grabbed

Plum Blossom's paws and rocked the kitten back and forth. When Zhada said, "Karlygash, where's Apa?" I pointed his paw toward Sister-in-law. When we all asked at once, "And Big Sister?" I pointed his paw at myself. Everybody laughed. Then Sister-in-law said, "Where's Ada?" I had to think about it for a second before lifting the cat high in the air and pointing his paw to the distant north.

Had Cuma been home, he would've snatched the cat by now and sung at him loudly in Mandarin, "Long, long tail, yellow, yellow eyes, where have I seen you before . . ." to the tune of a Mandarin pop song that was trendy at the time. We practically started every day with that song.

Had he been home, as soon as he woke up he would have been sitting in front of the tablecloth to announce some fake news. Such as: he would ride to Urumqi and return the day after next. Or: yesterday, he spotted seven puppies crawling through the desert. . . . In response to that, I asked, who left them there? He said maybe a dog gave birth while a family was migrating and they left the pups behind. That instantly tugged at my heartstrings.

But when I asked for more detail, he said it was nighttime. Only then did I realize that it was all made up!

Most of the time, his jokes were really lame. "Yesterday, when I was herding, I saw an airplane! I bet it was looking for you!"

I asked with a straight face, "Why didn't you invite them here for tea?"

"It was too high up, they wouldn't have heard me even if I shouted."

Sometimes, he would talk about government leaders. He envied them, always talking about how they must be living fine lives, not having to herd every day.

In the evening, there was no one who came home from herding, too tired to speak, until all of a sudden, he wrapped his arms around Sister-in-law and whimpered, "Old lady! I haven't seen you in eight hours. . . ."

And he would spend the next two minutes locked in a steadfast embrace with Sister-in-law.

Dinnertime was quiet as usual, even though the food was just as delicious as ever, even though everyone still ate a ton.

WHILE OUT COLLECTING snow during the day, there were several times when I clearly heard the sound of a car behind me. I was so excited that I threw down the sack of snow and charged up a sand dune. But after looking around for a long time, there was nothing.

By contrast, while sitting around in the burrow, the sudden whir of an actual motor felt like a hallucination. Whoever was speaking was cut off: "Shhh! Listen!" We all turned one ear toward the sound and waited. Yet, after the motor sound drew closer and closer, it gradually faded away into the distance . . . always only passing by. Always only a motorcycle.

Nowadays, many young people's preferred mode of transportation in the desert is a motorcycle rather than a horse. They don't care that gasoline is becoming more and more expensive or how tiring it is to ride through the sand.

Compared to the long night, dawn, dusk, and daytime in general felt fleeting. After quilting felt for a while, I suddenly noticed the light turn dim. When I walked out to check, the sun was already veering west.

I was reminded of a time when Cuma said that I was a quick sewer, "Like running on an asphalt road." Then, when I began sewing even more rapidly, he began to praise: "Like flying a plane!"

While he was away, I managed to finish a large, square orange *syrmak* with a basketball-sized pattern in the middle. Just wait until he comes back, how amazed he will be this time!

The felt was stiff. Toward the end, my right hand, which held the needle, was so sore that I couldn't make a fist and I had difficulty raising my right arm.

Needing to stretch, I went outside for a stroll.

During the days when Cuma was away, even though beautiful thick clouds padded the sunsets, most of the time the sky was clear. A week had passed without snow. To the west was a slim crescent moon and the faint outline of its missing ellipse.

Not far into my walk, I ran into Kurmash on the dune to the north. With a bundle of yarn and a felt mattress on his back, he walked slowly along the dune by himself. When he saw me, he slowly changed course toward me. When he came up to me, he asked where I'd just come from, and whether I had seen the horse. I said I hadn't. He asked when Cuma was coming back. I said didn't know. He then turned and walked away by himself. I hated not having seen anything, not knowing anything. . . .

28.

The Final Peace

IT WAS THE FINAL DAY of the lunar year. Not long after lunchtime, we were finished with all the chores. I decided to head north for a long walk. Though the weather was overcast, there was a hazy sun in the sky so I wasn't likely to get lost. The temperature was rather warm, only twenty-four degrees.

I remember that when we first arrived in the wilderness, Kama had pointed in this direction and told me that the graves of four people were out there! I had been thinking about it ever since and was determined to take a look when the weather was right.

I was so curious—what would a grave in the desert look like?

Kazakh graves are made in a unique traditional style. After the corpse is buried, four walls are erected around the mounds. In the meticulously built cemeteries found in suburban areas, rows of graves resemble little courtyards, each fitted with a colorfully painted wood door and windows, their walls decorated with colorful patterns and trimmings. As a result, each cemetery looks like a bustling village. Mountain graves are a little simpler, but still require logs that are stacked into beautiful and durable pyramids. Even the graves in rocky deserts, built with stone or mud bricks, were lovingly decorated. But in the desert, there was nothing but soft, flowing sand. What material was there that could be used to construct a grave?

I walked for a while before turning to check the sun's position in the sky to make sure that I was going in the right direction. After roughly two miles, I began to approach a long row of dunes that marked the end of this stretch of desert. Climbing up a dune, I scanned the world and saw nothing but yellow sand and white snow, without a hint of perturbation, much less graves. I wondered if I hadn't gone far enough or if I had veered off course. Perhaps it wasn't in the cards for me to see the graves that day. But the day was still young, so I wasn't sure where to go next.

At that point, I spotted an even taller, darker dune to the east of me. There, an enormous white-winged black bird was perched at the top of the dune, gazing west in complete stillness. So I descended the dune I was on, and with my eyes fixed on the bird, began to approach and climb the dark dune. When I was halfway up, the bird spread its wings and rose to the sky. After making a few circles overhead, it disappeared into the emptiness of the white sky. When I finally reached the top of the dune, I turned in circles to look. And then, suddenly, I saw the graves not far to my east.

What I approached wasn't a sand dune but a low plateau in the desert. The farther I walked, the more I felt the earth change—the patches of earth poking out of the snow became redder and redder. I realized that this area wasn't just sand but also dirt! I came to a sudden realization that when we first arrived at the burrow settlement, Cuma and Sister-in-law must have come here with a camel to collect dirt in order to renovate the dilapidated burrow. I also realized why those people from time immemorial would choose this specific location to build their graves, because holes dug in dirt do not collapse easily.

As I walked, the world came to a hush. The closer I got to the graves, the smoother the ground became, unmarked even by footprints. Not only the flock, but even the scattered cattle, sheep, and camel had not trespassed. There were only the occasional tracks of a pair of gazelles or similar wild animals arcing across the land.

It wasn't until I reached the edge of the graveyard that I could see there weren't four graves as Kama said, but perhaps seven of them. Some had collapsed, leaving twigs strewn all over the place, which made three grave mounds appear as one. From the looks of them, these graves had been there for a long time.

The two most striking graves were fenced in using short, winding branches from the desert poplar tree. Compared to the grand graves made from thick and straight pine logs found deep in the mountains, these seemed quaint. Yet, in spite of their simplicity, they were grand too—to find this many precious poplar branches in the vast desert, who knows how far the grieving family must have traveled in their wagon! I for one hadn't see a single tree in the hundreds of miles I had traveled from north to south.

There were also three slightly smaller graves that were surrounded by saxaul branches that had been stuck into the ground to form spiky cones, as if someone was setting up a bonfire. They were so simple that they couldn't even aspire to be beautiful; the structures simply served as markers: somebody sleeps forever beneath. Though these twig graves looked loose and flimsy, they had to be pretty sturdy. Just think of all the windy days across all seasons! They still huddled tightly together, pointing deep into the earth: somebody sleeps forever beneath.

It was the desert after all, but no matter how deprived or constrained you might be, you should not shortchange the dead. He wore the stars and the moon, walked in the wind and the rain, shuttled across this earthly loom from north to south and back. Then, one day, he died. He never had to move again, never had to migrate with the herd again. He would stay here forever. This was his true home, the home of a lifetime, an eternal resting place . . . building a final dwelling for this parting soul was the last thing his grieving family could do for him; of course they had to bring their full resources to bear.

Think about it: because of a person's death, all the thick branches and dry twigs from a hundred-mile radius gathers over his resting place—how grand, how colossal that death must be!

I stood there for a while. Even though the sky was high and the earth vast, I felt a tightness in my chest. I thought about the skeletons deep below the earth, about how they too had followed their horses across this very desert before their eyes had shut, their flesh had withered, their palms and faces had shrunk . . . and I thought, those in this world who had known them, who had missed them, were perhaps all in the ground too, buried somewhere far away from there. Then I thought about all the names and faces that will one day disappear, about how each of us will come and go without a trace, no different from the plants and the birds . . . but he really was once alive and walking across this stretch of land!

Why is there always so much peace and quiet in the world? Perhaps it is because too much death has accumulated, and the dead will always outnumber the living.

They had found their peace and quiet, and those who mourn them will gradually find theirs too. The quietest thing in the world isn't nothingness, or the passage of time, but people . . . people who will be alone in the end but whose hope can never be silenced.

I turned to go back, aiming straight for the hazy sun slanting to the west. At some point, the western sky had cleared up into a stirring blue and white. Far in the distance, beneath the sky, were ten or so wandering camels.

As I was walking, I suddenly turned as if I had seen a ghost! A white jeep was approaching! I hadn't heard a thing! While I was still getting over the shock, the car came to a quiet stop next to me. I immediately saw that it was Cuma in the front passenger seat—I didn't expect Cuma to find a car to bring him back! It had been five days since I last saw the guy. His hair was buzzed and his outfit ironed. He looked real spirited. He seemed especially pleased to see me. I was happy to see him too, even though he was always making noises at night and keeping people up, and incessantly working during the day whether he needed to or not. There was a big wound on his face, likely the result of having fallen when he was drunk.

The driver was a familiar villager who rolled down the window to greet me. I leaned on the window frame to look inside. Nur, my neighbor from Akehara, was there too!

Taking a closer look, oh boy, including the driver, the five-seater sat seven adults and a child. One big fellow, who was curled up in the trunk, grinned at me.

Since my destination was on their way, I squeezed into the car without a word. After the door slammed shut, we were squeezed so tightly that each passenger only had one foot touching the floor.

The driver asked me, "What are you doing walking all this way?"

My answer: "For fun."

"What's fun here?"

I smiled but didn't say anything.

Then he asked, "You walked all the way out here and didn't say anything to the people down below?"

"I did."

"What did you say?"

"I said, 'Hello!'"

Everyone in the jeep laughed: "No!"

I asked Cuma, "When are those graves from?"

He said, "Maybe seventy or eighty years ago."

The driver said, "No, no, at least a hundred years!"

The passenger next to me said, "When my grandfather was a kid, someone told him it was already a hundred years."

I was skeptical. "How can a few graves made of little tree sticks survive for that long?"

Cuma said, "No, no, there used to be at least twenty graves and more than twenty people buried there! Slowly, year after year, the graves collapsed, faded away. . . ."

The driver said, "Nonsense! The place has been used for hundreds of years, there's got to be at least a hundred people down there."

Whatever the case, what I saw were the last remaining graves. In the wind and sun, they'd melted back into the earth. They were the last traces of a once-large cemetery.

Cuma continued by explaining that that was a different time, not at all like now, when people have cars and can quickly take the deceased back north to the Ulungur where the ancestral graves are. As Muslims, Kazakhs customarily bury the dead as soon as possible, which often means finding some place nearby. But "nearby" could easily be dozens of miles away. As a cart carried the corpse slowly across the land, the family's grief slowly dragged on.

This was perhaps the only patch of dirt in this whole stretch of desert, and probably the only graveyard. After all this time, how many herders who could no longer march with their flocks had been left there? Now that people no longer used this ancient graveyard, it would be abandoned forever. Cuma said, "All thanks to the great improvements in transportation . . ." But as far as I was concerned, the "improvements" so far had about as much impact as a wooden mallet against an iron beam. Nevertheless, the impact had already shaken this world to its core.

PART

FOUR

Last Things

29.

Year of the Blizzard

CUMA ONCE ASKED ME whether I preferred winter or summer. I thought about the winter's long nights and short days, about being able to sleep in, and how milk production is low during winter, so there's no need to make dairy products, no need to break your back every day turning the skimmer machine or whipping yogurt, so I casually answered, "Winter's better!"

He said, "Then why didn't you come last winter?"

I was stumped. The previous year, 2009, had seen snowstorms of rare proportions. The region's livestock production was hit hard. Many flocks were completely wiped out; only the herders had managed to survive. Even I was nearly buried by the snow!

Cuma added, "If the weather was as good as today every day in winter, that would be nice! But when you run into situations like last year, you may survive this winter but it'll get you the next winter! The whole family kaput! What's good about winter? Can't be better than summer!"

IT'S TRUE—THIS WINTER, the snow came late and, when it came, melted quickly. Though it was a drought year, though we experienced more than a month of extreme cold weather, overall it had been a calm winter.

The weather last year was bad enough as it was, but what made it worse was the fact that Cuma's family was the only one in this whole pasture. When the snow reached its very worst, the family of three struggled to cope. As soon as they were out of bed, the whole family went into battle, carrying shovels out to clear a path—there needed to be at least one path by which the flock could come in and out the burrow settlement, a way for them to climb over the dune to the snow-covered wilds where they could graze.

Snow wouldn't stop falling, as if the sky was broken. In Cuma's words, "Old Man Sky dropped it for two days and rested for one."

When it wasn't snowing, the wind blew the dry, powdery snow into the dip that was our burrow settlement, where it compacted and hardened. At that point, a person wouldn't be able to dig more than a few yards by hand, so Cuma drove the camels and horses through to tread out a path.

But whether dug out or trampled, the path didn't last for more than a day. The wind was too strong. The path that was cleared in the morning was filled in by the evening, sealing them in.

Every morning, after a path was cleared, Kama herded the flock and Sister-in-law did housework and tended to the cattle as usual, but Cuma led the camels to a distant dirt road to wait for the government's emergency relief: corn. The relief corn cost one yuan for two pounds, fifty cents cheaper than the market price. Each burlap sack weighed a hundred and seventy-six pounds. But buying relief corn required luck—herders from every corner of the wilderness waited up and down that stretch of road, which was often impassable. Even though plow trucks and bulldozers dispatched by the Livestock Office worked day and night clearing the road, they still couldn't keep up with the speed of the wind and snow.

Cuma did eventually buy corn a few times. Thanks to two feedings of this supplementary corn, the sheep and larger livestock managed to survive. Yet, even though it was enough to appease their appetites, it wasn't enough to keep them warm. Fewer than fifty sheep made it through the end of winter.

In total, fifty ewes, eighty big lambs, two cattle, and two calves died.

One day, during a brief moment of leisure in the murky twilight hours before the sky went dark, Kama led me over the eastern sand dune, along a stretch of the ridge to where it sloped down. There, still visible, was a pile of sheepskin half-buried beneath the snow with white bones jutting out. Kama told me that these were the sheep that didn't make it through the long winter (Muslims don't eat animals who die of natural causes and hadn't received the prayer). There were sixteen sheep in this pile. Farther along were several more piles in which I could see the larger bones and skeletons of cattle and horses.

I thought of the piebald cow that lost its child to the cold and adopted the calf that had lost its mother to that same cold. They relied on one another to survive. And the patch-faced cow that survived against all odds, whose three udders had frozen. To this day, those three udders cannot produce milk.

LIKE FINDING A HOLE in the roof on a rainy night, the mount had to choose this of all moments to go missing.

Cuma said, "It was three months before we got it back!"

I was shocked. "Three months! What did it eat for three months?"

Before he could reply, I quickly realized the answer: "Of course, grass." Horses eat grass. They're not like people, who'd starve out there in the wilderness after a day or two.

Cuma found it hilarious and translated my question for Sister-in-law, who laughed too.

In theory, horses don't get lost, which was why Cuma wasn't worried at first. But the family's one remaining mount had been whittled down to nothing but skin and bones. Even a modest journey left it teetering. On the coldest days, it was so weak that no amount of whipping could get the horse to move. As a result, after having received the relief corn, Cuma decided to go look for the missing horse on foot.

The first time he went out, he walked east for ten days. The second time, he walked west for half a month. Along the way, he asked for information and followed the clues. Whenever he found a burrow, he asked for lodging . . . like that, a month went by without success.

For Sister-in-law and Kama, who stayed home, it was a difficult time as well. In the morning, there were only two women to clear snow. Without the horse, Kama had to herd through the deep snow on foot. The snow buried the desert, growing ever thicker and harder. The sheep could no longer dig through the snow to find grass. All the scratching only bloodied their hooves. But they were too hungry, so they kept digging. . . . By that point, much of the flock had already perished, and of the cattle, only two pairs of mother and calf survived.

Finally, Cuma bit the bullet and offered a three-hundred-yuan bounty. It worked. Two months later, someone rode the horse back from more than two hundred kilometers away. It had somehow run all the way to Red Flag Commune! (Yup, we were still using place-names left from the Cultural

Revolution like Eternal Red Commune, Happiness Commune, Peak Commune . . .). The family that found the horse knew that sooner or later, the owner would arrive at their door, so they might as well return it right away. But during those months, the pitiful horse was poorly fed. It continued to serve as a mount without any extra nutritional supplements, reducing it to a haggard state.

Because the snow was too thick and melted too slowly, and the flock was too weak, a long journey became impossible. In the spring of that year, Cuma's family wasn't able to migrate back north until the end of April, a month later than usual! Normally, by the end of April, the herders were already done lambing in the spring pastures north of the Ulungur River and were preparing to enter the summer pastures in the Altai Mountains.

Last year, the snow in the mountains melted slowly as well. At the end of May and beginning of June, the mountain passes were still frozen shut. The entire livestock industry was stuck in the foothills, unable to advance. Once the grass there had been consumed, some of the herders had no choice but to retreat south again to the banks of the Irtysh River and the Ulungur River basin to graze. This had rarely happened before.

But thanks to the excess of snow that winter, the next spring had an abundance of water. As soon as the grasses were eaten, they grew right back up. What was typically rocky desert scrub was suddenly transformed into a lush prairie! Never-before-seen grasses appeared. They were so unfamiliar that not even the cattle and sheep dared to eat them—it was uncanny (my good friend Erjiao thought they were planted by aliens).

Even though that winter was long behind us, the very mention of it still drew heavy sighs from Cuma, followed by repeated complaints: "So much snow, so much . . ."

AS FOR ME, I had spent all that winter at home by myself in Akehara, where I often stared out the window in a trance: an all-engulfing storm where the flakes didn't drift down but came shooting down like bullets. Especially during the first two storms, the clumps of wet and heavy snow the size of pigeon eggs could leave a painful bruise on your face.

At the end of that December, after a whole night of snow, my windows were halfway buried, and the door was completely blocked.

Actually, not being able to go outside wasn't such a big deal. The house where I lived was once a rabbit hutch, a hundred sixty-five feet long and plenty wide. Stored inside were several tons of sunflower seeds, over two hundred pounds of dregs from pressing sunflower oil, a sack of cracked wheat, and three sacks of wheat bran. The chickens, ducks, cats, dogs, and rabbits were in no danger of going hungry. As for me, though there were no vegetables, I had a sack of flour, a sack of rice, and plenty of salt, so I wasn't going to go hungry. The coal had already been moved inside. There was more than a ton of it, enough to burn for over a month. Water came from a well pump directly into the room. It would run as long as there was electricity. And the number of days without power weren't many. If I hadn't the need to use the toilet, I could have stayed inside that building until spring.

But how can you not use the toilet! Besides, as soon as the snow stopped, you had to figure out a way to get outside, or else, with the wind blowing and the snow settling and hardening, that door will never open again! So, in the morning, as soon as the snow stopped, I threw myself into battle. First, push as hard as you can against the door (it opened outward) until it opened wide enough to stick a finger through. Then, stick the iron poker for the stove through the crack and jiggle it around until the snow around the crack loosens. Then push again until the crack is as wide as a palm. Then, I used the small shovel for scraping ash to dig at the snow, then pushed again until the opening was six inches wide. Finally, I could reach out to shovel. . . . When the door was open a little more than a foot wide it was enough for me to squeeze out. . . . Throughout this whole process, I took regular breaks to warm myself up by the stove.

Once out the door, I spent a few more hours digging a path to the toilet through the waist-deep snow, then another path to the courtyard gate. But by the time I had cleared the snow that blocked the gate, and opened it (good thing the gate opened inward), I couldn't believe my eyes—there was a wall of snow taller than me. That gate faced the wind, trapping all the snow that had blown this way. . . . I gave up, I didn't have a shred of energy left. In the end, the courtyard gate remained shut for two months. No one in Akehara knew that I was home. They all assumed that behind the snow was an empty house.

Because I was slim, the two paths that I dug were only a foot wide, just enough space for me to pass sideways. But when my mother returned home, she was furious. She was too fat—so she got stuck.

My infinitely resourceful mother just happened to know a road-maintenance worker. So, when the heavy-duty loader passed through Akehara clearing paths, it went out of its way to come to my house to dig me out. As wide and tall as that loader was, it still had to make more than twenty trips (how much fuel must that have required . . . I didn't pay a cent). The mound of snow dumped by the loader to the west of the house was almost two stories tall!

WHEN EVERYBODY HEARD my story, they all gasped. They asked, "Is that something you will write about too?"

I said, "Of course," before opening my notebook to write it down.

Kama pondered for a moment, then asked me for a sheet of paper and a pen. With a flashlight in hand, she lay on the felt mat on the bed to reflect and write. During evening tea, she held the sheet filled with words and read it to us out loud. Bowls in hand, everyone listened intently. Afterward, everyone said, "Very good." Then, after a silent pause, Sister-in-law took the paper to read again, quietly holding the flashlight. The light was dim. The solar-powered flashlight was only three watts.

I asked Cuma what Kama had written. He was too lazy to translate. "Whatever you wrote, that's what she wrote!"

Later, when the party branch secretary from the elementary school visited, Kama brought out the paper once again to read to him. The teacher also said it

The flock braves the snow in the pitch-black of the snowstorm.

was well written before turning to tell me in Mandarin that she'd written about her own experiences. It talked about how, after Big Sister went off to school, life became challenging for the family, so she had to drop out from her first year of junior high school and herd sheep. Even though she felt sad about not being able to go to school, what other choice did she have? Then, she wrote about last year's snow and how much everyone had to endure. There were also some passionate passages about Kazakh herding traditions . . . it really was just like what I had written!

Anyhow, we were all grateful for how peaceful this winter had turned out. Everyone agreed, "Thank goodness this year's not bad!" Even though daily life was still a challenge—in the middle of every night, Sister-in-law had to wake up and rekindle the fire for the rest of us, and Plum Blossom was always so cold that he was always trying to burrow under our bedcovers.

30.

What I'm Experiencing

IN ORDER TO RAISE a telephone antenna, Shinshybek brought three ten-foot poles made of pine into the desert. He tied one on top of another and used it to raise an antenna sky-high in the sand next to the burrow. Although it only received a signal once in a while, it always attracted all the cattle to scratch themselves.... Of course, the pole didn't stand a chance against a big cow belly! So, the two men next door were constantly scrambling to save the antenna pole.

I asked Cuma, "Why do we have a television but no telephone?"

He replied, "I don't have any wood, so we can't raise an antenna."

I said, "So what if you had wood, don't you see how much trouble it is for Shinshybek's family? You might as well hang the antenna on top of that metal structure on the sand dune, it's tall and sturdy!"

He retorted, "But it's so far away, wouldn't you need a sixteen-hundred-foot-long phone line?"

I insisted, "Just let the line hang there and when you want to make a phone call, carry the telephone over, plug in the port, and when you're done, unplug it and carry the phone back."

He said, "*Koychy!*" Then he began to contemplate it seriously.

Sure enough, Cuma traveled to Akehara soon after and returned with a wireless landline telephone, which he set up as I suggested. And whaddaya know, our signal was much better than the neighbor's! And it didn't require daily maintenance. There was just one catch: we could make calls, but not receive them. . . .

This was the most helpful suggestion that I ever offered the family.

Come to think of it, it might be the only suggestion I gave all winter.

OTHER THAN THIS, what else did I contribute to the family? Only things like collecting snow, herding calves, herding sheep, embroidering, mending clothes, explaining TV shows . . . things that anyone could have done. In other words, the presence of someone like me had almost no impact on the family. On the other hand, I was deeply impacted. Especially when it came to speaking. Before I knew it, I was picking up Kazakh speech habits:

When studying Kazakh, I'd say, "Difficulties so many!" ("This is hard.")

At mealtimes: "Food to eat!"

Asking for help: "A help give to me!"

Announcing that I hadn't seen the sheep: "Sheep not seen!"

Meaning to say "neither hot nor cold": "Cold, it's not, hot, it's not."

I HEARD THAT AT FIRST, nobody had believed I would be able to persevere; they all thought that, after a few days, I'd call it quits. As time passed, they became more and more amazed. But as more time passed, they simply became used to my presence. They even began to worry about arranging for my return north in the spring—there were no extra horses. They thought of many possible solutions, and thought about my arrangements after the summer, entirely forgetting that I was only there to experience one winter.

In short, I was integrated into their lives and things weren't going badly. Even though they were never able to understand what I was doing there, neither did they reject my being there. I was a person after all, capable of hard work, capable of picking up social cues, so what was there to complain about? Whatever problems there were to speak of were generally of my own making.

How do I put this . . . my interest in the nomadic lifestyle is one thing, but the need to understand it and describe it is another matter. The more time passes, the more confused I feel. Here, no matter what I do, no matter how hard I try, it is never enough. No matter what I say, it seems impossible to get to the truth or to my purpose. I am, in the end, awkwardly superfluous. . . .

Still, though they say sensitive people are destined to suffer, I am more than happy to suffer rather than be any other kind of person.

CUMA'S MANDARIN WASN'T BAD, and basic communication wasn't a problem. Had I not been worried about bothering him and had I insisted on getting to the bottom of every question, I could have found out most everything I wanted to. But I did worry about bothering him . . . because it would have been annoying! Besides, life was already difficult enough, they didn't need an outsider chewing their ears off all day long, not only being of little use but also a constant distraction—I refuse to be that person. Plus, we had more than just a day or two together, there would be plenty of time and opportunity—better that I rely on my own experiences little by little and slowly try to learn.

I'm not sure if it was a problem with my approach or if Cuma just had trouble comprehending, but our interactions often faced the following obstacles:

I asked, "Some sheep have horns, some don't. Why?"

He answered, "Because they're different, so some have horns, some don't."

I asked, "When they're far away, horses, cattle, and camels look so small, they are only little black specks; how is it that you guys can tell right away which is a camel, which is a horse, and which is a cow?"

He replied, "Because their tails are different."

I just said they were little black specks—how could he still see their tails?

I couldn't understand him and he couldn't understand me. He was always complaining to me—apparently I always took pictures of him on his bad hair days. When he finally got a haircut and looked handsome, I stopped taking photos. In the middle of work, when he was dirty and ungainly, I snuck around with my camera clicking nonstop. But by the time he had washed his face and was sitting in a clean room, I stopped taking pictures. The complaining made me hesitate before taking any more pictures, unsure of what was appropriate.

Sometimes, after chatting for a while, we'd suddenly hit upon something that I felt was a matter of importance. For example, once, he suddenly said, "It'll snow in one week." When I asked why, he said, "In five days, the moon will be round and it will climb to the center of the sky."

I looked up a lunar calendar. In five days, it would be the fifteenth day of the winter month, the eleventh month in the lunar year, and in a week it would be the winter solstice! It couldn't have been a coincidence, right? Did the Kazakhs use the lunar calendar too? Amazed, I kept asking more and more questions. Seeing how interested I was, he answered many of my questions in earnest. He listed a timetable that had something to do with "eighty-one days," hoping to explain to me a way of calculating the progress of the cold weather, a tool not unlike the Han people's "Winter Solstice Table of

Nine." He mentioned a Kazakh saying that went, "The long shortens, the short lengthens," which seems to have something to do with the Nauryz Festival (vernal equinox), which in turn has something to do with the migration back north. I immediately felt like I was delving into this nomadic people's traditional lore; it was exhilarating! I grabbed a pen and paper, ready to conduct some serious research. . . .

Unfortunately, in the end I wasn't the rigorous type and Cuma was unable to express himself rigorously either. Our discussion quickly fell into a muddle, both sides too tired to function . . . in the end, I came away with no more than the ideas and fragments I began with. So I gave up. Anyway, I write essays, not dissertations, better to stick to the basics. . . .

OFTENTIMES, AS WE CHATTED, our conversation would turn toward criticizing the darker aspects of modern society, for example corruption (the town's family-planning commissioner collecting bribes), decadent youth (alcoholism), rising prices (mostly targeting my mother). . . . At this point, Cuma would become indignant, casting me as an agent of the enemy, insisting that I solve the problems immediately! Which left me feeling guilty.

He also had a habit of assigning me grave responsibilities. When Koktokay town's legend of "Amyrsana" came up, he ordered me to write down the story, then have it adapted into a movie. When he talked about the difficulties of relocating all the time, he told me to relay the situation to the powers that be: herding sheep every day is harder work than going to meetings every day!

IN REALITY, HE WAS MUCH more curious about me than I was about him. At first, I was thrilled to be living with someone who spoke Mandarin; life would certainly be more convenient. Whatever questions I had, I could just ask. But as it turned out, before I had found out much about him, he had already found out everything there was to know about me. Every time there was a pause in our conversation, he would gleefully put on his clothes, slide off the bed, then walk straight to Shinshybek's burrow to share his newest findings about me.

And in these reports, he let his imagination run wild. There was no limit to his creativity. As a result, in the eyes of the local herder community, I was by turns an unemployed vagabond out to steal herding secrets, a furloughed reporter from the county TV station, and the child of a high-level official banished to the countryside—I couldn't imagine what might have seemed high-level about my mother.

It was hard to know exactly where the misunderstandings came from either. Every time I talked about what I did for a living, he always asked for many details, and I always answered in earnest. Yet when all was said, he would always express his sincerest condolences and assure me that things will get better with time before personally adding an extra scoop of butter into my tea.

Cuma always had his own ideas about things. When it came to answering my questions, he was very selective. When it was too complicated, he didn't reply; too simple, he didn't bother to respond; too childish, he would make a joke of it. As a result, he hardly answered any of my questions. The worst part about it was that I had no way of knowing in advance if my question was complicated, simple, or childish. To me, they were all questions I didn't know the answers to . . . perhaps I was naive.

Slowly, I learned to be clever. Instead of trying to derive information directly from his answers, I paid attention to his reaction, attitude, tone, expression . . . analyzed them holistically and then came to a conclusion.

Once, I watched him remove the handle from a perfectly good shovel and replace it with a short handle; then, with that tool, a pickax, and a long strip of red purlin from the yurt in hand, he prepared to head out. It all seemed very mysterious. Needless to say, when I asked him what he was doing, I did not get the answer I wanted—and grabbing the horse's reins and not letting him leave wouldn't have worked, nor would taking his short-handled shovel away, nor would stomping my feet and whining. He only offered one answer: to dig a bear cave! When I asked, why dig a bear cave? He replied: for fun. It was like he was teasing a three-year-old child! How aggravating.

Once I calmed down, I made the following deduction:

A short-handled shovel only had one purpose: to dig pits; specifically, a narrow but deep pit. The pickax also served the same purpose. As for the thin purlin, when in association with a "pit," its use seemed clear: to erect a post!

But what was the purpose of erecting a post in the open desert?

To tether horses? No, it was too thin.

A marker? Possible . . . yes, it must be a marker, or else why use a purlin? Because it was bright red!

As for what kind of marker—that remains a mystery. . . . But since he rode a horse there, it must have been in a faraway place. A marker for a distant place, a boundary perhaps? Or a landmark for the lost . . .

Thanks to Cuma, I quickly became Sherlock Holmes.

Though more often than not, there weren't enough clues to deduce from—

When I asked why he added a ladle of water when rendering fats, he replied: to disinfect it.

When I asked where Sister-in-law went, he replied: Kazakhstan!

When I asked why he let the sheep out at seven that morning, he simply said: who knows!

Sometimes I wondered whether he was mad at me. But what had I done wrong? Likely, my mistake was endlessly asking him what he felt were inane questions. . . .

During a conversation with my big sister Yerkex Hurmanbek, she told a story. Someone once asked the wife of a family of Kazakh herders, "Since all your family sleeps together, is 'doing it' just a casual thing?" The woman replied, "Of course, we make love with whoever we want and whoever happens to be there." The person was both appalled and secretly pleased, repeating the story everywhere. But even an idiot should be able to tell that such a response was given out of contempt! Such boring, asinine, uncivilized questions don't deserve serious answers.

While Sister-in-law was rolling dough once, I asked, "What are you making?"

Cuma said, "Fried *baursak*." When I checked in again, it was clearly baked *nan*.

Perhaps this was what Cuma was driving at: What are eyes for?

SO, I EXERCISED CAUTION while observing life around me. I tried to be conscientious about my own ignorance and kept my mouth shut as much as possible. Anything I said might seem pointless, idiotic, or absurd.

For example, when Sister-in-law dyed felt, she completely ignored the instructions on the back of the package of the chemical dye (not that could she read them). All the stuff about "soak first in warm water for thirty minutes" and "dissolve dye and assisting agent in a large bowl, stir until a paste forms" and "gradually bring mixture to boil over thirty minutes" . . . was ignored. Instead, she poured the dye directly into a large aluminum pot (the instructions specifically noted to avoid using aluminum utensils . . .), stirred a few times, then started to drop in the felt pieces. I really wanted to correct her but it occurred to me she had probably dyed several tons of wool over the past few decades; she must have known what she was dyeing. I didn't need to be like the egg teaching the hen.

And of course, it turned out great! Whereas for me, when I tried dying old clothes at home, it was rarely successful—although I had scientifically followed the instructions every step of the way.

THE WINTER PASTURES were always too quiet. Whenever there were footsteps overhead, followed by the door swinging open, and strangers stepping inside the burrow with their greetings, in those moments, I too felt a genuine, happy surprise. But all I could do was examine our guests in silence. I didn't even have the courage to take out my camera to photograph them. Suppose I really was as important as Cuma had made me out to be, I could have used a professorial tone to ask them their names, where they lived, how far it was from here, the number of mouths in their family, the number of sheep, cattle, camels . . . except I wasn't stupid, I knew that these high-minded questions were actually quite silly. Had I asked them, they would've answered diligently out of politeness, but deep down, they would have found my naivety and pedantry contemptible.

Perhaps others weren't as churlish as Cuma, but their attitudes were strikingly similar: an average question received an average answer; a pointless question, a pointless answer; and a nonsensical question received, of course, a nonsensical answer.

In an environment like this, I was always in a passive position. Not that that was a problem; on the contrary, I depended on being passive. In such an unfamiliar environment, I relied on going with the flow. I had to avoid standing out and avoid causing conflict to gain their trust and feel a sense of security.

BEYOND NOT UNDERSTANDING each other, there were many other frustrations.

In order to faithfully record all I saw and heard, I borrowed a camcorder. But no matter what, the tape would get stuck after less than ten minutes of recording (might have had to do with the low temperatures). After taking out the tape, knocking it around a little, then reloading it, the camcorder managed to record for another ten minutes. But by then, I'd already missed everything.

Even more unfortunate was the fact that when I wanted to shoot the building of the yurt, they told me to watch the baby. When it was time to slaughter the horse, I was sent to haul snow. When I wanted to capture the dismembering of the sheep, they made me hold the bloody hooves, which occupied both of my hands—none left to hold a camera.

At first, a hi-tech toy like a camcorder earned Cuma's respect. But once it had been put to a side, it quickly became a joke to him. On several occasions, he offered to trade Plum Blossom for it, listing all the perks of having a cat. When he saw that I wasn't interested, he offered his binoculars instead, going so far as to point out their similarities: both had pieces of glass on the front.

At least my compact camera didn't have any problems. And it was run on AA batteries, which saved the trouble of charging. The only annoyance was how quickly the batteries drained in cold weather; that, and the broken battery cap, which had to be secured with tape every time the batteries were changed. If the tape was too loose, the batteries would spring out. But if the tape was too tight, some of the buttons jammed. It was frustrating . . . even the herders seemed skeptical of my taped-up gadget. Sometimes when I took my camera out to photograph them, they took one out to photograph me back—and their cameras were much better!

These one-thousand-yuan point-and-shoots required a lot of light. A little too dark and you end up with a blur. Out of politeness, I didn't want to use the flash. And everyone was generally most animated at night. After a busy day, the family relaxed under the dim solar-powered light bulb, dancing, embracing, eating meat, playing with the cat . . . I couldn't capture any of it.

THOUGH I WAS THERE physically, sometimes I still felt like I was a world away. On our way home with sacks of snow on our backs, Kama and I noticed a caravan of camels resting quietly in the desert to the southwest of us. The lead camel was crouched in the snow, sleeping, while a scattered flock of sheep grazed nearby. We dropped our sacks to observe for a while. Kama suddenly said, "There are two families traveling together, herders from Dopa village."

I didn't know how she could have known that. . . . I asked, "Why are there no people? Where did they go?"

She pointed to the direction of our burrow in the distance and said, "They're all having tea at my house! Two of them rode horses, two of them rode motorcycles. . . ." I still didn't how she could tell. I didn't see any horses or motorcycles. A moment later, she added, "One of the ones on horseback is a girl." I still didn't understand. . . .

During those long, quiet midday hours, everyone spent a long time quietly drinking tea. Without a word, Cuma suddenly got up, grabbed the horse's mask, filled it with corn, and walked out. I followed him out and observed from the top of the sand dune to our west. A stranger was bringing back our horse. Cuma approached to greet them. He fastened the mask on the horse before equipping it with the halter, saddle, and girth. I continued to stand in the distance, watching his every move. It was windy and quiet. Where would he be going at a time like this, and what would he be doing. . . . I felt indescribably far away.

One day, Sister-in-law brought out a parcel from the bottom of her suitcase that was wrapped in a headscarf. She unwrapped it, and inside were strands of light-green grass that didn't look quite like tea leaves. She said to me, "Medicine." She gestured for me to smell it. From one whiff I knew that it was lavender! At first I smelled nothing, but the moment I brought my nose close to it, the whole room was instantly filled with the fragrance. I could smell it for days.

Cuma had a cough. Sister-in-law poured hot water on the lavender like she was brewing tea. Once steeped, she added two spoonfuls of milk and handed the bowl to him. Noticing my fascination, she ladled me half a bowl too. I tasted it, and well, it wasn't bad.

Once, I got sick and lay in bed all day with a fever. In the middle of the night, Sister-in-law nudged me awake from the black pile of bodies clustered around the television and handed me a bowl of that same medicinal soup. When I took the bowl from her and gulped it, I felt both grateful and sad. As all the beautiful and romantic feelings associated with the lavender seeped into my miserably ill psyche, my mood instantly improved. Which at the same time made me feel distant.

Whenever the "Black Horse Trot" was playing through the speakers, Cuma couldn't stay still. Sitting cross-legged on the felt mats on the bed, he began to dance, arms gracefully bouncing to the rhythm. Kama gently swayed her shoulders back and forth. Sister-in-law clapped along and encouraged me to join the dance. My heart itched but I resisted the temptation. I sat there with a smile, motionless, afraid to reveal too many feelings. I was in a strange land; calling it pride would have been less accurate than calling it fear.

I used a black leather notebook to record everything that was happening in front of me. At the same time, I seemed to have used "recording" as a way of emphasizing something to everyone—a way of keeping my distance. I realized that I was never interested in writing when I was happy or excited. When I was happy or excited, I didn't even want to touch that notebook; touching it would have been an interruption—in those moments, I was only interested in the life in front of me. It was only during the awkward and lonely moments when I felt blue that I would reach for the notebook. I used it to write down all the happy and exciting things that had recently occurred.

LATER, I BEGAN TO OBSERVE the relationship between the moon's trajectory and its phases. I noticed that during the waxing crescent, the moon rose in the evening and did not drop beneath the horizon until daybreak. Then, as it continued to wax, the moon rose earlier and earlier in the day. By full moon, it was rising in the morning and descending at night, following almost the same schedule as the sun. As the moon waned, it rose earlier still. By waning crescent, it rose in the middle of the night and fell in the afternoon. Following that were two moonless days and nights.

I noticed that on dark, moonless nights, the sky exploded with stars. But as long as there was a moon—even if it was only a sliver of a crescent moon, the Milky Way faded into darkness.

I also noticed that since entering the wilderness, the sun no longer moved me, but the moon—it felt closer than ever before.

I also paid close attention to the reading on the thermometer. But after about a month, Panda Dog, bored, chewed a piece off the thermometer that was hanging in the passage outside the burrow. Luckily, the section that remained still worked, unless the temperature rose above seventy-five degrees Fahrenheit. But a month later, another section was angrily bitten off by the big black cow (we'd brought her newborn calf inside the burrow). This time, the thermometer could only read temperatures below negative fourteen degrees, making it quite useless.

There were always challenges, followed by more challenges. After a day of work, my muscles felt worn out, my stomach craved food and water. But after eating, I still felt hungry and thirsty. It was hard to tell what part of my body was lacking what . . . yet, when I really was thirsty—waking up in the middle of the night out of thirst, throat dry as smoke, I went outside to sit in the cold air for a moment before lying back down to ride it out in silence. After an hour or two, the discomfort eventually passed and I drifted off to sleep. By the time I woke up in the morning, the thirst was gone. Did the water in the body move from one place to another? The inside of my body had become confused; it was impossible to make any sense of it.

Plum Blossom had an upset stomach. For two days, the kitten left diarrhea wherever he went, including one particularly large pile on the rugs in front of the television. I crumpled up a sheet of newspaper to clean up the mess while Cuma laughed: "How did it know Li Juan sleeps there?" Everyone else laughed but I was distraught. I wiped the spot again and again and hoped that the cat would feel better in the evening. But in the evening, though he didn't violate my bedding, he continued to moan "ugh, ugh" all night a foot away from me on the manure and dirt ground near the TV. At the time I thought, I've had enough of this. . . .

But I had no intention of "retreating." Where would I go? Isn't life like this anywhere you go?

During that period, I must have unconsciously shown too much of my frustration, because everyone noticed. At breakfast, Cuma said to me, "Last night, I forgot to take a bowl of butter out before freezing the whole block in the yurt. Now it's too hard to scoop, so no butter to eat today." He added, "The rest of us eat tallow when there's no butter, but poor Li Juan doesn't eat tallow. . . ." As he spoke, he scraped up the last of the butter and threw it into my bowl.

On the eve of the Chinese New Year, I told Cuma that tomorrow was the Han "New Year." He didn't say anything, but started skipping from one song to the next on the stereo. Eventually, he reached a Mandarin song by Cai Yilin. He stayed on the track and said to me, "Every day is our song, now we play your song, a Happy New Year for Li Juan!" What more could I say?

I kept watching, kept on tirelessly discovering and witnessing. Every morning, I saw Kama refusing to climb out of bed. She complained that her own bedding was too cold and snuggled into her mother's. When her mother woke up, she immediately snuggled into her father's. When Cuma got out of bed, he told her to hurry, calling, "Child! Child!" again and again. Kama pretended like she couldn't hear.

Cuma pretended to be shocked. "Is she dead, has Kama really died?"

Eyes closed, Kama shouted, "That's right, I'm dead!"

Cuma leaped on top of her, squishing her, while shouting, "In that case, Dad is dead too!" Father and daughter rolled into a ball, refusing to move.

Squatting by the stove, Sister-in-law poked at the embers, while warning, "*Koychy!* Get up now!"

I WATCHED NURGÜN slowly maturing out of childhood. She was reaching the age when she should start learning the feminine arts. But in the process of learning, she made a mess of everything—the ram's horns turned into a crab's claw. The pattern-weaving stripes turned into dead snakes. All day long, she was mercilessly admonished and ridiculed. But no matter how many insults she received, the girl never gave up. She continued to put in the effort, fearlessly trying her best, and often with a smile—it was a self-deprecating giggle that was meant to appease. But even a smile like that made her mother angry. She'd say, "No smiling!" in such an angry tone that it sounded like she was going to stab her daughter with a needle. Even Karlygash was at risk of being drawn into the furor—in a tense moment like that, a baby couldn't cry. Crying would have provoked her mother's wrath.

I observed that nine-year-old Nurgün was Kama's only bestie and confidant. When the two chatted, you could hardly tell there was a huge age difference. Kama didn't speak as if talking to a child, and Nurgün didn't sound like a child either. Their conversations moved from embroidery to hairstyling, school stuff to village stuff, and even after an hour they still had more to say. At the height of camaraderie, Kama grabbed her purse and took out her treasures—they were nothing more than a few old hairpins and a rusty bracelet—and introduced each item to Nurgün, what this one was for, who had given it to her, how much it was worth, and where she'd bought that one, on what occasions she had worn it, and with what clothes . . . sharing the secrets and joys of womanhood.

For an outsider like me, looking in on such an intimate scene felt bittersweet. Oh, vicarious pleasures! I thought to myself, enough, that's enough. But I couldn't get myself to turn away. . . .

In a moment like that, a camera would have been a barbaric intrusion! My eyes captured the scene with more detail and vibrancy than any lens possibly could—the last of the nomads, the most quiet and remote way of life! But there

The horse skull that Kama found and that was perched on
the steel tripod, the highest point on the dune

was already much about the family that was no longer traditional; there were already the television and the trendy pop songs.

I saw the young boy Zhada begging his parents to buy him a computer, and further, suggesting that they install internet at the permanent encampment. I saw Sister-in-law sweep the floor, then put the litter directly into the stove— she no longer thought of it as an offense to the fire; this ancient taboo had long been abandoned.

But at the same time, I saw Kama, a young woman humming pop songs, walk in the dusk light, pick up a horse skull from the sand, walk to the metal tripod at the top of the dune, and rise on her tiptoes to hang the skull as high as she could . . . another ancient tradition, because an object as noble as a horse's skull must not be trampled upon, therefore it should be placed high up.

I also noticed that whenever Karlygash was going to be tied up in her crib, Sayna would first take out her lighter and wave a small flame over the bed to ward off evil spirits. This was also tradition.

And after washing her hair, the beautiful Kama melted a spoonful of sheep tallow to massage into her hair to make it oily, smooth, and glistening. What an interesting aesthetic, as well as method of hair care.

ON ANOTHER ONE OF those evenings beneath a perfectly round moon, a great southeastern gale filled the world with howls and hisses. But beneath the earth, it was as quiet as the bottom of the ocean, except for the occasional flapping sound made by the flimsy plastic covering the high window. Cuma drank his tea in silence. During those in-between moments when she wasn't serving tea, Sister-in-law embroidered. Zhada stared at his phone. Then, the door opened and Kama came lumbering in holding an unweaned calf across her waist . . . those moments profoundly triggered my curiosity. I wanted to know everything, but I didn't know where to start. I was only an outsider.

Whenever a curious visitor talked about me, they would ask Cuma, "What is she here to do?" Cuma's explanation always took thirty seconds or more, leaving the listener gasping in amazement. Then they'd ask, "How much longer is she staying with you?"

Cuma said whatever he felt like. "Probably another five months." The visitor let out an even more amazed gasp.

I swiftly corrected him: "Rubbish, I leave next month!"

It was true, I was leaving next month. What did that make me? How was I different from any other "cultural tourist"? They usually had a weeklong experience or a month at most. In that respect, I seemed to have them beat, having experienced a whole winter. But the difference was only marginal . . . I was still just a passerby.

Besides, just because someone has more experience with this way of life doesn't make them more knowledgeable. Quite the opposite: my confidence in what I understood only grew weaker with time. As time went on, I became more hesitant, more doubtful, and less courageous. After all the days and nights together, the thousands of feelings felt, the accumulation of shared moments . . . the more I thought I knew, the more I realized I didn't know. "Knowing" and "not knowing" grew out of one another. The world was opening up from both sides. When I thought the world was a tiny seed, the world turned out to be an apple; when I thought the world was an apple, it turned out to be an apple tree; when I thought the world was an apple tree, I looked up and saw the world around me—there was an apple orchard stretching forever in all directions. . . .

Even if I did catch a glimpse of the fate of the nomads and the desert, and learned to understand the basics, I still struggle to articulate it with my unwieldy and anxious tongue. The more I try to make sense of the big picture, the more I'm tripped up by the details. What's worse, the more I want to point out the most barbaric moments, the more I want to turn around and forgive human nature, especially forgive myself. . . . I really am no use. How I loathe my powerlessness. But at the same time, I would prefer to suffer this powerlessness . . . so, let's leave it at that for now. To be continued.

31.

Everything
Disappears Quickly

CUMA ALWAYS STAYED OUT on the pastures until dark before return-ing home, to allow the sheep to graze a little farther and eat a little more. The neighbors were not nearly as fastidious. Our flocks appeared near the burrows as soon as the sun set beyond the sand dune marking the horizon. This made Cuma very angry, but he couldn't bring it up openly. So he offered the following hint: when it was his turn to herd, he came back later and later until everyone began to wonder if something bad had happened in the dark-ness. He waited until people's imaginations began to get the better of them. Eventually, the neighbors took the hint.

But they still returned earlier than Cuma did.

Finally, Cuma complained outright. One night, when Shinshybek came for a bowl of tea, the two ended up in a long, serious discussion. The following day, the result was apparent: Shinshybek made up his mind and did not return until six o'clock! It had long been dark by then.... Bracing against the cold wind, Rahmethan and I ran up a nearby sand dune only to find the desert utterly still. Cuma was impressed: "At this rate, they'll let him join the Com-munist Party!"

For days afterward, the two men competed to see who could return the latest. By the time they finally reached home, they were frozen stiff.

Arms as stiff as a block of wood, Cuma slowly drank one bowl of tea after another. He sat for a long time without uttering a word. It had been an especially cold day. Even sitting next to the stove, his breaths came in thick puffs of white. Then, when he was finally warm enough to have command of his senses, he leaned over to tug my jacket sleeve and opened his mouth: "Is this new?"

I replied, "No, I've had it for five years." He looked shocked and impressed.

Then he tugged at the old military-style jacket that he was wearing and said, "This one, two thousand, ten years!"

At first, I interpreted that to mean he bought it in the year 2000 and had worn it for ten years. I quickly responded, "Wow, how does it still look so new after ten years? Great quality!"

He paused for a moment, then said angrily, "What ten years, not even three months!"

In fact, by "two thousand, ten years" he meant 2010.

If that jacket was only three months old, it definitely looked older than its age. . . .

Then he pointed at Sister-in-law's violet coat—the one that I'd spared no effort washing two days prior—and said, "This, worn for one year, cost two hundred yuan!" I said nothing. My cotton jacket only cost one hundred.

When I was washing Sister-in-law's coat, I had thought, I wonder how old this coat is, it's filthy! I never could have imagined that it was the first time it had been washed. After I washed it, the water was the color of chocolate! Or more precisely, the first wash left me with what could've been dark soy sauce, and the second left me with regular soy sauce; the third, I assumed, would have given me light soy sauce, but by then, I'd already been scrubbing for two hours (to clean four items of clothing! Each item was heavier than the previous one—I barely had the strength to wring them out . . .). I was exhausted, my hands were pruned, and there wasn't enough water, so I stopped at two washes.

Meanwhile, Cuma was still grumbling. "You wear it one year and it's useless. Two hundred yuan! Two pairs of shoes, gone, a hundred yuan! Inside, outside, up, down, yours, mine! It's all gone, how much money is that?! Herding sheep every day, leaving early, back late, and this is what I get for it!" What he meant was that considering how hard they worked for it, the money didn't last very long.

I didn't know how to comfort him. The few tricks I could think of in terms of caring for clothes were only really suitable in a sedentary lifestyle—a much more relaxed, stable way of life.

And who am I to suggest that they didn't look after their belongings? They patched their clothes again and again, and there wasn't a single pair of shoes that hadn't been mended. Clothes beyond repair were cut up to be sewn into durable bags and blankets for the camels or woven into sturdy ropes. The most colorful articles were cut into patterns to be sewn into the *syrmak*. Even the last remaining scraps were cut into even stripes and sewn back into a quilt to be used for cushion covers or cloth bags. . . . In short, even after a piece of clothing could no longer be worn, it still had a long life in the burrow, disappearing only little by little.

Shoes that were beyond repair weren't thrown away either. Instead, Cuma got rid of the soles and pressed the rest of the shoe beneath a rug. Once the material was flattened, it could be used to patch another pair of shoes.

A chipped ladle had its handle removed and affixed to an enamel bowl using a thin iron sheet to create a new ladle.

A broken square plastic kettle had the top cut out to make a square bowl for feeding the dog and cows.

Even an empty plastic bottle wasn't simply thrown away. It continued to act as a vessel for other things. At one point, it was a milk bottle that froze at night, so no milk would pour out. Kama placed the bottle next to the stove to warm it up, but the moment she took her eyes off it, the bottle shriveled, collapsing at one side to form a C shape. Still, they didn't throw it away. It just became a container for sunflower oil instead.

On our journey south, Shinshybek's lighter broke. After a long day of work, two men sat in the pitch-black desert night, shining a flashlight on the thing, and discussed how to fix it for a half an hour. They disassembled and reassembled it again and again without any success. I thought Shinshybek would throw it away, but two days later, at the end of our journey south, he took out the lighter and continued to try to fix it with the help of handy Cuma. It was only a one-yuan disposable lighter!

They never threw these disposable lighters away—even when the gas ran out. Next time, when another lighter broke, they could disassemble the empty one for parts to fix the broken one. . . . Somehow, it had never occurred to me that these lighters could be repaired.

But no matter how thrifty they were, everything continued to flow through the household at a rapid pace, like water. And no matter how this water continued to wash over them, the family, set in their ways, refused to budge.

Still, the water never stopped flowing. Discreetly, it would eventually wash everything away.

THE SECOND WEEK, after settling in, Cuma suddenly said, "Is the speaker broken? What's wrong with the sound?" Kama turned it upside down and shook it. A clump of dried grass fell out! She opened up the speaker and discovered another clump inside.

During the move, the speaker had been left in a pile of grass on the truck.

I asked, "Why'd you put it with the grass?"

Cuma said, "Who'd have thought it was a sheep? I didn't know it ate grass!"

In addition to all the items used in everyday life, the light-duty truck had also been loaded with over a dozen bags of ice and over a dozen sacks of fodder and grain for the two families. By the time the truck arrived, it wasn't just the speakers that had suffered a rough ride; the steamer pot was also bent out of shape, and Sister-in-law's bottle of osmanthus pomade broke. But compared with previous trips, the damage was negligible. In the past, they moved using camels. While the camels plodded, all the items weighing down over their humps bumped and scraped against each other. And if they had to travel over a mountain pass, there would be even more bumping involved. As a result, after every move, many things were broken.

In a life constantly on the move, these things were expected. And taking into consideration all the backbreaking labor, it was even more understandable. Even the highest-quality clothes didn't last more than a few months, and even the toughest rope didn't last more than two years.

The toughest ropes were made from leather. They lasted two years but took almost a year to make. After the summer slaughter, the cowhide is dried in the sun. When it has stiffened, it is cut into an inch-wide spiraling strip, measuring tens of yards long. It is then pressed, rubbed, and beaten until it eventually begins to soften. In autumn, once the flocks have wound their way down from the mountains into the wide-open pastures, herders attach these long, stiff strips to the backs of their saddles to be dragged along wherever they go. This was also to massage the leather, to let them bang on the earth until it gradually softened. This kind of work could not possibly have been done by hand. Across the autumn and winter pastures, almost all the herders rode with these long strips dragging behind them.

And throughout the long winter, time and again the herders would remove the strip from the saddle, lay it over a rock, and beat it with a hammer, inch by inch, to further soften it. Then, after lathering on some sheep grease, they wrap the still-hard strip around a pole and pull it back and forth to soften it further. By spring, it will finally be soft enough (though still tough, but at least it can be bent and twisted). On the spring pasture, a herder will cut the strip into four or five thinner strips and weave them together to make a braided rope about as thick as a finger. At this point, it is strong and supple, finally fit for use.

I said, "It will only last two years? That's not tough enough!"

Cuma said, "The plastic rope your family sells, eighty cents for three feet, two fingers thick, only lasts three months!"

LIKEWISE, THE FAMILY'S HEALTH was worn away, bit by bit. Years of strenuous labor had left Cuma and Sister-in-law with all sorts of aches and pains. At times, the pain was so bad they couldn't walk. As a result, they ate aspirin and painkillers like snacks, two pills, four to five times daily. It had been like this for almost six years already!

I warned them, "You cannot just keep taking pills like this, you must get proper treatment."

Cuma sounded exasperated. "Treatment? How? If we leave, what'll happen to the sheep? If we don't watch the sheep, where will the money come from for the treatment?" It was hopeless.

For the half hour after taking aspirin or painkillers, the pain is immediately relieved, much to everyone's satisfaction. Nearly every herder family maintains a large stock of these cheap drugs, much to my concern. . . .

Possibly due to taking too many pills, one day Cuma suddenly got a bloody nose that wouldn't stop bleeding. I wanted to help him stop the blood as best as I could, but he refused, saying that his head hurt and that once the blood had flowed out, it would feel better. So every time the blood clotted, he blew his nose as forcefully as he could to make it bleed again—it was horrifying to watch.

He admitted that the previous night, his knees were in extreme pain so he got up and took four painkillers.

My heart ached for him as I warned, "Don't take any more! Those things aren't good!"

He said, "I know painkillers aren't good. But aspirins are fine."

"Aspirins aren't good either!"

He said, "*Koychy!*" and went on to ignore me. Sitting at the edge of the bed, head drooping low, his nose continued to bleed.

IN ADDITION TO THEIR DEMANDING way of life, another factor threatening their health was certain unhealthy habits. I noticed that, after the women washed their hair, they immediately tied it, still dripping wet, into

braids and went outside to work in the icy cold. And they often went to bed
with their hair still wet.

When Sister-in-law asked me to help her scrub her back as she washed, she
told me to rub laundry detergent on her back! Afterward, the suds were never
fully rinsed (there wasn't enough water); she simply wiped the lather off with
a wet towel and got dressed. Didn't her skin burn? Didn't it itch? Frankly, I
thought her back was perfectly clean before, her skin fine and smooth; the only
thing dirty on it now was the laundry powder. . . .

Every evening, after her work was over, exhausted Sister-in-law crawled
onto the felt rugs and asked me for a massage, particularly around the calves.
After only lightly pressing on her muscles, she screamed in pain. Cuma had to
make a joke of it and wrapped his arms around her, pretending to wipe away
her tears. He sobbed in Mandarin, "Don't cry, it'll all be better soon, it'll all be
better soon. . . ." Something he learned from TV.

But when he was the one with a hurt leg crawling onto the bed, everyone
stayed as quiet as they could because the slightest chatter might annoy and
anger him.

Even fifteen-year-old Zhada grumbled about pain here and there. And he
had a persistent wet cough.

Only Kama could cheerfully announce, "I'm not sick, I'm healthy! I can do
this—easy!" She raised her arms high overhead.

"This—easy!" She bent over to touch her ankles.

"And this—no problem!" She huddled into a ball, crouching on the ground,
then jumped back up with ease.

These simple motions were beyond the older couple's ability.

But in reality, Kama wasn't all that healthy. Like Sister-in-law, her nails
were gnarled. But what could they do, they were hardly able to eat any vegetables all year (what little they had weren't fresh), and fruit was even scarcer.

The horse trader who had come to buy animals complained to me, "You
city folk, when you're forty years old you look like us when we're twenty! You
work by sitting inside every day, no wonder you're not sick!" I had nothing to
say in return.

THEN OF COURSE, there was the wearing away of youth.

Kama cut three holes out of her and her father's shared red gaiter to wear
as a balaclava when she went to herd. Yet even with most of her face covered,
she came back at the end of the day with cheeks that were red raw. Though
with her natural complexion as pale as it was, the rosy cheeks gave her an

extra bit of pep. But by the end of February, the rosy cheeks had turned deep red, and eventually into a soy sauce color. Gradually, her whole face had turned dark. She looked in the mirror and dolefully remarked, "Terrible! Winter is terrible!"

Kama's skin turned dark because she was out herding in the wind all day. So what happened to me? I did needlework in the burrow all day, at most going outside to collect a few sacks of snow, briefly herd the cattle and sheep, or take a walk. Yet somehow, at the end of winter, I was also so tanned that one glimpse in the mirror broke my heart. What's worse, I had a grown a bit of a mustache.

I noticed that children on the pastures always looked younger than they were when they were little, but as soon as they reached adulthood, they began to look older than their age. They matured so slowly but aged so quickly.

But it didn't just stop there. What that life also wore away were the children's hearts.

Aside from the cost of the school uniform, everything else at boarding schools was absolutely free. In other words, sending a child to boarding school took the pressure off the family. Other than special cases like Kama, very few children dropped out of school.

But this also led to a situation where there was a growing disconnect between the children and their families, their traditions, and their cultural environments. Children who have gone to school are clearly transformed.

When everyone sat around watching TV, the grownups wanted to watch exciting shows with lots of killing and fighting, but the children preferred urban melodramas that reflected modern life.

To express shock or disappointment or such, everyone exclaimed, "Allah!" whereas Nurgün said "*Aya!*" like a Han person.

Nurgün would sometimes blurt out, "What are you laughing at?!" in Mandarin, using frighteningly accurate accent and emphasis. It must have been some short-tempered Chinese teacher's catchphrase.

When I asked the kids what they would like to be when they grew up, Zhada answered repairman. Only a few years ago, he was happy to one day run a motorcycle repair shop. But as he got older, he became more ambitious. Now, he wanted to repair computers.

Kama revealed that she wanted to go out and find a job so that she could walk down the wide city streets, dressed in beautiful clothes, living a hip, independent, and trendy life. That was why she was working so hard on her Chinese.

The children next door giggled at the question, unable to come up with an answer. But being as intelligent and optimistic as they were, with a penchant to perform and a love of excitement, they were also unlikely to be satisfied with this lonesome way of life.

AND THE HERDERS' hearts.

My family has been living in Akehara for many years—the water from the wells has become harder and harder every year. Add to that the increasing number of shops that have been opening, increasing the competition, and business has become harder than ever. My mother and I have been discussing whether or not to move for some time now. Not long ago, a new settler village, Humuzhila (which means "lots of sand"), was built eighteen miles from Akehara. This was the place where I was invited to serve as the "village head's assistant." Situated on the north bank of the Ulungur, near several large sand dunes, seven thousand *mu* of land had been recently reclaimed in order to settle an estimated one hundred and twenty families. Mother and I rode over on our motorcycle to check it out. Even though not many families had moved in yet—making the place look desolate and barren—it otherwise seemed satisfactory. When Cuma heard about this, he tried to persuade my mother to drop the idea. He said the place was brand-new after all, and no one had lived there before, so there was no way to know if it was any good. Why not wait two or three years, then decide? He added, "Right now, there's no grass, no water, no electricity, nothing. Why go there?"

Even so, he'd been toying with the idea of settling himself. Though he usually liked to mock farmers for living pathetic, deprived lives, sometimes he'd let out a long sigh and confess that if only they owned fifty to sixty *mu* of land, there'd be no need to migrate; they could just grow all the feed they need for their cattle and sheep.

During some of our conversations, the metal tripod on top of the sand dune came up. I asked him, if there really was oil down there and they began to drill, then he would certainly receive enough compensation to never have to herd again—would that be a good thing? He said of course it would be a good thing. Only, that day seemed so distant in the future that he probably wouldn't be alive anymore by the time it came around. But if he did get that compensation, he'd buy a car right away so that he could make a living in transportation. What else could he do? Manual labor was out of the question, he was too old. As for opening a shop, he was afraid he lacked the experience.

Buying a car had been Cuma's dream. Besides, it might tempt his only son, Zhada, to stay at his side.

Only later did we learn that even without compensation from an oil well, the government subsidy for grassland restoration was more than enough for him to buy a car and live off it. He had been waiting for this policy to take effect for a long time.

ANY TIME THERE WAS a visitor who could speak Mandarin, I always asked the same question: Is settling a good thing? The answer was always in the affirmative, but they also always looked unsure.

The horse trader cut right to the chase: "Of course settling is a good thing! But then Kazakh will be over!" I didn't understand and asked him to explain. But he only spoke about the shortcomings of nomadic life in terms of health and education, and never explained what he meant by "Kazakh will be over."

No matter what, all life seeks security. Everyone hopes for equal footing in this world. The people must settle, the flocks must halt their migration. Not only the herders, but earth can no longer cope with it. There are too many sheep and not enough grass. Overgrazing was making the already fragile environment deteriorate even more rapidly.

Yet, balancing the livestock with the grass had long been a basic principle of pastoralists, their age-old creed. So, where did it all go wrong?

Regardless, going forward, the flocks must be kept from going any farther south and be forced to stay near the Ulungur through the winter. To enable their survival through the winter, large tracts of land along the river must continue to be reclaimed and put under cultivation, growing fodder; the river must be dammed to irrigate the fields; vast quantities of chemical fertilizer must be added to the infertile soil, and compound feed must be purchased. And without the flocks, the wilderness will also lose its vitality and slowly degrade . . . it's unavoidable. The sheep will continue to multiply and the people will continue to live as wastefully as they always have . . . and more than that I don't know how to talk about.

There are those who say that this was the final year that the flocks would be allowed into the winter pasture. I should count myself lucky to have witnessed the last hurrah . . . though I don't consider myself lucky at all.

AT DINNER, KURMASH CAME to ask for help with his phone again. Suddenly, he put on a video, which immediately roused everyone's curiosity. Cuma

said, "You can watch TV on phones?" It was a foreign film that no one understood, and there was no making sense of it just by looking either. Yet, we still
huddled around the phone as if we were all in a trance. Even Sister-in-law
couldn't resist, haphazardly tossing the noodles into the pot before rushing
back for a look.

When a Kazakh-language home shopping program played, they were
floored by the variety of compact and magical electronic gadgets, accompanied
by the salesman's mellifluous copy. They asked me if those things were real
and if everyone in the city had them.

I didn't know how to answer. I didn't know much about that world either,
but I knew that at least those weren't ordinary things.

Sister-in-law and Shinshybek braving the snow to clean the sheep pen; the
burrow choking with the smell of the dewormer (Cuma always tested the spray
nozzle inside before going out to spray the sheep); *syrmak* reinforced with new
layers, wrapped with a new hem, and sewn with ten thousand threads . . . were
these things any more ordinary?

Cuma lay in the center of the bed, smoking, with Kama resting her head on

Cuma's shoes, which he repaired himself

his knees, reading a Kazakh newspaper out loud. On his other side, Sister-in-law curled in a fetal position, her head resting on his chest, and listened intently with bright, curious eyes. Surrounded by the two women, Cuma was content. If cigarette ash happened to fall onto Sister-in-law's head, he flicked it off for her. Outside, the wind howled; the window's plastic cover flapped. It sounded like someone shouting at the top of their lungs into the wind: "Calm down, please, calm down!"

The news story that Kama read was about an elderly person named Abibao in Qinggil County who had raised ten orphans. Cuma said nothing for a while, lost in thought. Then, he said to me, "Where are there still unwanted babies? Me and Sister-in-law ought to go pick one up. . . ."

I said, "Once Zhada's grown up and married, will you want his firstborn?" It was an old Kazakh custom for the grandparents to bring up the first grandson.

Cuma said, "Of course, why wouldn't we?"

I said, "Then you'll have your own baby in six or seven years, no need to look for one!"

He murmured, "In six or seven years, will me and Sister-in-law still be around?"

32.

Herding Together

IN FEBRUARY, "THE LONG became short and the short became long." As the rotating globe gently tilted on its axis, the winter ebbed. Kama gradually took over all of Cuma's herding shifts. Until then, she only covered for her father a few days at a time when he was away or ill.

Face scrunched, she whined, "Herding sucks! My face is always black, my belly's always hungry...."

Despite her complaints, she never tried to shirk her responsibility. She was always planning for her days on the pastures, preparing an interesting Kazakh newspaper to read on horseback (carefully picked out of the stories she had already read). She charged her phone to full so she could listen to music the whole way and asked me to write down the lyrics of a Chinese song so she could learn the words and memorize it. After thinking it over, I chose a Taiwanese campus song with a simple beat, "Orchid Grass," and taught her the lyrics one character at a time, explaining the meaning and noting the pinyin as we went.

A little antsy, she asked, "What else should I take?"

I said, "Some *kurt* to eat when you're hungry."

Zhada said, "Biscuits and candies . . ."

I said, "Your thermos and a bowl . . ."

Zhada: "The tablecloth ..."

Me: "Cooking pot, flour, and veggies ..."

Zhada: "Your bedding ..."

Me: "And a mat and the tent frame ..."

Zhada: "Just pull a camel along with you ..."

Kama punctuated our every suggestion with: "*Koychy, koychy, koychy, koychy, koychy* ..."

In fact, Kama had been herding since she was fourteen—she wasn't afraid of toil and loneliness. In the past, the neighbor Shinshybek's family wasn't around, so Cuma was busy with all the heavy lifting and the task of herding mostly fell on the girl's shoulders. Only now there was more leisure time, which she wasn't quite used to.

When the day came, the girl donned her father's full gear and lumbered out the door.

On this day, those staying at home would begin to clean out the sheep pen. In preparation, Cuma woke up early in the morning to sharpen the shovels, rubbing a thin whetstone against the blades until their edges were razor sharp.

With temperatures rising and the wind picking up, the layer of sheep manure that was frozen solid began to thaw. Stepping into the soft and sludgy sheep pen, it was exceptionally humid. This wet layer (nearly a foot deep) must be removed or else the sheep would get sick. Though it was the same layer of manure that we dug in the early winter, it was now completely different. Back then, the manure had been baking under the sun for half a year. Hard and dry, the shovel could easily slice through and pry up large chunks. In its tofu-like state, though, it was impossible to pry the manure out (of course, it was still harder than actual tofu). Instead, we had to use the sharp shovel edge to cut the manure into ten-inch-square blocks, each of which we pried out with a spade. But being wet and heavy, the blocks couldn't be moved using the spades, so we had to lug them out by hand one piece at a time until the pen wall had grown by half a meter!

The wet manure blocks were too heavy, I couldn't lift them, so I was assigned to clean out the previous night's urine-soaked cow dung from the cattle burrow. But the window in the burrow was too high up and too narrow, so I didn't manage to throw the dung out. After digging a shovelful of dung, I aimed carefully and hurled it toward the opening with all my might, but in the end, it came falling back onto my head. . . . I had no choice but to do it the old-fashioned way, walking outside, one shovelful at a time—it was exhausting! I couldn't help thinking about Kama out on the pasture, who at that very moment was likely perched comfortably atop the horse, listening to music on her phone, while reading a newspaper and humming "Orchid Grass" . . . such a warm day with the sun beaming down, she must have been so comfortable.

But just then, I turned my head and saw Kama coming back! Tethering her horse already! How dare she, it wasn't even two yet. . . .

Resting against his shovel, Cuma casually said to me through the sheep pen wall, "She's hungry."

Sister-in-law dropped her work, peeled off her muddy coat, and followed her daughter inside. There was tea to pour and *nan* to cut for her hungry daughter! Zhada and Kurmash put down their tools to go round up the flock. I climbed up the eastern sand dune, where I saw the flock scattered across the land from north to east.

Neither Kama nor I liked to eat stir-fried offal. Whenever the dish was made, most of it ended up in Cuma's stomach. He said as he ate, "Kama, she's not eating now, but after one day on the pasture, she would finish this plate and then some!"

And he wasn't wrong! The girl had worked up an appetite herding. She drank one bowl of tea after another and ate five *nans* that she soaked in the tea. While she ate, she complained, "The sheep are full, but I'm starving!"

I asked, "Didn't you take some candy with you?"

She pouted, "Mom gave me three. They only lasted me a hundred steps. . . ."

For the rest of the day, the sheep were left to their own devices. The girl washed and dawdled, embroidered and swept. As dusk neared, Cuma rode out to bring back the flock himself.

Although Kama had only finished half her work, that evening at dinner, Sister-in-law still boiled some ribs specially to add to her daughter's rice and soup. When she served it, Sister-in-law made a show of placing it in Kama's bowl, drawing a sneer from Zhada. Normally, at dinnertime, mother was more likely to spoil her son.

IN THE FOLLOWING DAYS, Kama continued to return home at the same hour! There, she rested for an hour before heading back to the pasture.

Cuma said, with the warm weather, the flock could just move about near the burrow. There was no longer need for herders to follow them quite so closely.

When we first arrived in the winter pasture, the two men led the flock far, far away every day, all the way to the edge of the pasture. Once the flocks had eaten all the grass around the perimeter of the property, they began grazing closer and closer to the center. I assumed that this was to protect the territory: there was no iron fence that separated their pasture from the neighbor's, therefore if our sheep started grazing at the center then gradually moved outward, by the time ours got near the boundary, the grass might already have been eaten by the neighboring flocks.

One breezy, sunny morning at the end of February, as I was walking back alone through the snow having just finished herding the calves, Kama came riding toward me. She shouted, "Li Juan, want to herd together?"

After a moment of delight, I said with disappointment, "I'm not dressed for it!" I was only wearing a long down jacket and a light coat. I was wearing a hat but not a scarf.

She said, "So what? It's not cold."

I realized she was right. It had been very warm lately and Kama wasn't wearing a thick coat either, only Sister-in-law's brown cotton jacket. Besides, by noon, it would be even warmer. So I ran over to her horse, pulled myself up by the saddle, and sat behind Kama. The horse swayed its behind as it happily trotted ahead. We started to sing. Then, a large band of horses galloped across the western horizon, so we cheered and whooped. The sheep rested quietly beneath a sand ridge to the far north.

It took us a long time to catch up to the flock. While the sheep flocked close together when they were on the move, when they stopped to graze, they buried their heads to eat and quickly scattered. The herder's job was to constantly round them up and lead them to new pastures so that they don't walk in circles eating the same grass over and over.

Every so often we dismounted to sit in the snow and listen to music on the phone, all the while observing the flock's movements. I thought to myself, if this is herding, it is boring. . . .

In the distance, a figure on horseback was leading several camels westward. We watched him for a long time. Soon, the figure stopped his chase, reined in his horse, and turned to stare back toward us. Eventually, he turned his horse around and headed our way, leaving the camels behind.

When he was near, I realized that it was the old man I had seen the day before! He came to our burrow to drink tea and asked me whether or not I'd seen his camel—he had far too high an opinion of me, I couldn't even recognize our own camels.

Apparently, he'd found his camels.

The old man was our neighbor from a nearby pasture. He'd visited our burrow at least twice already so we were acquainted. I remember him asking me, "Aren't you Han people about to celebrate New Year?" I didn't know the word for "New Year" in Kazakh. He explained, "It's, well, you have this and that, all very delicious stuff that you put together on the table and eat as much as you want!" I understood immediately and was pleased.

I had been spinning a spindle, turning a ball of blue wool into a strand before combining three more strands into a yarn. The old man was beside himself with excitement. He called me a good girl and invited me to visit his home. He said his home was nearby to the northwest, only half an hour by horse or an hour on foot. He even described his three family members—himself, his old lady, and a son.

After he left, Cuma teased, "Be careful! His son isn't married yet."

But I found the old man rather charming, with his raggedy old coat and his cautious, considerate demeanor. His horse was a docile old thing too, blind in its right eye.

But for some reason, Kama was cold toward the old man. When he came to greet us, she quietly acknowledged him but was unwilling to stand up. She sat on the snow, playing with her phone, skipping from one song to the next. When the old man dismounted and sat down across from Kama, neither said a word. The flock stayed quietly in place. The horses sniffed each other's faces and went about eating their own grass. Kama kept to her phone while the man quietly watched her.

Like that, they sat silently for a long while until the man's camels began to wander off. Only then did he stand up, say his goodbyes, and get on his horse, ready to leave. At that point, Kama seemed to suddenly remember something and looked up to ask him a question. Sitting on horseback, he answered several questions in a serious manner. After a pause, noticing that Kama had no more to say, he said goodbye once again and rode his horse toward the camels.

Herding sure is lonely.

AS WE DROVE OUR flock northward, we saw another flock approaching from the east. But this was our territory! I asked Kama what was going on. She stared for a while and said, "I don't know."

Eventually, the young man leading the flock came into view too. As soon as he saw us, he turned his horse toward us and kicked it into a gallop. We sat on our horse waiting. It wasn't until he was quite close that Kama finally recognized him and said hello. His face was almost completely covered by his scarf and hat, leaving only a slit for his eyes to see through. Strange—it wasn't even cold, why was he dressed like that?

I thought: that's right, the winds were fierce this time of the year. Young people want to look attractive, so he didn't want his skin to turn dark from the wind.

But once he walked over and took off his scarf to speak, I saw straightaway— his face was already as dark as the night. . . .

He was young, twenty at most. His flock needed to pass through our pasture, so he came to let us know. After that was cleared up, he rambled on about

When Kama and I went herding together, she took this picutre of me.

all sorts of things just to stick around for a bit longer. He asked, "Where are you two going?"

At this point, Kama and I were already far away from our flock. She had decided to go with me to see the old cemetery on the red dirt again. We headed slowly in that direction and the boy followed along without a word. Even if he didn't know why we were headed that way, he didn't ask either. Once we'd nearly reached our destination, we halted the horses and the three of us stayed there quietly for a while. The wind picked up, rumbling like a mighty river, and we were caught in the current. . . . I looked back and saw that the boy's flock was drifting farther and farther away, yet he didn't seem to be in the slightest hurry to get back on track!

When we finally began to head back, we saw that our flock was slowly drifting northwestward as well. If we didn't hurry, the two flocks would merge together! The boy spurred his horse into a gallop and we followed him to help, shouting and yelping busily.

Before parting, he asked us again, "Where are you going?" still reluctant to say goodbye.

After he left, I asked Kama, "Is he a suitor?"

She laughed, "*Koychy!*" and said "little brother"—a distant relative perhaps.

At this point, it was past noon. We'd been out for two hours. I was wearing only a down jacket, with no scarf, and it was getting colder and my stomach was starting to grumble. We got off the horse and walked through the snow. The sheep were doing what they always did, head bowed, carefully searching for grass. How long must it take to fill up a belly on such sparse and withered grass! The wind continued to howl and the phone's tinny speaker continued to stubbornly play, to which Kama danced along. I looked around me: besides dancing Kama, besides our horse, besides the flock, there were only the sky, clouds, white snow, yellow sand, and nothing else. I thought: so this is herding.

33.

Visiting Neighbors

Entering February, the days lengthened and the temperatures warmed. After welcoming the first official visitors of the winter, Azila and her mother, our feet itched too. That night at dinner, everyone engaged in a discussion and drew up a schedule for visiting the neighbors, looking for the best days when we would set out one after another. First the young people would go, then Sister-in-law, and after her, Cuma.

In fact, as early as January, Kama and I had already made plans to visit neighbors in February. But why did it have to be February? Because in December and January, daylight would have flashed by so quickly that no matter how close the neighbor, we probably wouldn't have made it there and back on the same day. And we couldn't walk at night because there were wolves.

I'd been looking forward to a trip for a long time. Looking forward to it and equally anxious about not having a suitable coat, one that wasn't embarrassingly dirty! So dirty that it couldn't be washed. . . . But as February approached, everyone began to worry for me. I'd decided to wear my leather jacket, which didn't really fit but at least was clean. Their reaction was, "*Koychy*, you're not going herding." Too shabby.

I also considered my down jacket, which was clean and simple. Everyone said, "No way, it's too cold!"

I asked, "Hasn't it gotten warm already?"

Kama said, "When we go, warm. When we come back, cold." On our way back, the sun would have veered to the west, and the temperature would have dropped.

Cuma announced generously, "All right, all right, I'll lend you my mine!"

"*Koychy!*" I felt sorry for myself.

IT WAS FINALLY the day of the excursion. First thing in the morning, Kama reminded me that I must wear my freshly washed pants!

That day, it took her twice as long to wash her face, then another half hour putting on makeup and getting dressed.

I insisted on wearing my somewhat presentable down jacket, in spite of everyone's protestations. As a compromise, I wore my long down coat over it. I listened to their advice and planned to take off the outer layer and stuff it behind the saddle as soon as we arrived.

The original plan had been to visit one of Kama's classmates to the north, but being unable to find the horse delayed our journey. By the time we found the horse and were ready to leave, two figures on horseback appeared on the sand dune to the northeast—as they rode nearer, it turned out to be the very classmate and her mother we were planning to visit! That's what you call a suitable day for an outing. And that's what you call good friends too; great minds think alike....

So we dismounted from the saddle, took off our coats, and returned to the burrow for some serious heart-to-heart. Sister-in-law carved up a chunk of meat to cook *plov* for the guests.

When we saw them off, it was already midafternoon. Before going out to herd the cows, the tablecloth was relaid for a new tea session. We had another meeting and decided that the next day, we'd visit Kama's distant relatives in the pasture to the west. It wasn't far, only an hour by horse.

THE FOLLOWING DAY, after herding the calves to pasture, Kama spent another good part of an hour washing her face and getting ready. This time, we managed to set out without any complications. I still stuck with my long down coat over short down jacket. The frustrating thing was, the jacket was wide whereas the coat was slim. It took some effort to get my arms into the outer sleeves and zip up the front.

The two of us set out westward until we reached a sand ridge partitioning the desert, and there we turned and followed the sand ridge northwestward.

Slowly, we reached a chasm wedged between two sand dunes where there were clearly two rows of tire prints on the ground. We turned onto the car road, ascending and descending several sand ridges before eventually veering away from the road westward.

Whenever the road led us to the top of a dune, Kama would point to all sorts of directions, telling me who lived there, who was who, who was to whom, how far that who's whom lived from here . . . she made it sound as if the place was bustling with people, but one look around—there was nothing.

As we rode, the trail beneath the horse's hooves became more pronounced, busy with the footprints of more and more livestock. We slowly reached the top of another dune, and this time, I saw a small black nook wedged between the sand dunes ahead—we'd arrived! The desert was yellow, the snow white, the sky blue; the whole world was pale except for that single dark patch that animals and humans had called home, like a paperweight that pressed firmly down on the rolling land. On that black dot, the distance between sky and earth was farthest.

We slowed our pace as we drew near. All I could think about was how to escape from my dirty coat before anyone saw me . . . but the zipper was hard to pull! Just my luck, before we even got there, I was spotted. First, there were two kids standing outside the doorway staring at us with their mouths agape. When they finally recognized Kama, they screamed and ran toward us in joy. . . .

At that point, we had reached the flat ground at the edge of the settlement where the solid hitching post was. After dismounting, I tried to nonchalantly tug at my zipper, as hard as I could, and was eventually able to free myself from that dirty and slim coat. But the kids didn't seem to care. They stood quietly watching us hitch our horses and straightening out our clothes and hair. When we began walking toward the burrow, the kids rushed ahead of us to open the door. Noticing how slowly we were moving, they ran back to walk with us. When we were close to the burrow, they ran ahead once more to open the door. From beginning to end, nothing was said, only endless silent smiles.

THIS FAMILY'S BURROW was very deep, descending three steps down after entering the door, but it was very large. Once inside, there were dirt platforms on either side and behind the bed, where bedding and utensils could be stored. The stove was coated with mud. Square and spacious, one side was even made into an oven (no need to bake *nan* with manure charcoal). The whole place was clean, orderly, and well thought out.

Before padding the ceiling beams with hay, a plastic sheet was used to cover the dirt roof, protecting the space from dust. In contrast, in our burrow, whenever the dog walked over the roof, ash and dust fell into everyone's tea bowls and onto the tablecloth.

Kama said that this was a new home that was built only ten years ago! No wonder—our burrow was built twenty years ago. Back then, these thick, wide plastic sheets were hard to come by.

Because our burrow was so old, no one wanted to sleep under the beam at night, afraid that it might suddenly fall down. . . .

This new burrow even boasted sections of redbrick floor! Around the stove, they had built a low wall of red bricks to protect against fire. It seemed the family had spared no effort building this home. Transporting the bricks into the desert alone must have been an ordeal! They obviously intended to live there for many years to come. If their flock could never come this far south again . . . such a laboriously built home would be abandoned in the middle of the desert, what a pity that would be.

Though Kama had done all she could to prevent me from wearing only my down jacket for the journey, she insisted on wearing only pumps, the vanity! As a result, she was freezing the whole way, and the moment she arrived, she immediately took off her shoes and got into the bed. Hidden behind the stove, she pressed her feet firmly onto the warm red bricks as her teeth chattered. What else could she do? She only had that one pair of good shoes. . . .

None of the adults were home, so the older kid ran out. A moment later, she returned with a short woman full of smiles. Kama leaped to her feet and ran to greet the woman. The two shook hands then hugged. Kama introduced her to me: "This is my sister-in-law!" Then, pointing at the two children, she said, "These are my little sisters!"

Of the two kids, the older was eight years old but looked only six. The younger was six but looked only four. Moments later, the oldest daughter returned from herding. Kama said she was fourteen, but she looked like she was in her twenties. . . .

The oldest, named Sayragül, wore an army coat, felt overboots, a bright red scarf, and a weathered face. When she stepped through the door to find a room full of guests, she looked perplexed. Kama turned to me and ordered, "You, them, take picture!" The second eldest chirped excitedly at her big sister, "Picture! Picture!" So I had no choice but to take out my camera and begin randomly snapping away. It wasn't until the fifth picture that the oldest girl began to hedge. She said, "Wait! Wait!" before jumping onto the bed to rummage through boxes and chests looking for something . . . she needed to change into prettier clothes.

On the advice of Kama and her sisters, she selected a red wool sweater, red jacket, coffee-colored pants, and a clean pair of white leather shoes. She undid her braided pigtails and brushed her hair into a ponytail—her hair was thick and luxuriant! After washing her face, she could finally sit in front of the camera with confidence. She offered a shy smile but wasn't sure where to put her hands and feet.

Soon enough, the whole neighborhood arrived one after another to greet their new guests. Three families lived there, each with two or three children. There was a fifteen-year-old girl who, although a similar age to Sayragül, was much trendier and laid-back, full of confidence. Wherever she went, she carried a pink portable MP3 player with speakers the size of a Rubik's cube, with the volume always on full. (Though this nifty little thing clearly made Kama envious, she was too proud to bring it up. It wasn't until we were home that she gushed over how amazing it was and vowed to buy one herself in the fall. The return migration south in the fall is when the sheep are sold, so that is when the children "get paid." Last year, Kama received five hundred yuan and bought all sorts of things in the city. She once listed off all her purchases to me and relived the happy memories of shopping.) In front of the camera, she knew how to pose. Kama told me that she was Zhada's classmate. No wonder—the two shared so many similar attitudes.

So many children! I tired to count how many but I couldn't keep track . . . people kept going in and out, each time bringing a new child with a ruddy, tanned face that resembled the last.

With all the people and music, the kids all started to dance. Cuma's sister-in-law's second daughter danced the best, energetic and graceful. Everyone clapped only for her. The six-year-old, the third daughter, was shy, retreating to the bed after only a few moments of dancing, refusing to come back no matter how much people pleaded. It wasn't the timidity of a child but rather the bashfulness of a woman.

Finally, I managed to count them all—seven children. Plus us adults, ten people altogether.

WHEN THE OLDEST DAUGHTER returned from herding, her father showed his face for a moment. After that, there was no sign of him. Kama said that he had to herd the flock for his daughter. Besides him, and an older man who joined the dancing a little later (only for a brief moment as well), there were no other men around, only women.

Although there were three boys. Compared to the girls, they seemed more at ease, more talkative and opinionated, constantly arguing with each other quietly. And the littlest and darkest one was decidedly antisocial; whether it was dancing, drinking tea, or dressing up . . . everything annoyed him. But in fact, I could tell that deep down he really wanted to join in the fun.

At the height of all the excitement, the door swung open and in came another group. A stunningly beautiful young woman with an ordinary-looking baby in her arms was followed by an older couple. The older couple joined in the dancing the moment they came in, proudly and skillfully doing the Black Horse Trot. The beautiful young mother quickly handed her baby off to Cuma's sister-in-law and began dancing elegantly as well.

But the exciting performance by the three did not last more than a minute. They were adults after all; showing off for too long would have been improper. As soon as the music stopped, they placed their hands on their chests to thank their audience. Having had all the fun that they intended to, the older couple quickly bid goodbye while the young mother sat down to join us for tea.

Cuma's sister-in-law started to boil meat for us—to prepare a delicious meal for guests from afar is a necessary part of hospitality. While waiting for the meat to cook, the neighbors invited us to their burrow, so the whole troop filed into another burrow. This was the beautiful young mother's home, as well as the willful little boy's.

This child was the only spoiled kid I saw in the pastures, but also the most interesting. When everyone else sat around the tablecloth, he was the only one standing up (he was five, too young to sit at the main table), jabbing his finger at the biscuits, the candies, and the *kurt*. This mother gave him a little of each to make him go away. Food in hand, he sat down by himself in a corner and gobbled up everything like a little tiger! When he finished, he once again stood by the tablecloth pointing to this and that. . . . After three more rounds of this, his mother frowned and said gently, "Enough! That's enough! . . ." Maybe she was worried that he might get an upset stomach and maybe also worried about losing face in front of guests. The child stomped his foot and roared furiously in front of all the guests. Then, his mom grabbed a few raisins and handed them to him while softly scolding, "No more!"

After finishing his raisins, he ran to the kitchen, where there was a tin pot used to melt snow. He scooped out a ladleful of snow and water and gulped it down. After wiping his mouth, he pondered for a moment before resolutely reaching for a cloth-wrapped bundle from the cupboard. He unwrapped the cloth and took out a piece of *baursak*. Then he took out the big sheep bladder full of butter, scooped a big chunk of butter, and spread it generously on the *baursak* before fiercely biting into it as if it were his mortal enemy. After finishing the *baursak*, he hesitated for three seconds before scooping another finger of butter and putting it in his mouth . . . then he gulped some more ice water. While the rest of us, sitting before so much delicious food, ate politely and graciously. What was it like to be without restraint, to enjoy yourself that much?

THIS BURROW WAS a little on the small side, but it was clean and cozy. The bed platform was L-shaped, occupying the left side and back wall as you entered. The window was on the left side as well. They also had a redbrick stove wall situated in the center of the room. There was a half-embroidered felt mat on the bed. I picked it up and noticed that the needlework was beautiful and the color palate was elegant. From the looks of it, the woman of the house was quite talented.

At the table, she took out a photo album to show us. The first few pages were filled with group photos of young girls. Remarkably, the one with loose, flowing hair was her! Where I lived, almost none of the Kazakh girls wore their hair down. They usually either braided or tied their hair into a bun at the back. Let alone the pastures, even in the countryside, wearing your hair loose would be considered audacious—even frivolous.

But now, she'd been swept by life's currents into the desert's depths— married, had kids, herded sheep, milked cows. She still had her youth and looks, but she had become a most ordinary of wives, the most taciturn mothers. All her rebelliousness was there in the first few pages of that photo album.

Leashed to a corner of her burrow was a baby winter lamb. After having eaten and drunk his fill, the son was pulling at the cord around the lamb's neck to force it to stand up and face him. Kama said, "Li Juan! Quick! Take a photo!" His mother immediately ran to wipe his mouth and arrange his three tufts of hair, his only three tufts of hair. I said, "And the lamb!" She untied the lamb and shoved it into her son's arms. This time, the child didn't try to evade the camera. Arms around the lamb, even though he was still a little shy, he was no longer the wild child that he was a moment ago.

AFTER THAT, WE VISITED another burrow. This was the home of Zhada's female classmate, the daughter of the older couple from earlier. She also had two younger brothers. As expected, the visit consisted of tea and photo albums. Leafing through the pages, I came across a photo that I'd taken years back! It was of the adorable Kaziyman in the summer pastures. That year, after developing the photo, I'd given her a copy. At some point, she'd regifted it to these relatives of hers, and now the same photo appeared once more before my eyes.

After we'd drunk two bowls of tea, Cuma's sister-in-law came to tell us that the meat was ready! Everyone stood up and crowded into her burrow. The second daughter brought the kettle around for us to wash our hands, and the third daughter held the basin to catch the water beneath. Hands washed, we each sat down in our appropriate seats. The adults sat around one tablecloth and the children around another. It was cured meat that she boiled, and oh my, was it fragrant . . . but sadly, Kama had to eat like a good proper girl, which made me too embarrassed to eat as much as I wanted.

After we ate and took turns washing our hands, the pretty young mother popped in. It turned out her family had made a pot of pilaf for us too, as a token of goodwill. So the troops relocated once more to her burrow. Halfway through the meal, Zhada's classmate came to call: her family's meat and potatoes were ready, fresh out of the pot! Oh my, what a feast! No wonder everyone loved visiting their neighbors. . . .

COMPARED TO OUR SETTLEMENT, these three families were noticeably more well-off and sophisticated. But their communal sheep pen was somewhat lacking—with crooked walls built to an uneven height. Two of the families served tea with very little milk, too few cows perhaps? And one only had black tea, perhaps because they had no cows. But the food that these three families offered was copious, and there was a variety of dried fruits, *kurt*, and all sorts of fried flour dishes.

For some reason, Cuma's sister-in-law's second daughter was especially friendly with me, putting her arm through mine and following me wherever I went like a sticky honey candy. It was endearing, but I was unsure how to reciprocate her affection. As a result, even without Kama reminding me, I took as many pictures of her as I could, more than anyone else.

Regretfully, we had been in such a rush leaving our burrow that I'd forgotten to bring fresh batteries, and the old ones quickly ran out. Fortunately, the others were even more keen than me for a photo shoot, so Cuma's sister-in-law took out the batteries from the wall clock and handed them to me—they lasted for about ten photos. Then the pretty mother removed the batteries from her son's toy machine gun, which enabled ten more snaps. Then Zhada's classmate emptied her father's electric razor, which allowed for ten more photos. . . . How were they going to live their lives once I left? The clock wouldn't tick, the gun wouldn't *pew*, and beards wouldn't be shaved. What a shame.

When it was time to leave, everyone crowded around the horse and walked quite far to see us off. With everyone watching, I had to try to squeeze back into the slim jacket that was so dirty that it shone as if nothing was the matter. It was agonizing.

One more thing: Cuma's sister-in-law owned a cat that climbed onto the chimney to meow when it found itself locked out. When the children heard it, they went to open the door. Clever little thing, not at all like Plum Blossom, who would have squatted outside the door until someone happened to pass by.

When we got home, I pulled up the photos of the cat to show everyone. They all said, "Sayna's cat!" I took a closer look and they really were similar! Double eyelids and mottled noses.

When we reached the photos of everyone dancing, they all exclaimed, "So many kids!"

Cuma complained angrily, "The person in charge of the family-planning office is their relative. Have as many as they like! No fines!"

34.

New Neighbors

ONE MID-FEBRUARY MORNING, at around eleven o'clock, snow had fallen, the temperature had dropped, and having just returned from herding the calves, I noticed a caravan of camels inching across the desert to the southwest. I felt elated—the long-awaited migration had begun! The flocks were starting their journeys north! From now on, the vast open terrain north of the Heavenly Mountains would be crowded with sheep surging in like a receding flood, following the northward trajectory of the melting snow line. Before long, we would be leaving the desert too!

We stood together on the sand dune to our west and gazed at the approaching camels. Cuma said, "Seems like the snow to the south has already melted."

He added, "Without snow, there's no water, you have to leave."

Except what even Cuma hadn't foreseen was that this family wasn't simply passing through! The caravan, after its long journey, was headed straight for our settlement. They would stay there until the day we left.

So it was that a new family joined our settlement. There was a new yurt, a young couple, a young man, two children, a cat and two dogs, a large flock of sheep, a camel team, and two cows.

THEN I SAW A FACE that I hadn't seen since our initial southward migration—I realized it was Kulynbek's family! His home was to the southwest, two days' journey by horse from ours. As their relatives, Shinshybek and his family had apparently already known they were coming. By the time the camel team appeared at the edge of our pasture, they were already prepared to welcome the guests. When the camels reached us, they quickly rushed to offer welcome and to announce that food was ready. While the two families warmly reconnected, their dogs engaged in battle.

As soon as they arrived, a three- or four-year-old dark-skinned child ran to one of the camels when he was lowered to the ground. He pointed to a bag on the camel and begged for one of the adults to take it down. Kulynbek untied the bag and dropped it on the ground. The child unzipped it and started rummaging around inside until he found his tiny jacket and black cotton shoes. He found himself a nook sheltered from the wind and set about changing all by himself (he was wearing a heavy set of "armor," which was not conducive to mobility). Having made himself comfortable, the child happily ran inside Sayna's burrow to eat. He didn't trouble the adults at all!

Besides, the adults were too busy to attend to the little guy anyway. The horses had all caught up and the sheep hovered nearby. Faced with unexpected guests, Cuma was a bit surprised and annoyed, but he ran over to help unload the camels all the same. Zhada contributed his muscles just like any other grown-up. Sister-in-law and I helped carry luggage and clear out space.

Then, amid the hustle and bustle, there was suddenly the sound of a child crying. I looked over and saw that on the hump of a still fully loaded camel, in the middle of a mountain of household objects, was a little head! The kid had been securely fastened in the middle of the luggage. Around him were piles of bedding and over him was a thick felt mat, all wrapping him up in layers. . . . The goal of safety was certainly met but other than turning his head, the child was completely immobile. Just imagine, having set off at five in the morning, the child's arms and legs must have fallen asleep by now! The matron of the family quickly ran to untie him, removing one layer of protection after another until she could eventually lift him off the camel's hump. The child was around two years old, still a suckling babe.

AT DINNER, CUMA EXPLAINED to me that Kulynbek's family pasture was on flat terrain. Because of the unusually warm weather recently, all the snow had already melted. They were suffering from drought. They had no choice but to move early. However, it would still be a while before it was time for the flocks to move north en masse, as the pastures to the north were still covered in a thick layer of snow. So, for the time being, the sheep had nowhere to go. Shinshybek decided to host them on his land. He probably assumed that since he had already paid the rent, half the pasture belonged to him, and so he did not check with Cuma beforehand. Cuma was not happy, but he was too polite to say anything. When he greeted the new guests, he played with the children as he always did, invited everyone over for food, and helped the family with their work. Only when there were no outsiders around did he complain. He said, given the year's abundance of grass, making room for one more family wouldn't be a big loss. But this was a big decision. Not even talking to him about it was disrespectful.

But the family sure was unlucky—forced to leave because of lack of snow. Of course, as soon as they had set out, it began to snow. . . . Moving in the middle of a snowstorm must've been difficult, especially for the children.

This family of five, old and young, was each darker than the next! So dark that you could barely make out their nose or eyes; I couldn't wrap my head around it. They were all herders, so why wasn't Cuma's family that dark? And Shinshybek's family was all quite fair. Then I thought, of course! There was a water shortage where they lived! But what did a lack of water have to do with dark skin? As if they never washed their faces . . . how silly of me.

THAT FIRST NIGHT, the whole family squeezed into Sayna's burrow and made do for the night. Early next morning, after moving the sheep to pasture, everyone pitched in to erect a yurt. The men discussed among themselves before finally deciding to place the yurt in the clearing west of the sheep pen and east of Shinshybek's burrow. Although the ground there had a slight grade to it, there was no better spot.

I was worried. Staying in a yurt in such cold weather! Wouldn't they freeze to death? What about the children . . . ?

However, once the yurt was set up, it only took a short stay inside before I realized how hot and muggy it was in there! Turns out that between the latticework frame, ribs, and felt cover, they had added a layer of plastic.

The space inside was tiny, as it was built with one fewer lattice frame than usual. They stretched the lattice frames wide, which made the ceiling very low. This way, just one small steel stove was enough to heat the whole room.

They laid the *syrmak* directly onto the manure ground, on top of which they would eat and sleep. They kept only the bare minimum of items inside, as they didn't plan on staying for very long.

To show thanks, as soon as the yurt was up, the new family boiled meat and invited everyone over. It was already late so I didn't join them. I laid out my bedding and curled up for an early sleep. The next morning, Cuma startled me: "Why didn't you go? They were angry! Said you don't respect them. They saved you a big chunk of meat, white and fatty, they will be here any minute! They are going to watch you eat every last bit of it!"

With the addition of only one family, our neighborhood became five times more lively! The two newly arrived men, plus Shinshybek, Kurmash, and Rahmethan, as well as the two "foreign Kazakhs" staying at Shinshybek's, and Zhada and Cuma, added up to nine men in total! All day long the lot of them gathered in our burrow playing cards, gambling with one yuan at a time. They were always smoking, filling the room with a murky miasma and covering the bed in ash. And they took up so much room that Sister-in-law and I had nowhere to set the tablecloth for tea. Why didn't they go to Shinshybek's burrow? Because there was a baby over there. At least they were a considerate bunch.

IN ADDITION TO THE PEOPLE, the dogs also became livelier. The new neighbors had two dogs, one half grown and the other a two-month-old puppy, both plump and puffy. Most of the time, they were cute and well-behaved. Whenever their human mother appeared, they both leaped up and down, yapped, and scurried around her feet, gazing up lovingly, but one glimpse of Panda Dog and they entered battle mode without hesitation.

As soon as their caravan came to a stop, the two dogs swiftly assessed the terrain and decided to occupy the roof of Shinshybek's burrow (how remarkable, it was their first time there and they already knew that the roof was their "radiant flooring"). From this stronghold, they began to wage their long war against Panda Dog.

With foreign dogs invading, Panda Dog naturally felt that the full power of justice was on her side and immediately set to defending the homeland. As for her opponents, wherever their master went, that's where home was, so of course they didn't think they were in the wrong. Consequently, morale was high on both sides.

Though the neighbor's dogs were smaller, their greater number gave them twice the barking power. As a result, in terms of intimidation, the two sides were evenly matched.

So, day and night, they barked, they argued, they chomped. . . . Sister-in-law began to anxiously mutter, "Allah, Allah!"

What was there to fight over anyway? Neither side had any food.

I don't need to reiterate how the food given to Panda Dog wasn't enough to get stuck in her teeth. And I never once saw the new family feed their dogs! The little pup was always pathetically licking the sheep's bowl—they tied a winter lamb to the yurt and placed a bowl in front of it. The bowl was always empty, yet the puppy still returned time and again with renewed hope to double-check, licking the empty bowl until its bottom shined. Meanwhile, the lamb lay against the yurt, peering at the dog with a scornful look that seemed to say, "Even if there was food, it wouldn't be your turn."

That puppy reminded me of the saying: newborn puppies aren't afraid of big dogs. Despite its diminutive stature, when it was hungry enough, it could easily chase Panda Dog in circles!

The new neighbor's cat was very courteous toward our cats though, and even shook their hands when they met.

And as for the horses, the moment they arrived, they had gone off somewhere without a trace.

PERHAPS BECAUSE THEY WERE only staying for a short time, the neighbor's flock never mixed with ours. At night, they stayed by themselves in the clearing east of the sheep pen. In the morning, the flocks set out at staggered times and were led in different directions as much as possible.

For some reason, the new neighbors' flock didn't look right. There was something off about them, something out of place. But what exactly? After further observation, I realized that their legs were too skinny! Just look, these stout bodies supported by four spindly twigs, no wonder it didn't look right . . . but then when I saw our sheep, I found that their legs were just as skinny! Yet for some reason, our sheep looked just right.

Once they had everything in order, the first thing our new arrivals did was to place a dummy on the slope where the sheep slept. We already had a scare-wolf on top of the sand dune though.

EVEN THOUGH THERE WERE only two new kids, the moment I stepped outside, it felt like there were kids everywhere! Lined up, starting from Zhada, they formed five levels. They were always running back and forth with a flag, playing ambush in two teams. Then, in two new teams, they furiously dug traps in the sand. After digging a trap, they covered it with grass and broken plastic bags before covering it up with sand and going out to lure the other team to fall in. More often than not, the ones who fell in the pit had even more fun than the ones who dug it.

The older of the two was named Atakan. At first, I thought he was at most four years old, but when I asked, I was told he was five!

Though in general, most herder children are quite androgynous up until seven or eight years of age, Atakan wasn't one of them. He was obviously a boy. Everything about him screamed masculinity—he was brave to the point of reckless. He got to know everyone even before his parents, and soon enough was zipping in and out of both our burrows without any regard for boundaries. Grown-ups talked to him as if he were an adult, with serious words and sophisticated logic. He was able to carry a conversation for a long time, never shying away from talking back or even the occasional "*koychy.*"

His little brother was more timid, hiding from strangers for the first three days. I usually saw him alone on the sand riding a broom and cracking a whip, stumbling as he ran, with the look of a galloping warrior on his face.

Whenever his mother called round at our burrow, she brought the youngest son. The little guy sat next to the bed with snot hanging from his nose and mouth slightly agape, ever so still and expressionless. It wasn't until Plum Blossom appeared that his eyes lit up. He grabbed the cat and hugged him tight and squeezed his neck, forcing kisses upon him. He wanted to clean the cat's ears and even generously shared a piece of *kurt* that the grown-ups had given him. On account of the *kurt*, Plum Blossom gave in. After that, the cat would take a bite and the boy would take a bite. Everyone loved to eat *kurt* and they didn't mind each other's saliva.

The boy's mother was much less interesting, sitting at the tablecloth rigidly. While speaking quickly to Sister-in-law about this and that, she unwrapped and ate one candy after another like she had never tasted a candy in her life. The wrappers piled up in front of her.

THE CHILDREN WERE HAVING a blast! I couldn't help feeling envious. Rahmethan asked Atakan to collect snow with him and then tied two poles under his armpits. Seeing my bewilderment, he explained, "Camel!" I was delighted! Before loading up camels for a move, people would also tie poles to on the sides of the camel's belly and use those poles as support for loading up all luggage.

Atakan was more than happy to play the role of a camel, and was just as obedient. He even wore a rein around his neck and dutifully followed

Rahmethan's lead. They climbed over a sand dune and stopped where the snow had accumulated on the other side. Rahmethan said, "*Chök!*" (the command to make a camel sit), and without hesitation, Atakan knelt like a camel. Rahmethan untied the "rein" and kicked the "camel's" backside to signal that it was free to wander, so off the "camel" went to find a sandy spot to lie down and roll about in (this was camel behavior, so in character!). On the backside of the dune, Rahmethan started to collect snow. After filling one large and one small sack, he called "*mao mao*" (the standard way of calling for a camel!). Hearing the noise, little "camel" rushed over to let Rahmethan tie one sack onto the poles under his armpits. Once secured, Rahmethan reattached one end of the "camel's" reins and tied the other end to his own waist; then slinging his own sack over his shoulder, he began leading the "camel" back. Who would have guessed that only a dozen steps in, the "camel" couldn't take it anymore—the snow sack was too heavy! The little guy was only five after all. . . . As a failed camel, he felt rather embarrassed, admitting sheepishly, "I can't do it." Rahmethan had no choice but to untie the sack and empty just under half the

Helping our new neighbors erect their yurt. This was our busiest day since we had arrived at the winter pasture, yet from a distance, it looked so very quiet.

contents into his own. He then retied the lighter sack over the young boy's shoulder and the two got back on track. This time the little guy had no complaints. One in front of the other, attached by a rein, they carefully descended the dune and carried on homeward.

At the time, I was out gathering snow as well and saw the whole show from beginning to end. Only after returning home did I step in to unbind the little boy, and I took the sack from him while I was at it—still hefty, at least two kilos!

When the little brother saw his older brother playing a role, he was overjoyed. He led his brother the camel around the camp triumphantly. At midday tea, when the adults removed the "camel's" poles, the little one bawled furiously.

Yup, this was a game of labor. After that will come a life of labor.

35.

The Way Home

A T THE END OF FEBRUARY, as the new school term was beginning, Zhada, Rahmethan and Nurgün, were set to leave the winter burrow. After discussing it with Cuma, it was decided that I should go with them.

This year, the weather warmed earlier than usual. The snow would likely be gone by early March, and without snow, there was no way to sustain life. Therefore, this year, the whole herding community would migrate half a month early. Our family only had three riding horses, just enough for Cuma and his family. At that point, I didn't want to be jogging behind the camels, right?

During the migration south, Kama and I herded the sheep and larger livestock by ourselves, so there were enough horses, while Cuma and Sister-in-law had hired a truck. But now, not much was left of the heavy load that required a car to transport: the ice was gone, the bottoms of the sacks of corn and other feeds were visible, and the flour had mostly been eaten. So, there was no need for a truck—a couple of camels were more than enough to haul whatever was left of this home.

For me, that meant finding a car before the family began their move. I wouldn't want to wait and wait until after the camels had left and the whole house was empty, leaving only me alone in the desert, in a burrow with naked manure walls, still waiting for a car. Though it was nice of Cuma to offer to leave some bedding, a pot, half a sack of flour, and a handful of salt. . . .

In short, just to be safe, it was better for me to leave with the children.

Their transport had been contacted half a month in advance. The back-to-school season was peak period for every unlicensed taxi driver in the area. They went house to house asking if there were any students returning to school. Once you miss this period, finding a car was tantamount to winning the lottery. . . .

FOR THE FIRST COUPLE of days after deciding to leave, I put all my energy into organizing my sorry belongings. I gave a sweater and a scarf to Kama, and all my irreparable pants were set aflame, leaving me with one good pair that I wore.

Kama wanted to leave with us too because her sisters, the ones who had been caring for their grandma, also had to go back to school. Grandma had not fully recovered from her illness so she was still in need of care.

In addition, Shinshybek wanted to personally accompany his two children back to school. All of a sudden, six of us in total were set to leave the winter pastures at once! It was enough to fill an entire car. But for some reason, Cuma contacted two cars, splitting us into two groups. Regarding this decision, Cuma's explanation was especially incomprehensible. Only much later did it become clear that he was chummy with both of the drivers and wanted both of them to make a little money. . . .

But he went further, asking us to keep it a secret. Whichever car arrived first, those waiting for the other vehicle must keep their lips sealed and pretend like they wouldn't be leaving anytime soon. How exhausting . . . was that really necessary? But Cuma expounded, "We are all people who go up mountains and down winter burrows, we can't go around speaking carelessly, no way! I've asked the two of them to come already, if one were to turn up to find no one here, if that got out, who would ever believe us then? Afterward, if you died here, no one would come fetch you!"

Indeed, in the wilderness, promises mean more than responsibility toward others; they're a means of self-protection too. Especially for the people who go "up mountains and down winter burrows." For those whose existence depends on the vagaries of fate, with no other assurances, one's word was crucial.

Yet while we kept our word, the drivers didn't keep theirs! We waited day after day until a whole week passed by!

Every hour during the day, someone would climb up the eastern dune to scan the horizon. There was never any sign of a car.

Cuma and Zhada were getting impatient. They took turns carrying the phone to the tripod where they tried calling the drivers over and over.

The sky was clear and the wind was calm, so why was there no signal? When Zhada wasn't out herding (to earn some money while he still could), he was up the tripod waving the antennae around. But what use was that? It wasn't like a satellite dish that depended on the angle for the strength of its signal.

But no one was as impatient as I was; I had to leave right away! I'd run out of pants to wear . . . even my last good pair was starting to tear everywhere. . . . Strange, we were in a desert, not a forest, nothing but sand, what could they be snagging on?

Finally, one evening, the call went through. Only then did we learn that someone from a pasture to the east had just passed away. Burying the dead was clearly a higher priority than returning to school, so the drivers put us off and drove the mourners out of the wilderness. The soonest they could return was in two days' time.

Two days! But my pants couldn't last two days!

Cuma said, "Cars—there's others. They say there's one passing by here tomorrow, but it has eight people already. If you want to go, I'll call the driver!" If I had accepted, the other eight passengers would have hated me.

Just think about it: they had already stuffed eight people into a small four-seat Beijing 212 jeep. When the eight of them wanted to get out of the jeep, would they be able to unglue themselves? I'm afraid they might have merged together by then.

The most crowded ride I had ever experienced was in a minibus in the countryside. It was so crowded that they were throwing people out, but they couldn't throw me out so the driver let me sit on the dashboard next to the steering wheel along with two others. The three of us sat hunched, our backs to the windshield, facing a bus full of grimacing passengers. Every time the driver shifted gears, he shouted, "Leg!" and I lifted my leg as quickly as I could. Only when he was done shifting gears could I put it down.

In short, that's how bad it gets.

I WASN'T THE ONLY one anxious because of my pants—little Nurgün was devastated because she had been wearing her new red boots, which she had been saving all winter, thinking she might leave at any moment. She was terrified of wearing them out.

The most frustrated, though, was Zhada. Each day, he was torn between wanting to herd to make some money and the fear of missing the car. When evening came and it became clear that it was another no-show, he griped: if only he knew there would be no car, he'd have herded the sheep!

On those days, when Sister-in-law wanted to trick Zhada to get out of bed, she no longer said, "Guests are here," but instead, "The car's here!" It worked like a charm.

Nonetheless, during those final days of waiting, the burrow settlement was a hive of activity! All three mothers took turns preparing feasts, and with the weather warm and sunny, women and girls flocked from the neighboring pastures to our burrow settlement. On Sister-in-law's day to play host, she boiled meat in the white enamel kettle that she stewed tea leaves in, and she used tea water to boil it! The meat came out looking like it had been red braised, all dark brown and red, and the meat-broth-and-tea-water combo had an odd taste too. I eagerly observed everything that unfolded—I might have been there three months, but there would always be new things to learn, fresh experiences to be had. . . . Cuma noticed how avid I was and sighed: "Wait until Li Juan gets home with her mother to find there's no tea, no *nan*, no grease . . . it won't be a week before she thinks, forget it, I'm going back! She'll be back in the winter burrow in no time. . . ." I grinned ruefully but said nothing. A parting sadness was finally swelling inside me.

AT LAST, AT THE END of February, the long-awaited Beijing jeep arrived. Except . . . the driver was only twelve years old. He was making use of his winter vacation to earn some cash. . . .

Of the two groups that were leaving, I was in the first group with Zhada, but somehow I didn't feel especially lucky . . . that said, if the others dared ride in the jeep, why not me? There was nothing but desert and sand in any direction, with neither cliffs nor rivers to worry about. What was there to be afraid of, that the kid might drive the car into the sky?

Because the driver was too short, there were two thick cushions under his butt.

The kid was impressive. Not only did he have a car, but he also ran a little shop. Not long into our journey, he turned to ask if I wanted to buy some bubble gum, then after another stretch, tried to hawk me some biscuits. This was taking business to the next level!

Aside from me, Zhada, and another man (who I later learned was with the boy driver), there were no other passengers. I knew this couldn't be. And sure enough, along the way, whenever we came to a burrow settlement, we'd make a detour. Before long, we'd picked up a man, a girl, a young woman, two bags of things to be transported to Ulungur, and a few messages to pass on.

Every time we arrived at someone's home, whether there were passengers to join us or not, we all sat down for a couple bowls of tea first. If there was a *dombra* in the burrow, people took turns performing. It felt like we were traveling together, what a fun time.

At first, I felt uneasy. I was only a passenger, a total stranger to all these people. Eating their food along with the driver felt embarrassing, so I ate as little as possible even if I was drooling on the inside. Only later did I realize that my attitude was all wrong: by rejecting their kindness on the basis of unfamiliarity, I was implying that I'd already made my mind up to never repay them . . . that was selfish. In the wilderness, accepting others' help and helping others are equally important.

THE FAMILY THAT LEFT the deepest impression on me was the one that lived on an incredibly flat terrain. When I got out of the jeep to look around, I immediately thought, had I lived here, carrying snow alone would've been the death of me . . . smooth, open plains as far as the eye could see, barely a slope to catch the drifting snowfall.

But their burrow was incredibly cool! Amazingly, the walls were lime washed. And there wasn't a single crack in the door! When you closed the door, no wind leaked through.

And there was another home where a very beautiful, stylish girl lived. To me, having now spent a whole winter in the desert, she looked as fashionable as anyone in the city. She was even wearing high heels! Just sitting there, her beauty was striking, like a rose blossom in a bed of chives. She had put on heavy makeup, permed her long hair, and was drenched in perfume. Sitting quietly beside her, drinking tea, I sensed that it wasn't just me, but everyone was captivated by her.

When I learned that she was coming with us, my heart did a little dance.

No wonder she was so dressed up; like me and Nurgün, she was ready to leave at a moment's notice!

FROM THE START, I was prepared to be crammed into the car with six or seven people. But even as the journey was coming to an end, there were still only five of us! Not to mention we were all skinny, so everyone had plenty of room.

Skeptically, I asked, "Really only five? We're really not going to pick anyone else up?"

The man beside the little driver replied, "There's no one else, really."

Then he added, "But there are two horses . . . at the next stop."

My jaw dropped. I turned to look out the rear window at the truck bed. It was tight—a palm-sized space that was already stuffed with our luggage and the cargo that we'd been asked to deliver. Two horses? Not even two sheep could fit! Then what followed . . . was a real eye opener. I was struck with a profound sense of men's limitless strength.

It only required some discomfort on the part of the two horses, soon to be smooshed into one horse. . . . To celebrate the success of loading the horses, all the men who'd lent a hand gathered around the jeep to take a group photograph with the two horse heads.

While the men worked their brute force and wisdom to load the jeep, I was invited to join a sanguine old woman for tea in her burrow. Inside were a short-haired white dog with a black head, an unbelievably chubby baby with a lovely disposition, a filthy but happy child with an impressive appetite, and a young, shy mother.

Nestled in the warm burrow drinking tea, eating *baursak*, unwrapping candies . . . what could I do for my hosts in return? I had to take as many pictures as I could. Then I showed them the shots on my camera . . . seeing the joy on their faces made me want to give them the whole camera!

Before long, a young man, his wife, and two girls appeared one after another to check me out—and my camera. What a bustling settlement, it housed four families!

The four families lived by a massive sand dune. The sand dune was striking, towering over a flat expanse. Not a blade of grass grew on it, a magnificent edifice. When we drove past it earlier, the man in the passenger seat repeatedly pointed it out to me and suggested that I take pictures of it. He told me that this was the biggest "sand mountain" within a day's horse ride, an ancient landmark for herders.

Had I lived there, I would've climbed it every day to gaze out.

WITH THE HORSES LOADED onto the jeep, our journey continued without any further stops. The car cruised north.

The farther north we drove, the more snow there was. Gradually, there was no more exposed earth. At the same time, the road became more distinct, wider and straighter. This wasn't the same road that we'd ridden our horses along on our way south; it seemed to lie west of that.

Oh, and I was holding my Panda Dog pup the whole time. Cuma had promised to give it to me a long time ago. The young girl beside me occasionally reached out to stroke the pup's head as if she was worried it might die at any moment. The girl had chubby cheeks and wore brightly colored, pretty clothing. At about seven years old, she was only a little younger than Nurgün. Traveling alone, she seemed calm and brave.

This whole trip, Zhada was quiet and proper. Whenever folks were loading and unloading the car, he always helped. Whenever we arrived at someone's home, he rushed to help carry the luggage . . . how endearing! A completely different person than the Zhada I knew at home.

The well-dressed young woman didn't say one word the whole ride until finally, when her cell phone had a signal, she talked on it nonstop.

The two men chatted the whole time. The assistant driver seemed especially curious about me and kept turning around, asking questions and pointing out places like a tour guide, telling me the names of all the places we passed, how many families and pastures were located there . . . with such passion that it felt like he wanted me to pull out my notebook and write down every word, but I was far too lazy to bother. Little Panda Dog nuzzled softly against my chest, probably hungry. But soon, the life of drift and toil will be behind it. I had every intention of making up for all the hardship it had suffered that winter.

From setting out in the morning to turning onto the asphalt country road along the Ulungur's south bank, the ride took seven hours. As soon as we reached the road, the child driver switched places with the man sitting next to him. Obviously, the kid didn't have a driver's license. Although I suspected that there weren't any traffic police on this road anyway. We drove for another hour on the asphalt without passing another car.

All the goats we saw along the road had dirty butts that were hard to look at. Compared to the sheep in the winter pastures, these must have been living wretched lives indeed. The snow was so thick that no grass, not even withered grass, poked through. They had no choice but to become marauders, stealing hay from people's roofs and waiting outside shops. Whenever a paper bag or a cardboard box was thrown out, they pounced on it and munched.

We passed one snow-covered place after another—villages, fields, woods— like a dreamworld. Although the countryside was sparsely populated, I couldn't help but feel an ineffable sense of opulence. I thought long and hard about it until I finally realized that in fact, it was all the utility poles protruding from the ground.

My stop was the last one. The car was empty, the roadside scenery looked more and more familiar. It was Akehara. We reached the yellow building I called home. The jeep pulled up outside my family's shop. Even though the world before me was still engulfed in a thick layer of snow, white as far as the eyes could see, to me the winter was over. What felt like a long, interminable trial now felt ever so brief and cursory, much to my bewilderment.

The Little Panda Dog that I brought home from the winter pasture

Glossary

Ada: Grandpa

Apa: Grandma

aqyns: improvising poets and singers who practice the art of *aqyndyq*

ayak-kap: a small embroidered bag for storing utensils and knickknacks, which is often hung on the wall

bata: a ritual prayer made before slaughtering an animal, in order to make it halal

baursak: fried dough balls

bolangu: a two-faced drum with two pellets attached to cords. The pellet drum is played by holding the handle and twisting it back and forth, causing the pellets to strike the drum faces.

chök: the call to make camels lie down

Chulpan: Venus, morning star

dastarkhān: There are no tables as we know them in the earthen burrow, only a tablecloth laid over a wooden board in the center of the main seating area. Throughout South and Central Asia, *dastarkhān* refers to the main seating area where people eat.

irimzhik: cottage cheese made from sour cream

Jengetay: Sister-in-law

Kara Jorga, Black Horse Trot: a traditional style of Kazakh folk dance, as well as the name of the song played when practicing this dance

kazan: a large cooking pot

koychy: a versatile exclamation, often meaning "no way," "no thanks," "get out," "leave it out"

kurt: a hard cheese made by straining boiled yogurt

kuurdak: stewed meat (mutton or beef) and potatoes

nan: flatbread

oshak: a kind of stove or hearth for wood fires

plov: pilaf

sajayaq: a metal tripod used to suspend the *kazan* pot over a fire

suluv: beautiful

syrmak/tekemet: quilted patchwork carpets made from felt, which are often colorful. *Syrmak*, which are the more finely detailed of the two, are also used as wall hangings.

tary: dried wheat fried in fat, served with honey and hot milk

terme: band-weaving, the technique for making *baskur* or *zhelbau*. *Baskur* is a wide decorative band wove from about five different colors of wool yarn using a loom. *Zhelbau* is a thinner version of *baksur*. They are used to decorate a burrow or yurt, normally hanging in front of beams and around doorways.

toy: feast

tus-kiiz: embroidered tapestries made of cotton, which are often colorful

zongzi: a traditional Chinese dish made from sticky rice wrapped in bamboo leaves.

Goodbye, winter pasture! (The character in the snow reads "Argh!")

ABOUT THE AUTHOR

Born in Xinjiang in 1979, **Li Juan** grew up in Sichuan Province. In her youth, she learned to sew and run a small convenience store with her mother, living in a town where nomads shopped. Later, she worked in a factory in the city of Urumqi. In 2003, she became a public servant, until 2008, when she became a full-time author. Her writing career began in 1999, as a columnist for newspapers like *Southern Weekly* and Hong Kong's *Wen Wei Po*. Widely regarded as one of the best narrative nonfiction writers of her generation, Li Juan's writing has won several awards. *Winter Pasture* is considered her most popular and representative work.

Jack Hargreaves is a Chinese–English translator from East Yorkshire, now based in London. Specializing in literary and academic translation, his work has appeared in *Asymptote Journal*, *Paper Republic*, and *Los Angeles Review of Books China Channel* and includes writing by Zhu Yiye, Isaac Hsu, Yuan Ling, and Ye Duoduo. He translated Shen Dacheng's short story "The Novelist in the Attic" for Comma Press's *The Book of Shanghai*. Forthcoming translations include Yang Dian's flash fiction collection *A Contrarian's Tales*, *A History of Chinese Philosophical Thought* by Zhang Xianghao, and *Buddhism and Buddhology* by Hong Xiuping. Jack recently joined the *Paper Republic* team.

Yan Yan graduated from Columbia University in 2008 with degrees in English and religious studies. After working at the Alibaba Group in Hangzhou, China, his hometown, he backpacked around the world and eventually settled down in Brooklyn, then the Hudson Valley. As a freelance translator, he translated works by Hans Christian Andersen Award-winner Cao Wenxuan, including the Dingding and Dangdang series, *XiMi*, and *Mountain Goats Don't Eat Heaven's Grass*, as well as updated editions of *Grass House* and *Bronze Sunflower*, for China Children's Press & Publication Group. More recently, he has been translating works by the Chinese literary icon Wang Xiaobo, which include a novella collection titled *Golden Age* and an essay collection titled *The Pleasure of Thinking*.